PARENTS AND CHILDREN IN AUTISM

PARENTS AND CHILDREN IN AUTISM

MARIAN K. DeMYER
Indiana University
School of Medicine

1979

V. H. WINSTON & SONS
Washington, D.C.

A HALSTED PRESS BOOK

JOHN WILEY & SONS
New York   Toronto   London   Sydney

V. H. Winston & Sons, a Division of Scripta Technica, Inc., Publishers
1511 K Street, N.W., Washington, D.C. 20005

Distributed solely by Halsted Press, a Division of John Wiley & Sons, Inc.

Library of Congress Cataloging in Publication Data

DeMyer, Marian K.
　Parents and children in autism.

　Includes bibliographical references.
　1. Autism. I. Title. [DNLM: 1. Autism, Early infantile. 2. Parents. WM203.5 D389p]
RJ506.A9D45　　　　618.9'28'982　　　79-15208
ISBN 0-470-26733-X

Composition by **Marie A. Maddalena**, Scripta Technica, Inc.

TO MY PARENTS

Margaret Groenier Kendall
and
Wilber Lawrence Kendall,

who, by example, taught me
much of what I know about
good parenting.

CONTENTS

*With contributions by Dr. David Park.

FOREWORD FOR PARENTS

I write these words as a parent of an autistic child and direct them to parents into whose hands this book may fall. We tend to be a lonely minority. There are only about 100,000 autistic people in the whole United States, and except for large cities we are spread thin. Generally we know only a few other "autistic parents," and they are apt to have problems very different from our own. There are now several useful books on what autism is and how to manage it; this one also tells comprehensively what it is like for families and what happens as time goes on.

Since autistic people and their families vary so widely, no simple narrative is possible. You will find comparative data instead, based on Dr. DeMyer's study of 155 autistic children and many of their families and on comparison groups of normal children and children with other learning disabilities. You will from time to time very probably find yourselves in here: your child, your family, your problems. You will find what others in your situation have done: what worked for them and what didn't. You will find how they reacted to their problem and something of the range of outcomes you can expect. You will find what you already know: that life is a long road with few picnics but many others have travelled it before you and survived, and now that parents' groups and responsible and informed professionals are becoming numerous, you need not travel it alone.

As you read this book you will get an idea of what you can expect from a responsible and informed professional and what you cannot. You cannot expect a cure; you cannot expect him or her to act as if yours were the only developmentally-disabled child in the state. You can expect an open and frank discussion of your problems and prospects, though (s)he may decide that too much frankness at one time is more than you should have to bear. You should expect up-to-date knowledge of facilities and programs in your area. Above all, you should expect to find a friend, not in the social sense but someone totally free from any tendency to blame you for your child's autism. You will find in this book why no responsible and informed professional thinks that way anymore. If anyone tries to blame it on you, mention the data given here. If blame persists, walk out of the office—unless—but hope it is not true, that office contains "the only game in town." In that case you will have to make your accommodations, but never accept the guilt. You cannot except that the mental-health professionals you deal with will be instant experts in every rare condition that is brought before them, but you can expect that they will take an interest in new findings. Many are reported here.

Professor DeMyer has written her book with professional authority. This book will tell you much that you ought to know about how to live with an autistic child and what lies ahead.

David Park, Ph.D.*
Williams College
Williamstown, Mass.

*Prof. Park is Editor-in-Chief of the *Advocate*, member of the Board of Directors of the National Society for Autistic Children, and Editorial Board member of the *Journal of Autism and Developmental Disorders*.

AUTHOR'S INTRODUCTION

When infantile autism afflicts a young child, the parents must find ways of coping with problems in nearly every aspect of child development. Beginning in the first three years of life, the autistic child not only fails to relate happily to people or to communicate verbally, but has enormous problems in sleeping, eating, learning control of emotional expression and elimination, and acquiring such everyday skills as dressing and eating. As Bender (1955) pointed out in her study of the schizophrenic child, the autistic child also shows deficiencies in nearly every aspect of neurological and neurobiological integration. Later, Lorna Wing (1969) convincingly demonstrated the great similarities between autistic and perceptually handicapped and aphasic children.

For at least two decades after Kanner (1943) first described infantile autism, clinicians commonly assumed that parents had caused the disorder, despite the fact that he also favored biological abnormalities as playing a significant role. Increasingly, after the mid 1960s, investigators reported finding neurobiological irregularities in the children. In well controlled studies, they failed to detect any more mental illness or extreme personality types among autistic parents* as a group than among other groups of parents (DeMyer, 1975).

*This inaccurate expression, for the sake of brevity, will be used throughout the book.

Finally in the late 1970s, an investigative team (Cantwell, Baker, & Rutter, 1978) drew attention to the severe stresses experienced by parents in their struggles to deal with the symptoms of autistic children, stresses associated with loss of self-confidence and joy in life. Thus we come through a full circle of thought about symptom formation in the autistic syndrome.

Despite the evidence that parents do not cause autism any more than they cause well-marked neurobiological conditions such as Down's syndrome, these findings may be ignored in clinical practice. Also, many clinicians, because of the rarity of autism, may not appreciate the wide range of problems that parents must face in rearing their child. Certainly most clinicians have not experienced, as I have, the difficulties that parents encounter, year in and year out, in finding help for their autistic child and for themselves in the midst of the changes the child had brought into their lives.

Some parents manage to find the best help their communities have to offer and work in constructive tandem with physicians and teachers. Others flounder in finding services or antagonize most professional people, even those striving their utmost. While all parents experience severe stresses in caring for an autistic child, some falter as individuals and marital partners and others appear to develop increased strength. This book examines these issues and points out those professional and parental practices which help and those which hinder parents in their heavy task.

Most of the important aspects of autistic in contrast to normal development are described in detail so as to highlight the nature of the autistic child's learning disability and the difficulties parents face in their efforts to be good mothers and fathers. I have tried to add research findings and my own clinical observations to extend and supplement what the parents have observed and the conclusions that they have reached.

Many of the parents' observations about problems in rearing autistic children have been mirrored by parents of nonpsychotic children who were also failing to develop normally. These parents have had similar problems in finding help, similar emotional reactions to the developmental and social deviations of their children, and similar personal and family dilemmas arising from the fear that they were failing as parents. This book is also addressed to these parents and to those who try to help them care for their children. I would have liked to include more details relating to these parents' experiences and valuable observations in this book. However, because the problems of the two groups are so similar, I decided to focus on parents and children in autism.

This book traces the entire natural life course of infantile autism, which in most but not all cases ends tragically in an adult life of partial or total dependence. Most parents whose autistic children are still young will tend to deny that such a bleak future awaits their child. Such thinking is right and natural for a while and encourages all of us to search for more effective treatment; but autism is notorious for its resistance to clinical intervention, especially over the long run. Wishful thinking about treatment should not obscure our need to search for the causes of autism and for its biological and psychological links to other forms of learning disability. The final chapter makes suggestions for future research to locate causes and thereby find preventive measures. My overall purpose is to further the knowledge of all who try to help autistic people from infancy through adulthood so that their efforts can be based on the reality of autism rather than on its mythology.

Marian K. DeMyer, M.D.
Indiana University School of Medicine
Indianapolis, Indiana

REFERENCES

Bender, L. Twenty years of clinical research on schizophrenic children with special reference to those under six years of age. In G. Caplan (Ed.), *Emotional problems of early childhood.* New York: Basic Books, 1955.

Cantwell, D. P., Baker, L., & Rutter, M. Family factors. In M. Rutter & E. Schopler (Eds.), *Autism: A reappraisal of concepts and treatment.* New York: Plenum Press, 1978.

DeMyer, M. K. Research in infantile autism: A strategy and its results. *Biological Psychiatry*, 1975, **10**(4), 433–452.

Kanner, L. Autistic disturbances of affective contact. *Nervous Child*, 1943, **2**, 217.

Wing, L. The handicaps of autistic children—a comparative study. *Journal of Child Psychology and Psychiatry*, 1969, **10**, 1–40.

ACKNOWLEDGMENTS

My primary debt is to the parents who have opened to us their most private thoughts. They allowed staff members to examine and reexamine their children over the years. Many have called and written to keep me informed of the progress of these children. I thank my husband, William DeMyer, M.D., whose expertise in child neurology was manifested in the research from start to finish. His fine literary judgment and his generosity led him to comment constructively on every chapter.

Professor David Park of Williams College, Member of the Board of the National Society for Autistic Children, edited this book with superb skill. His search for verifiable case histories of autistic adolescents and adults yielded a selection of five (Elly, Terry, Bobby, Jean, and Mark) which he presented in Chapters 13 and 14. The sections on parental accomplishments and needs in Chapter 15 are also among his special contributions to this book which expanded considerably its value to parents and professionals alike.

Many colleagues have helped directly or supportively in the projects from which I have derived the information contained in this book. To all of them I am grateful. I would like to give special thanks to the following whose work with the Clinical Research Center for Early Childhood Schizophrenia extended over many years: John I. Nurnberger, M.D., then Chairman of the Department of

Psychiatry at Indiana University, whose able administrative and scientific efforts enabled the Research Center to be funded and to carry out its 12-year charter; Don W. Churchill, M.D., Assistant Director of the Research Center, director of the treatment program, author of landmark studies concerning autistic language deficiencies, whose wise head led to fruitful collaboration with his colleagues; James Simmons, M.D., coordinator of Indiana University Child Psychiatry Services, and Donald F. Moore, M.D., and Richard McNabb, M.D., administrators at Carter Memorial Hospital where the Research Center was located, who never refused a reasonable request and, unbidden, extended many a help; Joseph Hingtgen, Ph.D., whose wisdom and generous spirit made him a valued adviser and whose expertise in behavioral psychology helped elucidate the nature of autistic social and learning difficulties; William Pontius, M.A., and Ellen Smith Yang, Ph.D., with unfailing courtesy interviewed many parents, thereby facilitating completion of the intensive interview study; James Norton, Ph.D., a superb statistician whose patience with me and the data allowed conclusions to be reached; Joyce Small, M.D., a most careful researcher, whose expertise in electroencephalography led to valuable conclusions about the neurobiological basis of autism; Bette Joe Davis, Ph.D., a language pathologist, whose clinical work with the children and parents, was exceptional; Lois Hendrickson Loew, M.S., a psychologist who skillfully devised many of the ratings; Carolyn Bryson, Ph.D., a psychologist, for her penetrating criticisms, creative research, and hours of speculative talk; Gerald Alpern, Ph.D., for his innovative ideas about testing "untestable" autistic children; Bonita Watt, a secretary who talked to parents with exceptional skill, organized a busy office, kept the books of the Research Center, typed without error, and still found time to talk with me and do many extra kindnesses for me; and Sandra Barton, a research assistant with unusual skill in testing and understanding children and facility in data analysis, who listened intelligently to my ideas and commented on the manuscript. Zoe Manning, M. Mus, and Janice Hartman not only typed the manuscript but made valuable suggestions about content.

Victor Winston, publisher, has worked with my manuscripts over the years to make them clearer. His supportive comments have renewed my spirits. Also, a special thank-you to Hugh Hendrie, M.B., Ch.B., Chairman of the Department of Psychiatry, for allowing me to use most of my work time the past year to complete this writing, despite other pressing obligations.

My experience with day care programs for preschool autistic children came from consulting with a superior group of teachers, social workers, and psychologists at Noble School, a division of the Marion County Association for Retarded Citizens. My thanks go to them, particularly to Hazel Watson, teacher, and to Peg Goldberg, M.S.W., then director of special services, who also commented on the manuscript. The Association for Mental Health, because of the interest of Norman Skole and Joseph Brown, gave our group its start-up research funds and has remained supportive throughout the years. The Research Center was supported in part by Public Health Service Grant No. MH05154, PHS Grant RR-00162, by Carter Memorial Hospital, State of Indiana, and by Indiana University School of Medicine, including the latter's research computation facility. My thanks to all of these agencies.

I should like to mention a special debt to the leading authorities in the field of normal child development: Arnold Gesell and his associates from Yale University, Louis M. Terman, Psyche Catell, Nancy Bayley, David Wechsler, and others. Until I made myself thoroughly acquainted with their work, the nature of the autistic child's neuropsychological disabilities was unclear.

Last but not least, I thank the ward staff, teachers, and other therapists of the Clinical Research Center for Early Childhood Schizophrenia. I once sent a questionnaire to the parents to find out what they liked and disliked about our services. The superb care given to their children by the nurses, child care and therapeutic staff won the most accolades.

Marian K. DeMyer

Chapter 1

THE FAMILIES, DIAGNOSES
AND PROCEDURES

The information in this book was gleaned from the study of three types of children: autistic, normal, and those with various types of learning and intellectual disabilities. The period of most intensive work occurred during my 12 years (1961 to 1973) as Director of the Clinical Research Center for Early Childhood Schizophrenia[1] where 155 autistic and 47 learning-disabled children were studied. The Center occupied a wing of the Children's Service of Carter Memorial Hospital in Indianapolis. In addition, 700 normal children participated in one or more research projects by letting us see how they talked, socialized, played, and manifested their intelligence. In the years after the work of the Research Center, I have had the privilege of studying in various clinical settings about 35 other autistic people and about 75 learning-disabled children.

In the early years of the Center's existence, we screened all referred children to be as certain as we could that they had severe symptoms of social distance or emotional withdrawal. After 1965, when it became apparent that the young, socially isolated child had many biological and neuropsychological ties to the nonpsychotic learning-disabled child, we also routinely began to evaluate and enroll the latter type of child in our residential treatment program. Though our bed capacity was only 10, we treated about 58 children in all.

1

The mean age of the children at initial evaluation was 5 years and 4 months with a range of 22 months to 10 years. About 75% were male. Because we wanted to elucidate causes and the connection of infantile autism to early childhood schizophrenia, we chose to study children 7 years of age or younger. While a few children were older than 7 at initial evaluation, the bulk did fit into our initial specifications. Older age groups were seen during the course of follow-up studies. Nearly all children came from the State of Indiana and most were from the middle of the socioeconomic status range (see Tables 1 and 2 for details of demographic features). Because the state varied from place to place in its concentration of minority and socioeconomic groups, it is difficult to know how closely our population of autistic children represented that of the entire state. However, we received about 25% more than our expected share of autistic children from large urban centers, which may explain the somewhat high percentage of black children (autistic blacks, about 17%; blacks in Indiana, about 7%). The relatively low incidence of children from low-income families is harder to explain. No charge was made for diagnostic services, and no child was refused inpatient treatment for want of ability to pay. We must consider the possibility that autistic children as a group tended to come from higher-income homes, or else that referral services were not as readily available to low-income rural children. Also, scattered throughout the state, there are several low-income sub-cultures which reject professional services of all kinds.

While we accepted referrals from parents and lay groups, most autistic referrals came from physicians and mental health professionals. Since we solicited referrals of normal children and many subnormal ones, most of these children came from Marion County, a large urban-suburban area. For most

Table 1. Selected Indices of Autistic Children in the Study

Chronological age and sex	Years	Months	%	Race and sibships	%
Mean age				*Race*	
Child[a]	5	4		White	83
Mother	32	8		Black	17
Father	35	9		*Brothers and sisters*	
Sex				0	15
Male			76	1 or 2	61
Female			24	3 or more	24

[a]Range = 1 year 10 mo. to 10 yrs.

Table 2. Educational, Socioeconomic and Marital Status of Parents of Autistic Children

Education	%	Marital and socioeconomics	At initial evaluation %	At follow-up %
Below high school		*Marital*[a]		
Mother	19.0	Divorced-separated	13.3	25.5
Father	20.0	Spouse dead	2.0	2.0
High school graduate		Married	84.7	72.4
Mother	66.0	*Socioeconomics*[b]		
Father	40.0	Low	10.0	10.0
College graduate		Middle	70.0	70.0
Mother	15.0	High	20.0	20.0
Father	39.0			

[a] Years of marriage = 10.8 ± 5.5.
[b] Based on Warner's criteria.

comparative studies we matched the groups as closely as possible on important demographic features. We were most successful in matching normal and autistic families because we had such a large pool of normal children to draw from but this situation did not exist for the subnormal children in the preschool age range we studied most extensively.

The parents were likely to be in their third or fourth decade of life (mean age of mothers was 32 years and of fathers 35 years) and married 5 to 15 years (10.8 ± 5.5). The fathers came from all walks of life, including, for example, laborers, clerks, engineers, farmers, chemists, businessmen, teachers, scholars, lawyers, physicians, airplane pilots, salesmen, and military men. Some mothers worked outside their homes, but the vast majority had given up their jobs to become full-time mothers and homemakers; most of the homes had two or more children. Fewer mothers than fathers were college graduates or professionally trained, but 66% of mothers were high school graduates, many of whom had discontinued their higher education to marry and rear a family (see Table 2).

Historical Background and Inherent Problems of Diagnosis

When Leo Kanner (1943) first described early infantile autism, his diagnostic criteria were severe withdrawal from emotional contact, desire for preservation of sameness, and failure to use language for communication. He observed that the condition bore little resemblance to any known organic condition or to mental retardation. While he observed that parents were apt to be cold and obsessive, he also stressed that autistic infants came "into the world with innate inability to form the usual, biologically provided affective contact with people." Thus he initially favored a dual role of nature and nurture in producing infantile autism. Unfortunately most professionals of the 1940s and 1950s picked up only the parental personality factor of his hypothesis. Later Kanner (1968) reiterated that he never "pointed to the parents as the primary, postnatal sources" of infantile autism. He concluded that knowledge of cause was "extremely limited" and called for "much research, much curiosity."

Despite Kanner's apparently simple behavioral descriptions, the diagnostic criteria for autism have been the source of much dissention among different investigators for three reasons:

(1) The symptom of social distance lies on a continuum of severity, and it is difficult to measure this trait with precision or to define where on the severity continuum to place the point of psychotic withdrawal.

(2) Kanner implied that the diagnosis of autism required that the child have basically normal intelligence, and yet most diagnosticians said the autistic child was untestable.

(3) Eisenberg (1966) made the statement that signs of brain damage or neurological disfunction discounted the diagnosis of autism even if the child had every behavioral sign, and yet such organic brain malfunction is a difficult condition to rule out. Each child must be given a rigorous neurological evaluation and laboratory tests such as brain recordings done with care. In most reports, neurological evaluations were not thorough. Compounding the problem is the fact that even if the child has absolutely no signs of neurological disfunction in the traditional neurological evaluation, certain areas within the central nervous system may still be malfunctioning in an organic sense. Birth injuries, cerebral anoxia, or maldevelopment may leave the motor areas of the brain intact but seriously affect other areas such as the language centers or limbic associational centers without leaving a trace detectable in standard types of neurological examinations. Our population of autistic children would have been devoid of any with obvious neurological handicaps because of the prevailing view that such children were "really" not autistic. Professional people simply did not refer children with obvious neurological symptoms to us even though these children might possess classical behavioral symptoms of autism. Thus, it was apparent that the diagnosis of autism had traditionally been based not on the child's behavior alone but also on very rough estimates of the intactness of the child's central nervous system and of his basic biological intelligence.

At the beginning of our research in 1961, we too tried to comply with the dictum that we should sort out all "true" cases of infantile autism from cases that were "really" brain damaged or "really" primarily retarded. Then we began to find young autistic children with normal initial neurological examinations and EEGs who later, perhaps two years after treatment started, began to show abnormal EEGs or other signs of neurological disfunction. Some children who appeared "bright" on evaluation because of a splinter skill such as reading words were found later to have serious deficits in understanding what they read. These findings made it clear that we were trying to treat three separate aspects of the diagnosis of autism as if they were related in a known way, before their relationships were in fact clear or even confirmed. About midway in the research program we began giving every child three separate diagnoses:[2] a diagnosis based on behavior alone; a neurological diagnosis based on a neurological examination, history, and EEG; and an intellectual diagnosis based on intelligence testing, since we had found that we could test the children quite reliably (Alpern, 1967; DeMyer, Norton, & Barton, 1971).

This procedure allowed us to manipulate the three variables separately as we examined our data in order to discover not only their relationship to each other but also to other data such as socioeconomic status, parental handling practices, parental personalities, and even eventual outcome of the disability. In this way, we found that prognosis was most strongly related to the measured intelligence of the child even in his preschool years (DeMyer, Barton, Allen, & Steele, 1973). We also found that the autistic child had many signs of neurological disfunction which were not readily apparent in a routine neurological examination but became apparent in a searching evaluation, not only through traditional neurological examination, but by using multiple EEGs, studying learning patterns, and giving neuropsychological tests (DeMyer, 1975).

Description of Criteria for Behavioral Diagnosis of
Early Infantile Autism

The term *infantile autism*, as used at the Research Center, signified an early childhood psychosis (onset by the age of 3 years) characterized by all of the following symptoms: (a) severe and continuing social distance; (b) uncommunicative speech or muteness; and (c) nonfunctional use of objects. But even within the framework of the three principal diagnostic criteria, the autistic children varied considerably from each other. These variations assumed three principal patterns characterized by severity of withdrawal, level of speech, and presence of splinter skills.

(1) The highest functioning group was distinctive in having some islets of social relatedness in an otherwise withdrawn personality and a mixture of communicative and noncommunicative speech. Originally, we gave this group the name "early childhood schizophrenia" because we believed it did not exactly adhere to Kanner's criteria. Later, principally because of Kolvin's (1971) work, we dropped the term *schizophrenia* because this higher

functioning group had no prognostic ties either to later developing childhood schizophrenia or to adult schizophrenia. It did have many ties to the middle functioning group of autistic children.

(2) Middle functioning autistics were more severely withdrawn and used uncommunicative speech, or lacked speech. Like the high functioning group, the middle autistics exhibited some intellectual or perceptual-motor skills that approximated chronological age level.[3] Because of these splinter skills, many investigators have erroneously assumed that the high and middle functioning autistic children have a basically normal general intelligence.

(3) The low functioning group was similar to the middle group except for its failure to exhibit any kind of intellectual or perceptual-motor activity that approximated age level. Only walking and stair climbing stood above an otherwise uniformly low profile of intellectual and adaptive skills. These children, too, have in the past sometimes been regarded as having normal intellectual potential because of their relatively intact motor systems.

A splinter skill is defined as one that is considerably above the general mental age level of most other skills possessed by the child. In autistic children, the most common splinter skill was shown in a variety of assembly tasks such as fitting puzzles and form boards together. In speaking autistic children, a common splinter ability was rote repetition of words such as TV commercials. We might also speak of splinter disabilities. Autistic children, almost by definition, have their lowest mental age in communicative speech and in social skills. Rutter (1978) called attention to these splinter disabilities, saying that the social splinter disability is a necessary condition for diagnosis of autism. For example, the following mixture of high and low abilities was frequently found:

> Al, a 4-year-old autistic boy, had an overall mental age of 2½ years. His highest (splinter) skills were putting together a Merrill-Palmer mannikin (a jigsaw puzzle of a man) and recognizing colors and sizes at mental ages of 5½ and 3½ years, respectively. He could repeat words like a 4½-year-old child, but had the social age of a 12-month-old and verbal expressive abilities of an 18-month-old. These extreme disabilities in verbal communication and socialization were the hallmarks of his autism.

Table 3 shows the mean IQs of 121 autistic children. The relatively higher verbal and perceptual-motor skills of high functioning autistic children were reflected in their significantly higher IQ scores. Nevertheless, even high functioning autistic children, as a group, tested significantly below normal children in both verbal and nonverbal intelligence test items. Unfortunately, the splinter skills of most autistic children did not mean that other abilities of

Table 3. Mean Performance and Verbal IQs of 121 Autistic Children[a]

Diagnosis	At initial evaluation[b]		At follow-up[b]	
	Perform-ance	Verbal	Perform-ance	Verbal
High autistic	70	56	75	69
Middle autistic	57	28	49	41
Low autistic	37	19	35	37

[a] Significant differences: high autistic > middle and low autistics; middle autistic > low autistic.

[b] Mean ages: 5-6 years at initial evaluation and 12 years at follow-up.

the child were on the same plane. As shown in Table 3, autistic children tested at a mean age of 12 years showed the same order of verbal and perceptual-motor disabilities as they did at 5 to 6. As we shall see, subsequent chapters will indicate that social skills of the children also remained below average levels.[4]

Descriptive Examples of the Three Types of Infantile Autism

High functioning autism: The parents' chief complaints about Aaron at the age of 5 years and 2 months were that he could not "think abstractly as well as normal 4-year-olds," and did not socialize with children or converse with anyone. He was "slow" in motor development and in his first year seemed indifferent to people despite continuous family efforts to relate to him. He often averted his eyes when people called his name. In his second year, Aaron's mother noted he would allow more social interaction if she read him numbers from phone books. Thinking he was basically retarded, the parents finally welcomed his interest in letters and numbers. At the age of 3, he could read words and pronounce them phonetically without special instruction. Shortly prior to evaluation, he used minimal and rudimentary conversational speech mixed with much uncommunicative echolalia. He never played in a pretend game.

On examination, Aaron was small and thin for his age, with transparent tender skin and a tense and worried but uninvolved facial expression. His enthusiasm was reserved for numbers. Otherwise, his affect was flat, his eye contact less sustained than normal, and his acceptance of the examiner was one of indifferent tolerance. Aaron's adaptive ability was average or above when an activity involved size, color, form differentiation, or counting. He showed only one or two short instances of simple imaginative play and could not accept or assign a role in mutual play. His voice was high and "sing-song" in tone and cadence. Even though Aaron talked in full sentences, his ability to understand and use language abstractions was not above that of the normal 3 year old child. He could not answer why questions. His speech was full of immediate and delayed echolalia, generally without communicative features. When communicating, Aaron made frequent repetitive requests such as "I want to see the numbers. I want to see the recorder stop at the numbers." When asked about family relationships, he could do no more than name his parents. His gait was clumsy when he ran but within normal limits on walking.

Middle functioning autism: The chief complaints of the divorced mother were that Belinda was not talking and was unaffectionate. At 12 months, she used a few words but her speech did not progress. At 5½ years she said a few words (plus some jargon) and was thought by mother to understand simple speech. During infancy, Belinda was irritable and never smiled or followed mother with her eyes, but held out her arms to be picked up. The family tried to give her special affection during her first year of life. Mother taught her various affectionate responses, but Belinda remained aloof and withdrawn from most people, especially other children. She had little awareness of danger and no special fears. Her main ritual was tearing paper, occasionally spitting on it, and sticking it all over the wall. While she never crawled, she walked well at 9 months. From the age of 1 year and 4 months she jumped on her toes almost all day long.

At examination, Belinda was a small, blond wisp of a girl with a thin, unconcerned face. When excited, she jumped on her toes and flapped her arms. She ran gracefully. We caught only occasional fleeting eye contact, without expression. While Belinda seemed anxious when separated from mother and held tightly to her, there was no apparent warmth or affection in this clinging. She neither looked for nor accepted comfort from her mother and remained alone in her unhappiness. When other children came near, she glided away. Belinda seemed to know exactly what to do with some objects, such as keys, but rejected toys offered to her. Aside from responding to her name, she gave no indication that she understood words or phrases. While mute, Belinda at times responded to specific, communicative gestures. There were no indications of imaginative play or "inner language." She could imitate use of objects at about an 18-month level but could not do body imitations even at a level below one year. Her splinter skills were in object assembly tasks.

Low functioning autism: Cary, at 4 years and 3 months was

described as being so socially withdrawn that he did not seem to differentiate his parents from other people and totally ignored other children. As an infant, he paid no attention to the mother's attempt to get his attention while she breast-fed him. He never responded by smiling or looking and pulled his hand away as she stroked it where it lay on her breast. His characteristic reaction to both parents was to use their hands to get something that he wanted but to ignore them otherwise. He was late in motor development, not sitting up until 11 months and not walking until 22 months. Cary was a placid baby who seldom kicked off his covers. While he seldom used toys appropriately, at about 3 years he stacked some nests of cups together and on occasion, when the parents were not looking, rolled a toy back and forth on the floor. Until the age of 15 months Cary knew several words, but a few months later he had discontinued using them. At 4 years and 3 months, Cary's parents believed he understood the meaning of only four words and used none.

Cary, a somatically normal child, had large protruding ears. At the approach of adults he made no eye contact, avoided physical contact, and remained unresponsive to efforts at verbal and nonverbal communication. He never tried to put anything together or take anything apart but liked to run his fingers over uneven surfaces. His chief object of interest was a key which he carried and transferred from hand to hand, but he gave no indication of understanding its use. During testing, Cary performed only at infancy level in perceptual-motor tasks and demonstrated no splinter skills. While his walking gait was within normal limits, his running gait was clumsy.

Our three subcategories of infantile autism have been useful to us. Not only are they related to various descriptive features such as date of onset and follow-up status but also they have highlighted the relative scarcity of higher functioning autistic children (about 15% of all cases). As the description of autistic children unfolds, I will point out the great individual differences among them in ability to learn and use various skills. It is these individual assets and liabilities which provide the most useful bits of information for treating and educating the child, rather than whether he fits into any particular behavioral diagnostic group.

Psychotic Social Distance

Social distance exists on a continuum of severity. In nonpsychotic children, frequently there are found mild forms of social withdrawal, one type of which might be termed shyness. Mild forms of social distance generally are relieved by a sensitive social approach. In other words, the shy child can be reached through social means. The essence of a psychotic condition[5] in children is social isolation which is unbridgeable by usual social approaches of other children and only slightly reduced by approaches of adults in frequent contact with the child. The high functioning autistic child generally allowed more social contact than the lower functioning child and was frequently spoken of as a "loner" by his parents. The child with even more severe forms of social withdrawal was likely to be described as "living in his own world." The most severe form, found only in few members of the low functioning autistic group, was characterized by an inability to distinguish his parents from other people. As the child grew older, this failure generally disappeared.

Social distance of psychotic proportions is easier to sense than to describe, but typically was manifested in the young autistic child at the height of his illness as follows:

> The child did not habitually stay near people, especially other children. Eye contacts were brief; the child looked through people rather than at them. He did not imitate their physical actions or play with other children even though he sometimes hovered at the edge of a group. He did not respond to other people's attempts to engage him in simple conversation although at times he clearly understood simple speech, especially when it related to food or a favored object or routine. Parents often described this child as one who stayed in "his own little world," needing them mainly when in physical distress or if he wanted or disliked something. His signalling system under these conditions was rudimentary—only a cry, a tantrum, or leading the parent by the back of the hand. He did not signal by pointing or by serial pantomime as an aphasic child would. Between episodes of generalized and occasionally gross expressions of displeasure or pleasure, the child had a flat affect described by parents as a "don't care" attitude. At times, he "did not want his mother out of sight," and clung to her at every opportunity. If he talked, it was not to communicate. The child used objects and his own body repetitively and nonfunctionally but did not engage in role play.

Diagnostic Reliability

The behavior of children at initial evaluation was observed during two days and a night of hospitalization by ward staff, a speech pathologist, psychologists, and two psychiatrists. Also used were parental reports of current behaviors, which generally corresponded with staff observations. In most cases, the behavior of each child was fairly consistent among different observers. If the child was highly withdrawn from the ward staff, he was probably also withdrawn from the psychologist. If he used echolalic speech with the speech pathologist, he was echolalic with the psychiatrist. If behavior was inconsistent, we used the most prominent behavior to classify it.

About 8% of the cases presented problems in making a behavioral diagnosis. Sometimes a child would exhibit marked inconsistencies from examiner to examiner with respect to level of withdrawal or amount of noncommunicative speech. Sometimes a child's behavior overlapped two categories, most frequently the high and middle groups, such as when a child showed some emotional relatedness but had little or no communicative speech or vice versa. Because diagnostic features lie on a continuum, as nearly all human behaviors do, reliable diagnoses require constant feedback between diagnosticians as to the agreed-upon limits of normality and abnormality. In a series of 42 consecutively referred cases, two psychiatrists at our Center independently agreed in 97.6% of cases whether the child was autistic and in 92.8% on the subtype of autism.

In order to understand the degree of correspondence between our concept of infantile autism and those of other investigators whose diagnostic systems were widely used, we compared the DeMyer-Churchill classification system with four other systems (DeMyer, Churchill, Pontius, & Gilkey, 1971). While there were many statistically significant correlations among four different systems, the scores showed an overlap of no more than 45%. This means that a large proportion of children receiving high scores on one diagnostic scale would achieve low scores on another scale and thus be classified as autistic by one system and non-autistic by another. While questions may be raised regarding the compatability of various systems, our study served to suggest the degree of correspondence between the diagnostic systems of different sets of observers.

Diagnostic Features of Principal Control Groups

One of the crucial questions about autistic children was whether they were basically normal neurobiologically or whether they had some physical abnormality that affected the functioning of the central nervous system. If they were neurobiologically normal they should have resembled normal children neurobiologically. If they were neurobiologically abnormal, they should have been more like nonpsychotic subnormal children in their neurological signs and symptoms. Therefore logic demanded that we use at least two control groups of children: some who were behaviorally and physically normal and some who were subnormal in one or more intellectual skills but were not psychotic.

The criteria for normality were based on observations by the mother, teacher, and physician that the child's behavior was not appreciably different from that of his age-mates. A history of referral to a psychologist or psychiatrist was disqualifying. The child was then observed by staff members at the Research Center. Positive signs of normality were communicative speech commensurate with age level, relation with peers and parents free from serious problems, and at least average performance in school. Since many of our normal subjects were preschool children who had no nursery school experience, we substituted the opinions of Sunday School teachers and physicians about their intellectual and emotional adequacy. If a child's behavior deviated from normal, he was excluded from the study. The children were given adaptive or intelligence tests in many of our studies.

The diagnosis of nonpsychotic subnormality was made on the basis of subnormal performance in school or on pediatric observation that there was global intellectual defect or specific learning disorder, but no psychotic feature such as serious emotional withdrawal or nonfunctional use of objects. While about 95% of these children had some emotional problems, they were characteristically negativism or overdependency on their parents and immaturity in relating to other children. Parents often described them as wanting to play with younger children and liking to be with children but not knowing how to get along with them. Many had speech below age level in complexity but communicative in content. One additional requirement was that all psychotic and subnormal subjects in our study had to have the use of all four extremities, so that their life experiences with regard to motor activity were similar, and that the same motor and perceptual-motor tests could be used for both groups.

Additional Methods and Procedures

The methods of acquiring information were both formal and informal. Descriptions of the children's lives from gestation through about 4½ to 6 years of age came from a series of 9 semistructured intensive interviews with 33 couples who had an autistic child and with 33 couples whose children were developing within the limits of normality. The 33 normal index children were matched with the autistic index children for age, ordinal position in the family, number and sex of sibs, race, sex, socioeconomic status, and religion.[6] The average age of autistic children in the principal study happened to be 4 years and 3 months.

Interviews with parents were designed to gather information on most important aspects of child development (eating, sleeping, socialization, communication, play and toileting) as well as on their own personalities as individuals and marriage partners. While these interviews were structured so that the principal questions were asked in the same way of each parent, the interviewers were given some freedom in encouraging parents to talk by rephrasing questions and responding in an empathic way. When necessary, several attempts were made to elicit the required information. Most parents responded with comparative candor and ease to their interviewers, who were psychologists, psychiatrists, and a nursery school teacher. Mean interview time was 16.8 hours per parent couple.

Descriptions of the children's development from about 6 years of age to adulthood came from a formal follow up study of 120 autistic people and 36 learning-disabled children (DeMyer, Barton, Allen, & Steele, 1973) and from many "informal" consultations with parents when they or their children were having problems or, more happily, successes. For example, during the course of October, 1978, mothers of two young men who were first evaluated over a decade ago reported new events. One mother glowingly reported that her son was graduated from high school and had found a job. The other mother anxiously reported that her son was becoming "aggressive" on his job, and that his job supervisor had recommended consultation with a psychiatrist. Autistic adolescents and adults have talked to me about their successes and continuing problems.

The intellectual development of the children was studied not only through parental interviews but by extensive testing and retesting of about 147 children and adolescents (DeMyer, Barton, Alpern, Kimberlin, Allen, Yang, & Steele, 1974).

The statistical analyses for most of the data reported in this book have the form of chi square because of the discrete nature of most data. Where the data were continuous, paired t tests were used. In many cases, we collapsed adjacent rating items to avoid having too many marginal cells with an expected frequency of less than 5. The reporting of data in the text is as simple as possible as with rounded off percentages, in order to keep the narrative flowing. Significant features are indicated in most of the tables.

Extensive quotations from parents' statements are provided to illustrate the range of ideas and feelings expressed. In order to keep my promise to the parents that their confidences will not be revealed, some details that would have exposed the identity of parents had to be changed. All the children's names have been changed. Interrater reliability was 65 to 85%, being lower for subjective items. In all cases, quoted statements reflect the ideas of parents as closely as possible.

While no attempt has been made to be exhaustive in citing the work of other investigators, much of my knowledge has come from reading their works, and I have used some of their discoveries and insights to add to the observations of parents and the findings of our Research Center staff.

Notes

[1] A comment should be made about how the name for the Research Center was chosen. Before its establishment in 1961, Dr. Leo Kanner visited and talked with me about his views on the relationship of infantile autism to childhood schizophrenia. In his opinion, the relationship was not known. He suggested that I try to find out, preferably through study of both groups at as young an age as possible, whether or not infantile autism was the earliest form of childhood schizophrenia. At that time the staff had the

idea that a child with any communicative speech would not meet Kanner's criteria of infantile autism. Therefore we chose to call those socially withdrawn preschool children with some communicative speech by the diagnostic term "early childhood schizophrenia." As a working idea, we chose to think of infantile autism as the earliest form of childhood schizophrenia. Later, we found that nearly all our children, even those with some communicative speech, had the onset of their illness in the first 3 years of life. After Kolvin showed that the outcome of early-onset psychosis did not resemble the outcome of later developing childhood or adult schizophrenia, we changed our mind about the names of our three subgroups. On hindsight, it might have been more appropriate to have referred to autism rather than to schizophrenia in the name of our Center.

[2]This diagnostic system is similar to the concept of a triaxial diagnosis suggested by Rutter, Lebovici, Eisenberg, Sneznevsky, Sadoun, Brooke, & Lin (1969). The important exception is that in addition to a behavioral and intellectual axis, Rutter used an etiological axis, while our third diagnosis (or axis) was always a neurological one. We use the neurobiological axis rather than the etiological one because while evidence of neurobiological disfunction is found in most of our cases, the cause is usually unclear.

[3]In adopting the terms high, middle, and low function to identify three subgroups of infantile autism, the research staff changed the terms used in our publications prior to 1973. Most notable, the misleading term "schizophrenia" was replaced to bring our own terminology more in line with recent evidence and current usage. The change was in name only.

[4]Social age of children can be estimated using the norms derived by Gesell, Halverson, and Amatruda (1940). The Vineland Social Maturity Scale, which is commonly used to judge social age, is more appropriately thought of as a test of intelligence, since most items involve perceptual-motor and/or thinking skills.

[5]A question properly might be asked why more precise methods of measuring social distance were not devised, given the importance of the phenomenon in a diagnosis of autism. A project was initiated in the early 1960's in which 8 different types of social overtures were made by an examiner to autistic children. These included activities which typically interested children, such as ball play, doll play, drawing simple figures, and using preschool toys such as a ring stack set. After studying a group of autistic, normal, and subnormal children, I became less impressed with the productivity of studying social distance and more with that of studying the patterns of verbal and perceptual-motor assets and liabilities (DeMyer, Norton, & Barton, 1971). Other studies were pointing toward neurological deviations and a central language disability. Nevertheless, social distance remains an important diagnostic feature that needs to be measured, if for no other reason than to achieve diagnostic reliability between different investigators.

[6]A more complete description of the method can be found in Allen, DeMyer, Norton, Pontius, & Yang (1971). To satisfy the extensive criteria for matching the normal families, over 1,000 families were contacted. The clinical families were those consecutively referred to our Research Center over a 4-year period in the mid 1960s. We did not require that the parents be living together, but both parents had to be available in order to complete the interviews.

REFERENCES

Allen, J., DeMyer, M., Norton, J., Pontius, W., & Yang, G. Intellectuality in parents of psychotic, subnormal and normal children. *Journal of Autism and Childhood Schizophrenia*, 1971, 1, 311-326.

Alpern, G. D. Measurement of "untestable" autistic children. *Journal of Abnormal Psychology*, 1967, **72**, 478–486.

DeMyer, M. K. The nature of the neuropsychological disability in autistic children. *Journal of Autism and Childhood Schizophrenia*, 1975, 5(2), 109–128.

DeMyer, M. K., Barton, S., Allen, J., & Steele, R. Prognosis in autism: A follow-up study. *Journal of Autism and Childhood Schizophrenia*, 1973, 3(3), 199–246.

DeMyer, M. K., Barton, S., Alpern, G. D., Kimberlin, C., Allen, J., Yang, E., & Steele, R. The measured intelligence of autistic children: A follow-up study. *Journal of Autism and Childhood Schizophrenia*, 1974, 4(1), 42–60.

DeMyer, M. K., Churchill, D. W., Pontius, W., & Gilkey, K. A comparison of five diagnostic systems of childhood schizophrenia and infantile autism. *Journal of Autism and Childhood Schizophrenia*, 1971, 1, 175–189.

DeMyer, M. K., Norton, J. A., & Barton, S. Social and adaptive behaviors of autistic children as measured in a structured psychiatric interview. In D. W. Churchill, G. D. Alpern, & M. K. DeMyer (Eds.), *Infantile autism: Proceedings of the Indiana University Colloquium*. Springfield, Ill.: Charles C Thomas, 1971.

Eisenberg, L. The classification of the psychotic disorders in childhood. In L. D. Eron (Ed.), *Classification of behavior disorders*. Chicago: Aldine, 1966.

Gesell, A. L., Halverson, H. M., & Amatruda, C. *The first five years of life*. New York: Harper & Bros., 1940.

Kanner, L. Autistic disturbances of affective contact. *Nervous Child*, 1943, **2**, 217.

Kanner, L. Early infantile autism revisited. *Psychiatry Digest*, 1968, **29**, 17–28.

Kolvin, I. Psychoses in childhood—a comparative study. In M. Rutter (Ed.), *Infantile autism: Concepts, characteristics and treatment*. London: Churchill-Livingstone, 1971.

Rutter, M. Diagnosis and definition of childhood autism. *Journal of Autism and Childhood Schizophrenia*, 1978, 8(2), 139–161.

Rutter, M., Lebovici, L., Eisenberg, L., Sneznevsky, A. V., Sadoun, R., Brooke, E., & Lin, T-Y. A tri-axial classification of mental disorders in childhood. *Journal of Child Psychology and Psychiatry*, 1969, **10**, 41–61.

Chapter 2

GENETIC FACTORS, PREGNANCY AND LIFE FROM BIRTH THROUGH THE FIRST YEAR

Genetic factors, life inside the womb, birth, and the first year of life are critical to human development. A person can inherit an adequate or inadequate nervous system. During pregnancy and birth many events can damage the developing fetus. Unfortunately for the researcher studying this period after several years have passed, it is nearly impossible to obtain more than a hazy glimpse of factors which might have damaged a developing nervous system. For example, virus illnesses afflicting the pregnant mother which might have played a role can have the mild outward symptoms of a cold and be forgotten. Certain medicines may cause damage if taken at a certain time, varying for different drugs. Medicines, dosage and dates of intake are often unrecorded and forgotten. Moreover, medical science all too often cannot detect these untoward events even during on-the-spot observations. The damaging but overlooked event may be a mutated gene or a vascular accident or a "silent" infection. It is nearly as difficult to judge whether an infant illness has caused damage unless it is overwhelming.

The role of parenting in the critical first year is likewise difficult to study several years after the fact because we must rely on memories of people who made no systematic observations and who tended to be biased observers and reporters. Nevertheless, we combed the memories of these parents about the beginnings of their children's lives for the light they might shed on that vexing question: "Is infantile autism a result of defective nature or of defective nurture or even a combination of defective nature-nurture?" We knew we had to study the earliest medical and psychological events because the greatest proportion of autistic children showed deviations late in the first year and in the second year of life.

The results support the idea that most autistic children (about 88%) either while growing in the womb or during the first or second years of life, have probably sustained some neurobiological insult that impaired the function of the central nervous system. The results gain more importance when considered in conjunction with evidence from other studies showing similar impairment. Disappointingly, our parent interviews shed little light on the exact nature of the biological insult, except that there is some evidence of genetic defects in some cases and perhaps of viral illnesses in a few others. Some normal children also came from troubled pregnancies and difficult deliveries, but few of them showed signs of neonatal distress or unalert infancy.

We found no evidence that autistic parents differed from normal in planning for and accepting the pregnancy, in maternal response to the newborn, or in warmth, nurturance and appropriate stimulation during the first year of life. Nevertheless, autistic infants, like nonpsychotic handicapped infants, were less alert and less active than their sibs and their matched normal counterparts.

Similarities in Parental Attitudes Toward Pregnancy and Neonates

There were surprising similarities in planning for and accepting the pregnancies with the index children. We asked parents if it was a good time to have this baby, if they wanted the baby, and about the mothers' spirits during pregnancy. Unplanned pregnancies were reported in similar numbers for normals and autistics, namely 63%. After learning of the pregnancy, 60% of both groups said they mainly wanted the baby. Of parents who initially "didn't want" the pregnancy, all but 6% told us that somewhere in the course of pregnancy their feelings changed and they wanted the baby. Examples of types of parental reactions to index pregnancies are the following:

> Eva's mother: "I felt so good after the doctor told me I was pregnant that I bought a bottle of champagne. Gill and I gave a toast to her that evening. Eva was invited into our home."
> Donnie's mother: "My pregnancy was darned inconvenient. I remember how resentful I felt after the doctor told me. My husband was absorbed in business and money worries. We had let our medical insurance lapse too . . . He was shocked and angry after I told him

and I cried. We had one of our few shouting arguments. You know, it was a funny thing how quickly both of us got used to it and wanted him."

Another mother, representing the minority, reported the pregnancy "was the low point in our marriage. I was shocked at being pregnant. My husband hated it." Serious problems had marked the marriage of this couple since the birth of their first child and the marriage was a disappointment to both.

The reported mental health of mothers during pregnancies did not differ between the study groups. Four normal and 4 autistic mothers reported definite depressive symptoms. One autistic mother drank heavily and one mother of a normal child had at least a mild alcohol problem. In summary, there was no greater incidence of mental illness in mothers before their autistic infant was born than in mothers of normal children before the matched control child was born.[1]

Mother's Feelings Toward Neonates

Again, both normal and autistic mothers reported similar feelings on first holding the index infants in their arms. The raters found four types of maternal responses. The first and most common was a highly charged, positive feeling (autistic, 46%; normal, 39%). Barry's mother had difficulty putting the feeling into words, but the interviewer noted that a joyous expression filled her face as she tried to explain: "It was so big—I can't explain—oh, I just loved him so!" Eva's mother used the word "ecstatic." Other mothers said there was no other experience quite like it in their lives.

A more quiet positive feeling was recalled equally by both maternal groups (33%). Despite not wanting her pregnancy, even close to delivery date, Harold's mother had quiet but positive feelings for her newborn. She thought the feelings were about the same as for her other children, whom she had wanted. "I looked down at that little face and knew I wanted him," she said.

The third type of response (autistic, 6%; normal, 9%) was like that of Carrie's mother who felt rather distant when first holding the newborn. She said, "Oh, it always takes me about a week after I get home to feel motherly. There's nothing like caring for a baby to get me attached." Other mothers were worried about something and also needed the stimulus of taking care of the baby before they felt close. These characteristics show how important it is to have mothers care for their babies immediately after birth to facilitate the mother-infant bond.

The fourth type consisted of three mothers (autistic, 2; normal, 1) who were not happy to see their newborn infants and wished they had not been born. Mrs. A had just delivered her fifth baby and felt unequal to rearing another child. She reported telling the nurse who first brought the newborn to her: "I should say he is sweet, but we just have too many children."

Similarities in Parenting During the First Year of Life

If the nurture theorists were correct, we should have found important differences in parental attitudes and practices during that vitally important first year of life. Instead we found that autistic parents were much like normal parents in infant acceptance, nurturing warmth, and appropriate stimulation of the infant. For example, they reported a similar incidence of breast-feeding, talking and singing to the infant, rocking and cuddling, and exposure to outside social contacts.[2] Later we shall show how similar the autistic and normal parents were in approach to child rearing but how dissimilar the autistic and normal children were in response.

Evidence Against the Nature-Nurture Theory

Exponents of this theory assert that the autistic infant is born into the world physiologically "vulnerable" and that his parents fail to give him the extra emotional support and stimulation he needs. Such a lack of parental support is seen as causing the vulnerable infant to withdraw socially. To test this theory we used a third group of parents and their nonautistic learning-disabled children. If the nature-nurture theorists were correct, we should have found the learning disability parents to be at least as adequate as normal parents and more adequate than autistic parents taking care of the infant. Instead we found that learning disability parents put more pressure on their infant to wean, were less responsive to his crying, spent less time talking and singing to him, and were judged to be less warm. The failure to find specific parenting defects in autistic parents during that all important first year made the search for neurobiological defects, indirect as any such evidence has to be, all the more urgent.

Results Supporting Neurobiological Impairment in Autistic Children

The autistic infants had more signs of physiological and anatomical abnormality at birth than normal infants (see Table 4). To make these judgments we used physicians' and nurses' reports written at the time of delivery and in the newborn nursery. Autistic neonates as a group were less successful than normal neonates in feeding, breathing, oxygenation of the body, and neurological control. Two autistic neonates had seizures. However, only one autistic neonate was in such severe neonatal distress that the delivering physician was seriously concerned, and all but the three premature

Table 4. Physiological Problems in Neonatal Period

Problem	Autistic	Normal
Premature or low birth weight with complication	3	1
Premature or low birth weight without complication	0	3
Jaundice	1	1
Excess mucous	2	1
Ugly	4	5
Head molding	4	3
Blue, pale, anoxic	4	0
Seizures	2	0
Runny nose	1	0
Vomiting	4	1
Weak or absent cry	2	1
Too large	3	2
Not tolerate formula	2	1
Swallowing problems	3	0
Respirations difficult	1	0
Abnormal placenta or cord	3	0
Tumor	1	0
Clogged tear duct	0	1
Feeding problems	0	1
Excessive crying	1	0
Lethargic or frail	2	0
Excessive weight loss	1	0
Total number of problems	44	21
Cases reporting neonatal problems	22 (67%)	12 (36%)
Cases not reporting neonatal problems	11 (33%)	21 (64%)

$p < .02.$

infants came home in 3 to 5 days after delivery. The significant fact to note is that about two-thirds of autistic infants, in contrast to about one-third of normal infants had difficulties on a physiological level in becoming acclimated to life immediately after birth. It is also important to note that there was no clue from our data on how to distinguish clearly from physical examination records a newborn who would become autistic from one who would develop normally. Several normal neonates appeared to have had physiological problems immediately after birth of a type and severity equal to those of autistic neonates, although such judgment is again difficult to make from hospital records. There is a statistical relationship between neonatal problems and the development of infantile autism just as there is between prematurity and the development of learning problems later in life. These findings, while inferential, show that in the earliest days of life infants who later become autistic were more likely to have physiologically based problems than infants who developed normally.[3]

The neonates who later became learning disabled or mentally retarded showed about a 70% incidence of neonatal problems similar in character and type to those of autistic neonates. This incidence was not different from the 66% found among autistic infants.

The second line of evidence supporting neurobiological irregularity in autistic children came from parents' reports of differences between autistic infants and normal infants in alertness and activity. It is well documented that intelligence can be seriously compromised by an insult to the central nervous system during gestation, birth process, or formative years. Many nonpsychotic learning-disabled children have a history of an unusually irritable or unusually passive infancy. If we should find that autistic infants had less adequate intelligence than normal infants during the first year of life, such finding would add support for the nature causation theory especially since we found no significant differences in environmental factors (DeMyer, Pontius, Norton, Barton, Allen, & Steele, 1972). We asked parents if the autistic child was alert to and interested in his surroundings and if he understood the meaning of various events. Finally, we asked parents to compare the autistic infant with his siblings at the same age. We learned that autistic infants as a group were considered by their parents to be less alert and more passive than their siblings and normal controls.

Such finding by itself would have little import. First, it can be argued that the term "alertness" is a broad one and can be interpreted in many ways. Second, parents cannot be considered to be unbiased observers even when they are systematic, but they were our only observers of that important first year of life. The parental report is buttressed by the convincing detail of the autistic child's intellectual failures shortly thereafter in understanding the meaning of toilet training, of punishment, of rewards and of abstract speech.[4]

Searches for the Cause of the Neurobiological Disfunction

Since so many autistic children had physiological abnormalities immediately after birth and so many deficiencies of behavior and alertness in the first and second years, we searched for biological causes in genetics, pregnancy, delivery, and first and second year illnesses. Our search was rather disappointing, with the possible exception of genetic influences (see Table 5) and perhaps severe infantile illness in a few cases.

Siblings of autistic children did not have a significantly higher incidence of learning problems (plus speech problems) than siblings of normal index

Table 5. Incidence of Disabilities and Abnormalities of Possible Genetic Origin in 33 Families with an Autistic and 33 with a Matched Normal Child

Disability or abnormality	Family with autistic child		Family with normal child	
	Immediate	Extended	Immediate	Extended
Speech problems	4	5+	5	2
Learning disabilities or mental retardation	8	22	5	10
Down's Syndrome	2	2		1
Congenital anomalies		5	2	
Poor eyesight or eye muscle imbalance	3		1	
Coordination problems	3			
Seizures	2	5	2	1
Asthma	3			
Death in infancy	2	9	1	2
Miscellaneous	4	6+		1
Total	31	56	16	17

Family structure	Family with autistic child			Family with normal child		
	N	%	p	N	%	p
Immediate with abnormalities	15	45.4	$<.01$	9	27.3	$<.01$
Extended with abnormalities	23	69.7	$<.01$	10	30.3	$<.01$
Immediate *and* extended	11	33.3	$<.05$	1	3.0	$<.05$
Either immediate *or* extended	27	81.8	$<.05$	12	36.4	$<.01$
All siblings	59			67		
Siblings with abnormalities	21	35.6	$<.10$	14	20.8	$<.10$

children [autistic, 12/59 (20%); normal, 10/67 (15%)]. Three siblings of autistic children had moderate to severe mental retardation and the remaining nine had learning problems. All the learning problems of sibs of normal children were of borderline to mild severity. When we combined learning, speech, and physical defects, sibs of autistic children tended to have a greater incidence of such defects (autistic sibs, about 36%; normal sibs, about 21%). About 69% of autistic extended families were reported to have a member with a defect compared to about 30% of normal families. The differences was even more marked if we combined all members of all generations with defects (autistic families, 81%; normal families, 36%). Since we neither tested nor examined these sibs and extended family members, these reports must be considered as grossly approximate estimates.

Autistic parents in the intensive interview study were significantly older than normal parents at the birth of the index child (autistic mothers, 28.1 years; normal mothers, 24.6 years; autistic fathers, 30.6 years; normal fathers, 26.7 years). These age differences assume greater significance in view of the careful matching of index children to secure similarities in age of child and position in the family. It is well known that deficiencies in genetic material are more common with advancing maternal age. Several of the autistic mothers were in their late 30s and early 40s at the birth of their index child (Allen, DeMyer, Norton, Pontius, & Yang, 1971).

The most convincing evidence of a genetic component in autism comes from twin studies which were reviewed by Spence (1976) and by McAdoo and DeMyer (1978). The largest series of twin studies by Folstein and Rutter (1977) linked the basic disability to a cognitive-language disorder which in some cases appeared familial and in others connected with some kind of "biological hazard," usually perinatal in origin. They found a sample of 21 pairs of same-sex twins in which at least one twin was autistic. Eleven pairs were identical and 10 faternal. In four of the identical pairs, both twins were autistic, and in all except one pair, autism in one twin was accompanied by some cognitive abnormality such as unusual speech delay in the other. In all the pairs of fraternal twins, on the other hand, the nonautistic twin was perfectly normal. In the same study, autism was connected with perinatal insult. Of the 17 pairs of twins in which only one was autistic, there were 6 pairs in which the autistic twin had suffered possible or probable brain injury at birth, whereas in no case was this true of the nonautistic twin.

Folstein and Rutter conclude from their data that in some cases genetic factors seem both necessary and sufficient to cause autism, while in others the sole cause appears to be injury at birth. In the remainder, autism appears to result from a combination of brain damage and inherited cognitive defect. Spence's review (1976) hypothesized several specific genetic mechanisms, one of which is that certain aspects (or symptoms) of autism may be inherited while other symptoms may not.

If autism is inherited, according to Spence, the specific mechanism cannot involve a single gene or the chromosomes but would have to be polygenic or multifactorial. In conclusion, it appears that genetic inheritance can be involved in some cases but not in all, and that the insult to the central nervous system in other cases would have to come from biological hazards sustained in the womb, at birth, or in the first three years of life.

Pregnancy, Delivery Complications, and Childhood Illnesses

About half the mothers of both groups reported some pregnancy complication. However, in a larger series of cases (DeMyer, 1975), there was a

Table 6. Pregnancy, Delivery and Child Illness as Factors in Incidence of Possible Neurobiological Insults in Autistic Children

Factor	N	$\%$
Troubled pregnancy	16	48
Difficult labor	12	37
Illnesses in first year[a]		
Series of "cold-like" infections	3	9
Measles	1	3
High neonatal bilirubin	1	3
Illnesses in second year		
Measles	3	6
Severe diarrhea[b]	4	12
Illnesses in third year		
Butterfly rash	1	3
Nephritis	1	3

[a]Followed by change in behavior.
[b]Dehydrating.

difference in that mothers of autistic children reported more and, we believe, more serious illnesses during pregnancy than did those of normal children. This aspect of a medical history is the most difficult to obtain and to evaluate after the fact because fetal damage depends so much on the type, time, and severity of the maternal illness. Mothers of autistic children tended to have more complicated deliveries (autistic, 37%; normal, 27%). Here we relied not only on the mothers' memories but also on physicians' and hospital records though they varied in completeness. Again, this kind of evidence must be evaluated during delivery in order to be of use in finding the nature of the biological insult.

Biological irregularities in sleeping, eating, and elimination were more common in autistic than in normal children.[5] There were no significant differences in incidence of first year illness in the infant groups. However, at least three autistic infants had a series of infectious illnesses followed by a definite change in social behavior and alertness, although none of these illnesses were identified as ones that directly attack the central nervous system as do, for example, meningitis and encephalitis. In the second and third years of life, an additional 27% of autistics sustained an illness (apparently viral in most cases) followed by change in behavior.

In conclusion, we could identify a possible biologic cause for autism in

Table 7. Possible Neurobiological Insults per Autistic Case

Cause	N	%
No putative	4	12
One putative	7	21
Two putative	7	21
Three or more putative	15	46

about 88% of cases by looking at genetic factors, pregnancy, birth, and the first three years of life (see Table 7). However, after-the-fact study of such questions is grossly unsatisfactory. Society must mount solid research into ongoing events in order to locate specific biological causes of autism as well as of other types of learning disability and mental retardation. The value of the present gross studies is to direct our attention to the factors and period of life that must be studied.

Infantile Behaviors that Herald Autism

We were interested in the earliest heralds of autism and asked parents to use their hindsight to recall the earliest behavior they recalled as unusual in

Table 8. First Differences Noted by Parents of Autistic Children[a]

Symptoms during first year[b]	N	Symptoms during second year[c]	N
Slow or unusual motor development	6	Isolated self from people	2
Unresponsive socially	6	Stopped talking	2
Too placid	5	Hypersensitive to sound	2
Too irritable	4	Too irritable	2
Eye muscle imbalance (squint)	3	Excessive bouncing	1
Rocked/bounced excessively	3	Poor balance	1
Liked to be in one place always	2	Stopped walking	1
Poor sleep	2	Unusual fears	1
		Ran from mother in stores	1
		Over interested in books	1

[a] Retrospective observation (hindsight).
[b] 69%.
[c] 31%.

the infant or child. Most parents (about 69%) recalled these behaviors as occurring during the first year; the rest occurred in the second year. While there was a risk of getting parents to dredge up trivial behavior with such a question, actually most reported deviant behaviors seemed significant (see Table 8). They involved, for example, social unresponsiveness, unusual emotional responses, motor deviations, unusual apathy, and language problems. In many cases, such behaviors were not the first abnormal ones, but the important conclusion to draw from the parental observations is that an important behavioral abnormality was noted in each case during the first two years of life and often before the full-blown syndrome appeared. Such a finding, considered in conjunction with the high percentage of cases with neonatal abnormalities, made it imperative that we look for the cause or causes of autism in the earliest stages of life.

Depth of Parental Worry During the First Year

The first year of life was recalled by most parents as being the best of all years in the autistic child's development. About 88% of parents recalled either mild concern or none at all. Only 12% said they felt seriously worried about their infant's development. True, 40% of autistic parents felt mild worries, but in general the first year of life was experienced as the most worry-free year. Most parents on hindsight and after detailed questioning revealed differences from norms in the autistic infant's development, but few saw at the time major deviations from sibs' first year of development.[6]

One mother recounted a typical recollection of an autistic child's first year: "We thought he was the sweetest and perfectly normal. After his brother was born, we saw some differences. His brother was more demanding and active, but Rinny was cuddly and smiled and sat up and walked well."

Evan's mother said: "He used to stand in the corner of his playpen with his arms hooked around the railing and jiggle his feet. We though it was cute then, but I think now he must always have been abnormal." Evan was also more placid than his sibs.

This relatively worry-free first year was soon to change, for the autistic children were to reveal, in the second year of life, gross deficits in socialization, emotional equilibrium, language, and intellectual ability. Parental worries then began in earnest.

Notes

[1] The mental health of these parents will be discussed more fully in Chapter 10.

[2] Details of this study can be learned from DeMyer, Pontius, Norton, Barton, Allen, and Steele (1972).

[3] Barbara Fish, in a classic longitudinal study (Fish, Shapiro, Halpern, & Wile, 1965), followed 16 neonates, 3 of whom had physiological difficulties and "uneven neurological

28   MARIAN K. DeMYER

development." One infant in this group, whom she following into late childhood, developed childhood schizophrenia.

[4]These failures are described in detail in subsequent chapters.

[5]These will be discussed in detail in subsequent chapters.

[6]These deviations will be discussed in detail in chapters devoted to language, intelligence, socialization, eating, sleeping, elimination, and motor skills.

REFERENCES

Allen, J., DeMyer, M., Norton, J., Pontius, W., & Yang, E. Intellectuality in parents of psychotic, subnormal and normal children. *Journal of Autism and Childhood Schizophrenia*, 1971, **1**, 311–326.

DeMyer, M. K. Research in infantile autism: A strategy and its results. *Biological Psychiatry*, 1975, **10**(4), 433–452.

DeMyer, M. K., Pontius, W., Norton, J. A., Barton, S., Allen, J., & Steele, R. Parental practices and innate activity in normal, autistic, and brain-damaged infants. *Journal of Autism and Childhood Schizophrenia*, 1972, **2**(1), 49–66.

Fish, B., Shapiro, R., Halpern, F., & Wile, R. The prediction of schizphrenia in infancy: III. A 10-year follow-up report of neurological and psychological development. *American Journal of Psychiatry*, 1965, **121**, 768–775.

Folstein, S., & Rutter, M. Genetic influences and infantile autism. *Nature*, 1977, **265**(8), 726–728.

Folstein, S., & Rutter, M. Infantile autism: A genetic study of 21 twin pairs. *Journal of Child Psychology and Psychiatry*, 1977, **18**, p. 297.

McAdoo, W. G., & DeMyer, M. K. Research related to family factors in autism. *Journal of Pediatric Psychology*, 1978, **2**(4), 162–166.

Spence, M. A. Genetic studies. In E. R. Ritvo (Ed.), *Autism: Diagnosis, current research and management*. New York: Halstead/Wiley, 1976, pp. 169–174.

Chapter 3

SECOND THROUGH FOURTH YEAR OF LIFE

As the autistic infants in our study grew into toddlerhood, parental worries grew apace. A host of abnormal behaviors began to appear or worsen or to take on a new significance in minds of parents. For example, infants who rocked and banged their heads generally continued these activities into the second year and failed to learn new and more complex behavior. Parents were not concerned by infant body rocking but they worried about the 18-month-old who spent most of his time rocking. The few repetitive words uttered by some autistic infants failed to develop into useful speech or disappeared altogether. Those children not already showing signs of social isolation began to go to their rooms, to ignore their families and shun other children. Hyperirritability, hyperactivity, destructive and messy behaviors appeared. Each child developed some simple repetitive behavior with an object but didn't use it symbolically or as intended by the manufacturer. They flipped, spun, tapped, and mouthed their toys instead of pretending with them. Sleeping, feeding, and toilet training problems became prominent. Parental concerns and frustrations grew with each passing month as they found no way to help their autistic children "be normal."

Parental Reactions to Early Symptoms

Despite our asking detailed questions about the ages of appearance of individual symptoms, we found that many parents had difficulty remembering when a troubling individual symptom first appeared or worsened. Part of this uncertainty came from the slow onset of symptoms, part from the carry-over of symptoms from the first to second year, and part because experienced parents expected a 12- to 18-month-old to be emotionally labile and somewhat self-absorbed. In some cases, parents were inexperienced and didn't recognize behavior as abnormal. In other cases, experienced parents rejected what their senses told them and would not consider the early behavior to be abnormal. Most of these latter parents realized later how they had hidden the real import of the early symptoms from themselves. Here is how the parents of Albert (aged 4 at interview) discussed their early perceptions of his difficulties. The mother was a professionally trained woman who had worked several years with children and they had older, normal children.

Question: When did Albert's problems begin?
Father: Well, I guess they have probably always been.
Mother: But we didn't realize then—but I think in the back of our minds we knew.
Question: You say they have always been.
Father: Well, from the time normal children are supposed to do things, he didn't and you couldn't get him to do it. He ignored us.
Mother: He has never been able to play with children at all, and he has always fiddled with things. And when he was a baby he was almost too good, but he kicked his feet all the time. He tore up things with his feet because of the kicking. Noises scare him—he puts his thumbs in his ears.
Question: When did you first notice oversensitivity to noise?
Mother: I can't remember, but it's been a long time.
Question: How did you first begin to know something was wrong for sure?
Mother: My mother and his sister said so.
Father: Now, we kind of knew he was slow.
Mother: Yes, but I know children grow in spurts and I thought he was in a slow period and would come out of it. I guess you kid yourself. But my mother took me aside and said that she and his sister were sure something was wrong. I was furious at them for awhile, but then I finally realized they were really concerned and we went for help. The doctor said he was sure something was wrong too, and we came here. We were surprised and shocked at what we learned.
Question: Even though you had some idea before?
Mother: It was subconscious, because it was really a shock.

Through subsequent similar interchanges, Albert's parents revealed a host of other problems such as repetitive echolalic speech, eating dirt, running away, spinning the wheels of his tricycle rather than peddling it, and periods of frantic crying. They revealed their deep worries about the future if he didn't start progressing soon and their puzzlement about the best way to handle him.

As the raters examined all the parental accounts of onset of illness, there emerged three chief types of history. The first type was exemplified by the children like Albert who had "always been different" (about 35%). A second type had a "turning point" or setback (about 45%) as typified by Jerrold, aged 5½ years at interview time.

Question: Tell me when Jerrold's problems began.
Father: I'd say about 2 years old, I guess. He wouldn't talk the way he should. Before that he looked normal.
Mother: Until you start looking real close. There was nothing outstanding but something happened to him, maybe about 15 months. There was a turning point. (Jerrold had measles about one month before onset, but mother never connected this illness with the onset, and of course, it would be conjecture for us to do so.)
Question: What was the first indication you noticed?
Mother: Well, first he seemed too quiet, but so was my first child—but Jerrold would go off to the bedroom by himself. He was such a little guy. I would go look and maybe he would be just sitting up asleep. And this was the turning point, where he was going off by himself. He sat down and quit walking. It seemed like something frightened him so bad. And he kept looking up and hiding his eyes. But thinking back at 15 months—it was just little things. Then at some time he started spinning everything and ignoring us.

In the third type of onset (about 20%), the children seemed to have had a fairly normal first year but then failed to keep up with normal milestones. Kitty, age 5 years, typified this type of onset. Her mother said:

She was so much like the others until—oh, I'd say about 2 or maybe a little younger. It's hard to remember. But I noticed she just didn't do the things she was supposed to do; and then she didn't play with other children and had those screaming spells that lasted and lasted.

To date the onset of illness for each child, which again was difficult to do, the raters read several interviews in addition to the first one of the series which dealt specifically with the onset and progress of symptoms. The reason for so doing was that many parents seemed overanxious in the first interview and genuinely could not remember certain details that emerged more clearly in later interviews when they were more relaxed. In many cases, going back to a subject a second time, as we did for important topics, facilitated recall. The raters used social withdrawal and unusual emotional responses as major criteria to rate onset during infancy, as infants could not be expected to demonstrate distinctively noncommunicative speech and nonsymbolic use of objects. For the second and third years of life, the latter two criteria were also used. The age of onset for the greatest proportion (about 44%) was between one and two years and the next was in the first year of life (about 31%). The remainder (about 26%) were between 2 and 3 years of age or "around" 3 years at onset.

Course of Symptoms

The autistic child was generally perceived by his parents as being most severely disturbed between the ages of 2 to 4 years (about 78% were so reported) (see Table 9). Several factors beside the severity of the autistic child's symptoms seemed to determine parents' response to the question: "Was there a time in your child's life when his or her problems were worse than at other times?" The parents' own uncertainties, anxieties, and feelings of helplessness with respect to effective action for their child appeared to color their responses. During periods when they felt alone and without prospects for help, they seemed to experience their child's problem as the most severe. The accuracy of their recollections is also questionable because they tended to lose track of when events occurred, months to years in the past. Despite these qualifications, it does appear that the autistic child is most likely to be at his worst symptomatically

Table 9. Age of Onset and Symptoms at Worst in Autism

Chronological age[a]	Age distribution at initial evaluation and intensive interview of child		Age of onset (%)	Symptoms at worst (%)
	N	(%)		
0–1			31	3
1–2			44	8
2–3	3	9	22	46
3–4	10	30	3	32
4–5	9	27	0	8
5–6	6	18	0	3
6–7	5	15	0	0

[a] Median and average age = 4 yrs and 3 months.

Table 10. Onset of Serious Parental Worry

Period of onset	N	%
First year	1	3
Around 18 months	6	18
Around 2 years	7	21
Between 2 and 3 years	9	27
Around 3 years	7	21
Between 3 and 4 years	2	6
Around 5 years	1	3

between the ages of 2 and 4 years with respect to speech, social relatedness, and general disposition. It is also the period during which the parents have become painfully and irrevocably aware that their child is not going to "snap out of it."

The median age of the children when we intensively interviewed their parents was 4 years 3 months, and this too affects the data given in Table 9. If 50% of the children at the time of initial evaluation were 4 years and 3 months and below, then at least 50% of the sample would have to have had their worst period below that age. In actuality, 89% of the children were reported as being at their worst before the fourth birthday. Ninety-five percent of this sample of autistic children were reported by their parents as being noticeably and globally different from other children before their third birthday and 75% before their second.

While no two children were exactly alike in appearance and course of symptoms, it is possible to summarize these events for the group roughly as follows: Onset of initial symptoms was insidious and occurred in the latter part of the first through the second year of life. The symptoms became more severe over a few months to a year and then improved slowly as the children approached and passed their fourth birthdays. Seven children (21%) were reported to have become worse or more difficult to handle the older they became. About 70% showed improvement after a "worst" period. Nine of those children showing improvement were seen by the parents as undergoing remarkable improvement in speech or emotional response during a few months or a year before we saw them for the initial evaluation. Despite improvement, each autistic child still displayed severe social isolation, severe language defects, and nonsymbolic use of objects.

Parental Reactions to Worsening of Symptoms

There was a nearly universal response to symptom worsening. The parents worried. In contrast to the first year of life, when parental worries were mild or absent, by the time the autistic child was 3 years of age about 91% of the parents were definitely worried that their child was seriously different from other children his age. For roughly half of the parents, their serious worries started before or by the time their child was 2 years old. Only two sets of parents began their serious worrying as late as 4 to 5 years of age and only one set after the fifth birthday. One couple claimed that they really never seriously worried about their autistic child but came for treatment only at the urging of other people.

The following account of growing parental concern is fairly typical of most autistic parents. Mickey's parents were a little more graphic than most, but the chief worry elements of this story were expressed by all parents at one point or another.

Mickey's mother:

When Mickey was a real little baby he didn't sleep much but he was happy and smiled and cuddled and gained weight. I think even on hindsight he was not much different from our other children at that age. However, on hindsight, I think we should have begun worrying when he was 10 months old, but he was our first. His grandparents gave him a teddy bear, and they put it on his high chair tray so that he could play with it. He gave a loud agonized shriek and picked it up by the ears and deliberately dropped it to the floor. We thought that was funny then. He always actively shunned that teddy bear. I think he didn't like its face.

About that time, he paid less attention to us and turned his face when we talked to him. By the time he was a year old, we were definitely worried and so was our doctor. By the time he was 18 months old, I was frantic with worry. Our doctor was concerned about Mickey's hearing. Many times he acted as if he didn't hear, and we saw a hearing specialist who said he could hear. We had so hoped a hearing aid would be all Mickey needed.

After that, we had a series of appointments with various kinds of doctors. My husband and I became more alarmed after each specialist saw him. We could see that each doctor was seriously concerned, but nobody could tell us what to do. One doctor said we were the cause, but wouldn't even discuss how we caused it. Each time we saw another doctor we became more confused. Also Mickey got progressively more withdrawn that year and screamed a great deal. Somewhere around his second birthday, he became very destructive. My husband and I look back on his second and third years with wonder that we didn't go mad or end up divorced.

Parental worries of the typical autistic mother in the second and third years grew by leaps and bounds until finally thoughts about the autistic child crowded out most other concerns. We discovered this degree of maternal concern by asking the following questions: "What do you think about most of the time? Is there any thought you can't get out of your mind?" Nearly 75% of autistic mothers reported that the autistic child and his problems were never far from their thoughts. In contrast, few of the autistic fathers or normal parents so reported. This question was designed to uncover obsessive thoughts. Only one autistic mother seemed to have genuine obsessive thoughts. The others were reacting in a predictable way to a situation in which a child was developing abnormally and for which they could find no satisfactory solution.

The mother of Stan said, "Stan is what I think about the most—what I can do to help him. I have four other children and a job that I think about too. No matter what else is on my mind, I know thoughts of Stan are just under the surface."

Most mothers began to worry earlier in the child's life than the fathers did, and they worried harder, probably because they spent more time with their children and were more knowledgeable and sensitive to deviations from developmental norms. Mack's mother: "I knew something was wrong with him. My husband just kept telling me that everything was all right. He didn't see all the things I saw all day long. I felt so alone in my worry."

What kinds of infant and child behavior caused so much worry in parents of autistic children? In the first interview, the psychiatrist asked for a description of all the problems that led the parents to seek help. While nearly every aspect of child development caused concern, the following abnormalities were named for each autistic child: inability to relate to others in socially appropriate ways, inability to communicate and learn through language, unusual emotional expression, and abnormal play. The first three topics are discussed in later chapters of this book.

Abnormal play of autistic children involved omission of three features routinely found in the play of normal children 2½ years old and older: acceptance of other children, ability to pretend, and ability to understand rules. Autistic children spent most of their time in endless and solitary repetitive activities. About 80% of the children would do such things as rock, bounce, stare at their posturing hands, flip, spin, tap, or mouth objects (see Table 11).

Robin's mother said, "In the spring time, he goes out in the yard and picks up a long piece of grass or an iris leaf and waves it in front of him. Oh, how he hates to be interrupted in this. He'll just carry on if you try to get him interested in something else."

Rupert liked to rock and bounce. His father said, "He wore out a couple of rocking horses." Other children sat on couches and rocked vigorously, hitting the back of the couch with their backs and heads or stood up and rocked sidewise from foot to foot.

Jeremy walked around in a circle looking at his outstretched hand which he

Table 11. Incidence and Severity of Repetitive Bodily Behaviors

Type of repetitive behavior	Autistic		Normal	
	Incidence %	"Very much" of the time %	Incidence %	"Very much" of the time %
Non-hurtful[a]				
Rock or bounce	78	36	33	3
Mouths objects	75	24	48	0
Stare at hands/lights/objects	70	21	9	0
Masturbate	63	6	45	0
Circle, whirl, pace	61	12	27	0
Hand-arm posturing	57	21	3	0
Flip, spin, tap objects	54	27	9	0
Toe walk	54	12	33	3
Suck thumb	24	3	27	6
Self-hurtful[b]				
Bites nails, pulls out hair	21	3	18	0
Bang, hit head	45	12	9	0
Mutilate body	42	12	3	0
Accident prone	60	3	69	0

[a]71% engaging in one or more non-hurtful behaviors "very much" of the time (vs. 6% for normals).

[b]8–24% engaging in self-hurtful behaviors "very much" of the time (vs. 0.0 for normals, $p < .01$).

put in strange positions. Stan "sighted down the slats of his crib or down any horizontal object like fence rails." Such unusual play made a child appear odd to other observers and impressed on the parents "how different he was from other children." No two autistic children were exactly alike in their repetitive activities, but all lacked the three elements of normal play. The parents described the missing elements thusly:

> Harold won't have anything to do with other children. He ignores them. He simply doesn't understand how to play house. All he wants to do is line toys up in rows. Then he sits down and rocks and stares at his lines of toys.
>
> Other children don't mean a thing to Joan. She just wants to be left alone to talk to herself and look at her catalogues. They try to make

her play like at a tea party, but she just cries or walks away. She can't even understand a game of tag and yet she loves to be chased at times.

Thus we see that parents described both social and intellectual failure, the latter involving failure to symbolize and to understand rules.

Destructive Activities

Among the most worrisome of repetitive activities was destructive behavior. Some children "literally got the house in a shambles" by pulling down drapes or picking things to pieces that had a defect in them. Most of the destructive behavior was a by-product of other repetitive activities such as pulling, pounding, throwing, or shaking things. Some children repetitively threw things down stairways or out of windows, apparently just for the love of throwing. No parents, even those whose children threw things, saw their autistic children as destructive with conscious intent. As Rupert's mother said, "He doesn't do those things on purpose. He isn't mad. He just pulls on anything that's loose—he'll pull on the drapes or on the tablecloth. He's so active that he'll hit a lamp or stumble over a cord, and there goes another lamp." Intense rocking could destroy high chairs, beds, and sofa backs. Most parents felt punishment was useless to curb these activities and they "child-proofed" their houses.

Most keenly felt by the parents were the self-destructive acts which in a few cases were so severe that they were life-threatening. Eliza, in her worst periods, picked bleeding sores, banged her head on walls, and kicked her legs with her feet. Her mother observed that she looked like descriptions she had read of a battered child. Larry hit his chin as much as several hundred times an hour and it swelled "to the size of a red grapefruit." These cases required hospital treatment and even then control was only partially successful. The parents' reaction was to try anything that would help protect the child. Eliza's parents found that it helped to hold her for hours during her worst periods. Tying Tim's hands lightly behind his back with a single length of string helped him control himself even though he could easily break the string with one tug. The parents' psychological position was described by one mother as "just hanging on." That is as good a description as I can think of. There comes a point where parents need relief from trying to manage severe self-destructive activity just to preserve their health and that of their other children.

Most children's self-mutilative activities were not severe and could be dealt with by ignoring them and being careful not to reward them. We found that about 45% of autistic children banged or hit their heads or mutilated their bodies. In about 15% of cases such mutilation was a moderate problem and in only about 6% a severe problem. When severe, however, there is no worse problem for the parent or the doctor to try to relieve.

Differences from Normal Children

We did find that normal children engaged in every type of repetitive activity that autistic children used. However, only three normal children were scored by their parents as doing something repetitive "very much of the time." In contrast, 85% of autistic children were scored as performing one or more repetitive routines "very much of the time." Those repetitive behaviors mentioned most rarely for normal children (9% or less) were putting hands in strange postures, staring fixedly at lights or objects, self-mutilation, head banging, and flipping, spinning, or tapping objects.

While masturbation was more common in autistic than in normal children, it was seen as a "real problem" in only 6%. One 6-year-old autistic boy "constantly" handled his penis. His mother said, "I get pretty tired of it. He does it everywhere."

What Happened?

After exploring the changes that occur in autistic children after the first year of life, one wonders what caused them. What happened to convert these unusually placid, good babies into overactive, overirritable, unsociable young children? We have already seen that in the first year of life the autistic parents as a group were no less warm or stimulating than parents of normal and nonpsychotic handicapped groups of children. Could some change have occurred in them during the second and third years? Did they approach their autistic children differently or did the difference in the autistic children elicit a different type of parental response?

In chapters to follow, I will explore these questions, choosing as subject matter other main aspects of early child development: social-emotional behavior, speech, eating, sleeping, toileting, general intelligence, graphic activities, and music. In each section, parental responses to problems and approaches to solutions will be described. In each chapter, comparisons of normal and autistic children will be given in detail, for such comparisons allow the neuropsychological handicaps of autistic children to stand out in bold relief.

Chapter 4

PROBLEMS WITH SPEECH AND COMMUNICATION

Speech and communication problems were uppermost in the minds of most parents of autistic children when they were interviewed by a psychiatrist at initial evaluation. In nearly every case, parents named communication difficulty as being one of the main reasons they came to the Research Center to get help for their autistic child. In 36% of cases the parents reported it as being the problem that worried them the most. In our scientific work at the Research Center we have come to the conclusion that the central problem of the autistic child is his language difficulty. Even if he has many imitative words at his command, the autistic child probably lacks the central neurological language equipment to generate creative speech or understand more than the simplest of verbal abstractions. The parents were right to be concerned about the autistic child's lack of useful speech and his inability to converse. They were right to be puzzled if their autistic child could echo TV commercials but not talk to them. This chapter focuses on parents' description of their child's speech development and on parental reaction to the frustration of not being able to talk with their child. It will instruct parents and professionals in the uncertainties that parents have to live with as an autistic child develops or does not develop speech. Perhaps it will teach all of us some realism about autistic children without causing us to give up hope and will spur us to new research for locating physical causes and preventive measures since treatment is not as effective as we would like. The best treatment will probably be prevention.

Character of Infant Crying

Crying, the first vocal signal of the infant, is in the first weeks merely a reflex response to discomfort; then it becomes also a conditioned stimulus or a planned signal. We asked parents about three aspects of infant crying: its character, amount, and sending power. Overall, when parents remembered a difference in the amount of crying it was in the direction of less crying than sibs (autistic, 21%; normal, 15%). About 9% of parents of an autistic child thought his crying was excessive, while only 3% of parents of matched normal children thought so. Most autistic parents (70%) said there was no difference in amount of crying.

When we analyzed the differences in sending power of the infant cries, we found that about 27% of autistic mothers remembered that they could not "read" the cries of their autistic infants as well as they could those of their other children at the same age. Furthermore, these mothers reported that they felt it was not their inexperience that led to the deficit.[1] If it was a first child, the mothers were apt to blame themselves at the time; but, on hindsight, after the advent of their second child, they realized there was a difference in the sending power of their autistic infant's cries.

The deficit seemed to stem from three sources. About 9% of autistic infants "almost never" cried in their first year. The mothers relied on the clock or close observation for dirty diapers, for example, as these infants also did not use any body signals to indicate distress. The other autistic infants had one type of cry for everything and often could not be comforted no matter what the parents tried. Joan's mother said, "Joan has always been less expressive than the others. Her cry was more like a scream and she cried a lot, especially in the middle of the night. It was frustrating because we couldn't tell what was wrong or comfort her." Herbert's mother said, "He never cried—never. I had to watch him close for feeding time and changing him. He wouldn't let me know if he hurt."

Many parents in both groups were uncertain about remembering these characteristics of infant cries but most tried to answer the questions. The premature infants of both groups were described as crying less at first than their sibs and then crying the same amount after the first 3 or 4 months of life. One premature autistic infant never did cry much. It must be emphasized that about 60% of autistic parents recalled no differences in amount or character of autistic infants' cries. However, only two normal mothers reported a normal infants' cry that seemed to be innately hard to interpret.

One normal infant seldom cried but when he did it was a "frantic" cry which was difficult to soothe.

In summary, autistic infants tended to be different from normal infants in that more of them were reported as innately lacking in the sending power of their infant cries. This lack was manifest in infrequent to almost complete absence of crying and no substitute body language, in having one cry for everything, and in being very difficult to comfort when crying. No normal infant was described as being almost completely without crying and only two normal infants were described as being so deficient in sending power that the mother could not understand what they wanted.

Infant Babbling in Comparison to Siblings

Speech has its roots in the babbling of infancy which starts with cooing and crowing and progresses to more complex babbling until, at about the age of 11 months, most normal infants begin to say a few recognizable words. Despite the mother's doubts about the accuracy of their memories of infant babbling (about 50% of both groups felt quite uncertain),[2] we asked them to answer to the best of their ability whether their autistic infant babbled as much or as complexly as their normal infants did.

Table 12 shows that about 52% of autistic infants were different in some way from their sibs in babbling, while only 9% of normal infants differed from their siblings. Most mothers recalled that their autistic child babbled less than his sibs. Only 15% of autistic parents recalled that the babbling was different in character; e.g., that it was less varied or, for example, "a high-pitched squeal." One mother said one of her normal children acted "happier" when she babbled, but 79% of normal infants were recalled as being about like their normal sibs in amount and character of babbling.

We asked parents whether they imitated the babbling of their infants. About half the parents could not remember at all and would not hazard a

Table 12. Infant Babbling in Comparison to Babbling by Siblings

Infant babbling	Autistic		Normal	
	N	%	N	%
Amount higher	1	3	3	9
About same in character and amount	10	30	26	79
Amount less or of different character	17	52	3	9
Did not remember at all	5	15	1	3

$p < .01$.

Table 13. Milestones in Normal Speech Development from 1 to 6 Years

Chrono-logical age (months)	Expression	Comprehension
11	Uses 1–3 *meaningful* words.	Comprehends "no".
18	Uses 10–15 words.	Comprehends simple one-step commands ("Give me"; "Sit down").
24	Uses 100–200 words (25% intelligible). Connected phrases of 2–3 words used for a purpose ("Go bye-bye"; "Want cookie"). Verbalizes immediate experiences. Pronouns appear. Asks "what" questions.	
36	Uses 300–500 words (50% intelligible). Three words per speech attempt. Carries on simple conversation and verbalizes past experiences. Asks "Where" and "Who" questions.	Comprehends prepositions and two related commands.
48	Uses 600–1000 words (100% intelligible). Four words per speech attempt. Asks "why and how" questions.	Comprehends three related commands with practice. (54 months)
60	Articles appear. Asks meaning of abstract words.	Comprehends abstract dependent clauses introduced by "if," "because," "when," "why".
72	Uses 1500–2000 words. Uses compound and complex sentences.	

guess. Of those that remembered, about half said they did. Several normal parents and two autistic parents emphatically said they never imitated babbling because "We don't believe in baby talk," fearing that parental babbling would encourage infantile or poorly pronounced speech. About half of the autistic parents believed their autistic infants never made pre-speech imitative sounds, while only two normal parents gave this response. However, again about half of all parents could not recall the pre-speech, vocal imitative skills of their children.

In summary: Despite about half the parents saying their memories were hazy on the subject, we can conclude that autistic infants as a group probably babbled and imitated pre-speech sounds less than their sibs in the first year of life.

Adequacy of Early Speech Development
(From about 11 months to 3 years)

In hearing parental accounts of earliest speech development, one may get a strong impression that many autistic children have once "talked normally." In light of parents' intense desire to have their autistic child turn out all right and their belief that learning to talk is one of the important keys to normal development, it would not be surprising if parents inflated the adequacy of any early speech.

The interviewer who hears the statement from parents that their autistic child once "talked normally" must take a detailed history of when the infant first said recognizable words, how many words were said in the second year of life, when two words were first put together, and the first appearance of sentences. After so doing, the interviewer can then compare the autistic child's first speech with that of norms developed by people such as Gesell and Amatruda (1965). Table 13 can be consulted for important early milestones of speech development in normal children as the following section is read.

In order to evaluate early speech development, we asked detailed questions about the age speech developed and how it developed during the second and third years of life with respect to number of words, sentences, meaningfulness of speech, and communicative properties. We also asked about auditory characteristics and sounds not amounting to speech. A detailed analysis of parents' responses failed to confirm the parental hope that the autistic children may have normal speech locked within them because they once talked normally. The following abnormal characteristics of early autistic speech were described:

(1) In the first year of life, the average normal infant says 1 or 2 words plus "mama" and "dada." These words are used meaningfully. About 75% of autistic infants failed to reach that milestone. About half were definitely late in saying their first words; i.e., they spoke not until the second or third years or not at all (see Table 14). Terry's mother said, "The only thing I recall her saying was at 13 to 14 months, 'night-night,' 'bye-bye,' and 'eyes.' Then she quit saying any of these things, as best as I can remember, from 18 months on until about the age of 3½ to 4 years."

Table 14. Parental Recollection of Age when Autistic and Normal Controls Uttered First Words

Period	Autistic[a]		Normal	
	N	%	N	%
Before 12 months	5	15	23	70
Around 12 months	11	33	4	12
13 to 18 months	9	27	4	12
19 to 24 months	2	6	1	3
After 2 years	2	6	1	3
Never or highly doubtful if ever	4	13	0	0

[a] $p < .01$.

(2) In about half of autistic cases the first words lacked meaning but not in any normal cases. Jack's mother said, "He said a few words at about 12 months, but I never thought he connected them with anything."

(3) In the second year of life, the normal child at 18 months of age knows and habitually uses about 10 to 15 words. By 24 months, he knows and uses about 200 words, a number the average parent does not bother to count. Only one autistic child met this normal standard, and his speech was noncommunicative. About 89% of autistic children acquired 15 words or fewer during their second year, a grossly deficient number (see Table 15).

As the normal child acquires more and more words, he seldom loses previously acquired words. The autistic child who developed 15 or more words in his second year may not have this stepwise increase in number, as Merrill's mother described:

Table 15. Number of Words Used by Autistic Children in Second Year of Life

N of words	N	%
None	4	13
Only 1 to 2	13	40
3 to 15	12	36
16 to 60	4	13
Too many to count	1	3

The thing that stands out most in my mind about him in his second year was that he didn't build on his vocabulary like the other kids. They would start out with a few words; then close to 2 years of age their speech would blossom. Merrill learned a few words at about 14 months. Later he got a few more words, but he stopped using the words he learned earlier. He had favorite words like "train" which he used a lot for a few weeks; then we never heard it again. We waited for that flowering of speech and when it didn't happen we were definitely concerned. He never stopped saying words completely, but he never improved either.

Charles' mother replied this way to the question, "When was it that Charles made sounds you could identify as words?"

He started at 1 year saying "baba" for bottle and "toast" for breakfast. He also said "mama" and "dada," but he never called us that—these were words he mimicked for awhile. These words disappeared and he seldom picked up any more, but he went into jabbering. At 2½ to 3 years, he wasn't talking any better than at a little past a year.

(4) Combining of words into phrases and sentences was delayed for nearly all the autistic children in this sample. By 21 months of age, normal children habitually put 2 words together. By the age of 2½ years, the normal child habitually uses 3-word creative sentences (see Table 16). About 45% of autistic children never used a sentence in their lives. Those sentences used were almost always echolalic. Some could repeat long sentences of other people but never used language creatively.

(5) Conversational speech begins in the normal child at about 2 years of

Table 16. Sentence Use of Autistic Children

Sentence use	%
Never uses sentences	27
Used an occasional 2-word phrase	18
Echoed one sentence only	9
Echoed several sentences	9
Echoes occasional sentences	9
Uses sentences at least several times a week: echolalia and echo-communicative	15
Uses sentences as in item 6 and occasional 3-word original sentences	12

age. By 3 years the normal child habitually carries on simple conversations. None of the autistic children could converse.

(6) Nearly all autistic children with enough speech to rate had one or more of the following abnormalities: reduced frequency of speech (about 90%); poor diction (about 50%); disorder in rhythm, tone, or stress (dysprosody, about 75%); and too fast a rate of speech (about 13%).

(7) At the age of 24 months, the normal child begins to use pronouns correctly, which demands that he be able to think abstractly. None of the autistic children could use pronouns at the usual age.

Progress in Speech Development Between the Ages of 3 and About 6½ Years

In the interim between the earliest speech development and interview time (mean age of children 4 years 3 months), we found that some children had made some progress in their speech. Unfortunately, the progress was limited and generally featured an increase in the number of words repeated by rote. The speech features the parents most longed to hear, namely the ability to converse and to verbalize thought processes, did not materialize. In a few instances, some autistic children used brief simple speech to communicate an immediate need or created a 3-word sentence, but most parents remained intensely concerned about speech disability. Let us examine the specific nature of the progress.

Of the 16 children who had stopped using words, only 4 (25%) had regained use of words and made some progress thereafter. There were 12 children who did not entirely cease using words and 9 of them (75%) had made some progress by interview time (see Table 17). This means that roughly 40% of the sample had made some kind of progress in speech.

The entire group of children could be divided into three major groups with respect to useful speech at interview time (see Table 18):

Table 17. Types of Autistic Speech Development after First Words Were Heard

Type of speech development	%
Word use stopped. Not regained by evaluation time	36
Word use stopped and regained with slow progress by evaluation time	12
Word use remained at about 12 month level during second year of life, then slow progress	27
Word use remained at infant level	9
No infant words and no subsequent words gained	13

Table 18. Autistic Children's Speech at Evaluation Time[a]

Type of speech	%
No words	27
Infrequently says a word or noncommunicative echolalia	37
Frequent noncommunicative echolalia and infrequent communicative echolalia	24
Combination of communicative and noncommunicative echolalia and 3-word creative sentences	12

[a]Mean age = 4 years 3 months.

(1) About 64% had no useful speech at all; i.e., essentially, they used no speech to communicate their immediate needs. Of this group, a little less than half never spoke a word and the rest infrequently echoed a word or a short sentence.

(2) About 25% used echolalia fairly frequently and in some instances used it communicatively. An example of this type of child was Evan (age 4½ years) whose chief speech was murmuring to himself bits of poetry, songs, and some words used by his family. On occasion, however, he would communicate to his family in the following way: "He might go to the door and say, 'Do you want to go outside?' He says it just like a question, but we know he's telling us that he wants to go outside." This was the first way Evan told them that he wanted to do something other than by screaming or simply standing in front of something that he wanted. Evan's mental capacity was not advanced enough so that he could perform the necessary mental operations to understand the meaning and proper use of pronouns. He was, however, beginning to understand that speech could be used communicatively. Another child substituted the echolalic sentence, "He wants a drink." for his previous behavior of standing in front of a sink when he wanted water.

(3) The least common pattern was found in only about 12%. The difference from pattern #2 was that communication was more frequent, although echolalia continued to be dominant and the most often used communicative mode. In addition, these children occasionally said a few, simple creative 3-word sentences. Ken, age 6 years 10 months and the oldest child in the sample, began to use some creative speech at close to age 6 after he had stopped using words altogether in his third year. His mother responded this way to the question: "How much difficulty does he have in expressing what he wants?"

Now he doesn't have too much. Before (up to about age 4½), we couldn't tell what he wanted. Between the ages of 4½ and 5, we could tell some. Then between 5 and 6, he got better. Now he says, "I want ice cream" or one word like "ice-water." He still doesn't put sentences together very good.

None of the children were considered by the parents to carry on true conversations with anyone. By age 4, the normal child can carry on a long and involved conversation. Walter's mother said, "Up until a year ago, all he did was repeat words. Now (at age 6) he may ask for things, but he doesn't converse with us. His speech is an incessant mimicking of things other people say or of TV commercials." Martin's mother said, "Marty can't converse. He may ask for something very simple like a drink. If he hurts someplace, he can't tell me where it is. I have to guess. He can't answer a question and so any kind of conversation gets stopped at the beginning."

The capacity for abstract speech was still very underdeveloped. Only one child answered simple "what" and "where" questions and none answered simple "why" questions. One parent said, "She can say almost anything and she can answer a question like 'What is that?' or 'Where are you going?', but if you ask her a question about something intangible, she won't answer you." Only two children used pronouns with even partial correctness and only one, the oldest child, used them correctly most of the time.

Even so basic a conversational tool as the concept of "yes" was not understood by 90% of the children. "Yes" is a word used by normal 3-year-olds. Breon's father described this problem: "Sometimes he says 'yes,' but we don't know if he really means it or even really knows the meaning of 'yes.' I asked him if he wanted to go to the store with me and he said 'yes.' When I put on his coat, he acted like he didn't want to go." Breon's mother thought he often did not understand what his parents were talking about and would reply in a hit-or-miss fashion. Most of the children were not as advanced as Breon, who could at least say the word "yes." Others did not use the word or even nod in agreement.

From these descriptions, we found that autistic children also did not understand the concept of time or other abstractions commonly used in conversations by normal 3-year-old children. Their thought content as expressed in speech was limited to simple wants such as hunger and thirst and keeping their simple repetitive activities going.

Comparison of Autistic Echolalia with Normal Echolalia

Echolalia is a routine feature of the normal child's speech development beginning at 8 months with imitation of sounds such as a cough or clicking the tongue. According to Sheridan (1960), echoing the speech of others is a prominent feature of the speech of the normal 18-month-old infant. According to Gesell, Halverson, Thompson, Ilg, Castner, Ames, and Amatruda (1940), the 21-month-old child repeats a single word said to him or the last word of a phrase addressed to him. At 2 to 2½ years of age echolalia persists, but by 3 years of age, none of the child developmentalists include echolalia as a feature of normal speech.

We hardly notice the echolalia of normal young children because they so frequently talk to us in nonecholalic fashion. In contrast, the preschool autistic child's echolalia is highly noticeable to the listener because it is generally the only kind of speech he had beyond single words. In autistic children, echolalia frequently increases after 3 years of age, just as it drops out in normal children. The autistic child may use echolalia beyond his sixth birthday.

We have no examples, nor do the child developmentalists give any, of normal children using echolalia to express immediate needs. The normal child doesn't need to do so because creative speech (developing concomitantly with echolalia) is so much more effective. In contrast, Churchill (1978) has shown conclusively that autistic children lack the power to create speed on their own. DeMyer (1975) has shown that the most common speech splinter ability on formal tests is repetition of words and numbers, while the most common speech disability is poor performance on language tests requiring abstract language skills. Therefore, we can conclude that evidence supports the idea that the neurological connections mediating word production are relatively intact in many autistic children, but the language processing centers are not intact. The autistic child can't think with language and he can't create language of his own. The mothers who said the following were essentially correct: "My child can say anything we can say, but he can't do anything with it." "She can probably say anything she wants—she can repeat anything she has heard—she can count and say her ABCs, but she can't convey any idea of her own."

Ability to Understand Speech

The parents' perceptions of their autistic childrens' ability to understand speech were not as clearly expressed as were their descriptions of expressive speech. Only about a third of the parents thought their autistic child understood little or nothing of what was said. About 36% thought the child understood most speech while the remainder thought there was partial understanding, as shown in Table 19.

Sometimes the parents' reports were colored by the reason the parents ascribed to the cause of the expressive speech deficiency. Lucius's mother

Table 19. Receptive Speech of Autistic Children

Understanding of parents' speech	%
Little or none	30
Some	33
Most	27
Everything	9

thought he really understood speech but "pretended not to." Jerry's father said, "I think he knows what we say, but he shuts you out when he knows you want him to talk." Howard's mother said, "He ignores us. He's a real master at that." Thus, in general, the parents spoke more positively of the children's receptive speech than of their expressive speech. In formal testing, we found that autistic children as a group tested a mean of 10 IQ points higher on receptive speech than in expressive speech.

Creak (1972) noted that autistic children showed increased autistic withdrawal when they failed to understand a verbal request and increased compliance when they understood. She concluded that "much of the time the autistic child is neither simply unwilling nor uninvolved but wholly at a loss" and retreats from a situation and the words he cannot understand.

How the Autistic Child Expresses Himself

If the autistic child does not use speech, how does he express himself? We asked the parents to describe this phenomenon and how well they understood. Answers indicated that there were stages to self-expression. After the first year of life, the normal child typically uses a combination of words and crying. The autistic child during the second year of life typically used only crying, which in many cases was frequent and loud. During this early period, autistic children added no other discriminatory body signal and parents were left to guess at the exact nature of the child's need. Gradually most autistic children began to substitute some simple body language for screaming. Nearly all of them took a parent by the hand and led him to the object. They did not point to objects, however. If they wanted a drink, they stood in front of the sink. For food, they would sit in the chair where they were habitually fed.

By interview time, most parents felt they understood quite well what their autistic child wanted. Many had doubts that other people unacquainted with the child would know because signals were so general that no one but mothers could read them. Other signals were inadvertent facial changes that the child was not sending as a conscious communicative device. Lucius's mother said, "I understand him better than most people because I have been with him constantly. If he has to go potty, he gets real quiet or looks worried, but someone else wouldn't know this."

Some children remained in the screaming stage and this posed a problem. Jana's mother said, "I anticipate her needs. Since she doesn't talk, I'm extra careful that she's fed. We guess and work on a timetable." Jerry's parents remembered how upsetting the screaming was at the dinner table when frequently Jerry screamed during much of the meal because the parents could not guess quickly enough what he wanted to eat. It is obvious that screaming was used as a gross signal that the child wanted a thing or that he was uncomfortable, angry, frustrated, or fearful. Parents gradually learned through other body signals and environmental contexts which condition the screaming signaled.

Some children expressed negative wishes by throwing themselves on the floor. At home, these tactics could be ignored, but on shopping trips, they could be a problem for a mother who had to deal with her other children and her packages at the same time. Very few parents said their child shook his head in negation.

One mother expressed sorrow that her child was so easy to read. "He really wants so few things—doesn't want to do much but play with his blocks. If he's hungry, he sits in his chair. I can always tell what he wants. I just wish he wanted to do more."

Parental Response to Speech Development Problems

No parent expressed worry that the infant didn't babble because none were aware of its importance as a prelude to speech. For those autistic infants who said words at the end of the first year of life or shortly thereafter, the parents did not worry about speech in and of itself until one of two subsequent events happened: Either the child lost the few words he had learned and became virtually mute, or he continued to use a few words but infrequently, and failed to enlarge his vocabulary or use sentences or meaningful speech. The dropping out of word use occurred most frequently between 18 to 30 months of age and was gradual in most cases. In one case, cessation of speech occurred totally after a pleasant visit to relatives and 3 weeks after a case of measles.

During the period of speech loss, parents were puzzled and slightly concerned. Most were lulled by their own expectations that speech would "start again soon." Most were told the story of some friend's child or family member who was late talking and was now a person of great capability. Ronnie's mother said indignantly, "I bet I've been told 10 times that Einstein didn't talk until he was 5 years old!" A few parents professed no concern at all until relatives pointed out that the child should be talking.

The period between 2 and 3 years of age was a time of mounting concern. As Eddy's mother said, "I got panicky that my child wasn't talking." In that period, most of the parents were seeking professional help. Around 2 years of age or shortly before, most parents had consulted their family physicians about speech. The most common results were either a wait-and-see approach or "Mother, you are worrying too much." Parents would return home temporarily lulled, only in a few months to begin worrying about speech again. Of course, during this period other alarming symptoms of social withdrawal, excessive irritability, hyperactivity, and excessive messiness also worried the parents, but lack of speech or odd speech was usually the focus of parental worry.

On their own, parents often consciously tried to teach speech by asking for a word before a toy or food was given. Terry's mother said, "I tried every way I could think of and decided I wasn't any good at it. She didn't say a thing." Other parents tried talking more to the child: "We thought maybe we hadn't talked to him enough and talked more to him. We never tried to sit down and teach him."

By the age of 3½ to 4½ years, several children had been evaluated at speech or child guidance clinics and in every case parents were told not to try to make the child talk. Parents agreed to these requests.

> A year ago I read about the reward system of getting kids to talk. I made Howie try to say "up" before I picked him up, which he liked me to do. He learned to say "ah," which I would accept and then reward him by picking him up. Then we started at the guidance clinic, and they thought we shouldn't do that. They thought when he was happy and well adjusted that he would just learn to talk naturally and so we stopped.

Parents, with two exceptions, thought their efforts to teach the children formally were without effect. As Jana's father said, "Her sister has very consistently and patiently tried to help her speak. It hasn't done a thing." Mack's mother felt she had scored a real victory when she had taught him to indicate "yes" or "no" by a word or a nod. "Mack just wasn't talking to us. I didn't know where to start to help him, but I knew what was lacking—he didn't talk to us. He didn't know 'yes' or 'no.' I taught him that. Do you know you can have a conversation with a child if they know just those 2 words? If he doesn't know them—well—he can't converse at all!"

Professional Efforts at Speech Training

By and large professional people have not been successful at training autistic children to speak. We know that if a child does not learn to use speech for communication by the age of 6 to 7 years it is unlikely that he will ever develop useful speech. We have not learned how to train a child to utter words if he does not learn first on his own to do so. Churchill (1972) was able to teach some autistic children to use an artificial 9-word language in the laboratory, but I know of no instances where any such speech was generalized to deal with the everyday environment. Even with formal conditioning procedures, Churchill met with failures of varying degrees in some of the children.

Creedon (1973) has taught simple sign language to autistic children between the ages of 4 and 10 years while simultaneously teaching them words. She used operant conditioning techniques of rewarding first partial and then correct performances with food, desired objects, and social approval. Parents also were taught the method. According to Creedon: "All the children . . . have used signs for their immediate needs and affective states. They have varied in acquisition rates and ability to combine words in sentence form." Pronoun use was facilitated by signing. Whether such a method will facilitate more and better speech in the usual, everyday environment is a matter for further study.

Teachers of young autistic children find that getting face to face with the child and using a firm tone and simple phrases or sentences facilitate attention and understanding. Formal drilling to teach words and phrases can be used by parents who are willing to consult with speech therapists. For the most part, parents should talk to their child slowly and simply about people and things the child likes. When and if the child makes some consistent sounds for actions or people or things, these sounds should be rewarded with hugs, praise, food, anything the child likes. If the child's central language mechanism is capable of enough neuronal growth, then some creative, conversational speech will follow.

Notes

[1] There is an interesting study which adds support to this observation. In London, Derek Ricks and Lorna Wing (1975) taped the vocalizations of infants brought up in households speaking seven different languages. The situations were the normal ones in that the infant was expressing frustration, greeting, and pleased surprise. They found that for normal infants the surrounding language was immaterial. Swedish parents could correctly interpret the sounds of a Pakistani baby, and so on. But when the child was autistic, it seemed not to share this universal language of infancy. It seemed to have made up its own language, comprehensible to its own parents who were used to it, but to no one else.

[2] Dr. Irene Stephens reports a better way of obtaining a babbling history from mothers than we did. She imitated the progressive stages of infant babbling for the mothers which stimulated their memories better than did our questions. In each of four cases, she obtained replies indicating their autistic children did not babble with a normal quality.

REFERENCES

Churchill, D. W. The relation of infantile autism and early childhood schizophrenia to developmental language disorders of childhood. *Journal of Autism and Childhood Schizophrenia*, 1972, 2(2), 182–197.

Churchill, D. W. *Language of autistic children.* Washington, D.C.: V. H. Winston & Sons, 1978.

Creak, M. Reflections on communication and autistic children. *Journal of Autism and Childhood Schizophrenia*, 1972, 2(1), 1–8.

Creedon, M. P. *Language development in nonverbal autistic children using a simultaneous communication system.* Chicago: Michael Reese Hospital, 1973. (ERIC Document Reproduction Service No. ED 078 624).

DeMyer, M. K. The nature of the neuropsychological disability in autistic children. *Journal of Autism and Childhood Schizophrenia*, 1975, 5(2), 109–128.

Gesell, A., & Amatruda, C. S. *Developmental diagnosis.* New York: Harper & Row, 1965.

Gesell, A., Halverson, H. M., Thompson, H., Ilg, F. L., Castner, B. M., Ames, L. B., & Amatruda, C. S. *The first five years of life.* New York: Harper & Brothers, 1940.

Ricks, D. M., & Wing, L. Language, communication, and the use of symbols in normal and autistic children. *Journal of Autism and Childhood Schizophrenia*, 1975, 5(3), 191–221.

Sheridan, M. D. *The developmental progress of infants and young children: Ministry of Health reports on public health and medical subjects.* London: Her Majesty's Stationery Office, 1960, No. 102.

Chapter 5

PROBLEMS WITH FEEDING AND EATING

Feeding and elimination comprise a large portion of the infant and toddler's life. How mother and child experience each other depends in some measure on how well they get along during these daily encounters. The mother's satisfaction with herself as a mother of any given child depends on how successful she perceives herself to be as a giver of food and as a social guide.

Early in the autistic child's life, generally in the second year, mother and child encountered difficulties in feeding and toilet training far more severe than those encountered by the "average" normal child and mother. Fathers suffered directly because of family upheavals at mealtime and indirectly because of the emotional pain of the mother. Both parents worried about the child's developmental failure and felt intense frustration as mealtime and toilet training problems continued past the third birthday. When an autistic child passed the 3½ year mark and was still not toilet trained, his father tended to blame his mother and tensions between the couple mounted. Our interviews, however, revealed that autistic parents and normal parents reacted similarly to severe problems in the index children, and that the two parent groups were not significantly different in basic attitudes and approaches to problems of eating and elimination.

The major differences were between the autistic and normal children themselves. Autistic children intellectually and verbally were not ready for toilet training as early as normal children. Perceptual-motor and communication problems delayed the autistic child in learning how to eat neatly and behave properly at the dinner table. Also, physiological elimination problems interfered more often with toileting in autistic than in normal children. As a result, difficulties with eating and elimination posed serious problems during the ages when the total problem of autism was reported most severe, the second through fourth years of life. Parents reacted at first with active efforts to cope, followed by a sense of frustration as their measures failed, and then finally felt great relief at about ages 4 to 5 years as the eating and toileting behaviors improved. This chapter and the following one detail the findings that led to these conclusions.

Feeding Problems in First Year of Life

Autistic babies did not differ strikingly from normal ones in number or kinds of feeding problems, although there was a slight tendency for autistic babies to have more feeding problems (on the average, 1.52 per autistic child, 1.40 per normal one). Also, more autistic (21%) than normal (6%) infants were felt to be eating too little. An intriguing report of "huge appetites" in 9% of autistic infants was not matched for any normal infant. No normal infant had difficulty in chewing, swallowing, or sucking, while these problems were reported for about 18% of autistic infants. Such difficulties may imply a delay in motor integration of mouth, jaw, tongue, and swallowing muscles.

All other infant feeding problems were reported in nearly equal measure for both groups and consisted of frequent or copious spitting up, frequent vomiting, "food allergies," and too frequent or prolonged feedings (see Table 20).

Relationship of Breast Feeding to Autism and to Infancy Feeding Probelms

Several members of the LaLeche League asked whether there was a relation between breast feeding and infantile autism. These women suspected that autistic children are breast-fed less than normal ones, apparently because these women believed in the "nurture" theory of autism. There were in fact no significant differences in the amount of breast feeding between autistic and normal groups (about 36% of autistic and 42% of normal children). Also, there was no relation between the incidence of feeding difficulties in the first year and breast feeding in either group (see Table 21).

Table 20. Infant Feeding Problems

Type of problem	Normal[a]		Autistic	
	N	%	N	%
Too little food intake	2	6	7	21
Difficulty to chew/swallow/suck	0		6	18
Frequent or copious spitting up	5	15	5	15
Frequent vomiting	5	15	4	12
Frequent formula change	5	15	4	12
"Allergic" reaction or food intolerance	2	6	4	12
Huge appetite	0		3	9
Gained poorly or lost weight	1	3	1	3
Too frequent or prolonged feedlings	1	3	1	3
Total problems	21		35	
Incidence per infant	1		2	
N of infants with problems	16	49	23	70

[a] $p < 0.1$.

Changes in Eating Problems from Infancy to Childhood

After the first year of life, the incidence of eating and feeding problems increased in both groups (autistic, from 70 to 94%; normal, from 48 to 59%). Despite this increase in feeding problems, food intolerances, food "allergies" and regurgitation of stomach contents virtually disappeared except for two cases. As infants passed the first-year mark, parents increasingly expected them to eat alone, even if sloppily. As toddlers neared their second birthdays, parents expected at least the use of a spoon, more neatness in eating, and the development of better table manners. Normal children largely met these expectations. Autistic children largely did not. They were slow to master utensils, played in their food, left the table frequently, and had problems in delaying gratification and in making their wants known. They could not participate in sociable eating. Parents observed that autistic children tended to become "picky eaters" (in infancy, 21%; in childhood, 47%); i.e., they did not eat enough food or a wide enough variety to suit their parents. While some normal children displayed the same picky habits, not only was the problem less frequent, but it was usually less severe and less long lasting than that in autistic children.

Table 21. Relationship of Infant Feeding Problems to Breast Feeding

Feeding pattern	Normal		Autistic	
	N	%	N	%
Difficulty present in first year	17	52	23	70
Incidence of breast feeding				
Yes	14	42	12	36
No	19	58	21	64
Breast fed infants[a]				
No problems	8	57	3	25
Feeding difficulty	6	43	9	75
Infants not breast fed				
No problems	8	42	7	33
Feeding difficulty	11	58	14	67

[a] $p < 0.1$.

Types of Problems after the First Year in Autistic Children

About 72% of autistic children were described as having some kind of food intake problem, chiefly involving too little food eaten (30%) and too restricted a variety (39%). Conversely, a voracious appetite was reported for about 12%. Other intake problems were a variable appetite, irregular eating times, and frequent vomiting after meals, seen in 3 to 6% of cases. Other mealtime problems involved behavior at the table. The normal children talked too much or too loud while autistic children seldom or never talked at the table. While some normal children were restless (21%), they seldom left the table during meals. In contrast, autistic children not only were restless but left the table frequently, in addition to frequent screaming and messing.

Differences between Normal and Autistic Children's Feeding Problems

We first noted a large difference in the incidence and severity of problems in feeding. Autistic children had on an average 2.97 feeding problems per child while normal children had 1.30. Mealtime in about 49% of autistic homes as compared with about 15% of normal homes was seriously disrupted because of the eating and feeding problems of the index child. About 39% of normal parents said they had virtually no problems, while only about 6% of autistic parents so reported. One rater remarked, "Normal parents don't know

Table 22. Feeding Problems after First Year of Life

Type of behavior at table	Normal[a]		Autistic	
	N	%	N	%
No problems	10	31	2	6
Problem with food intake	7	21	24	73
Problem using utensils	6	18	20	61
Consistently messy (plays, throws, dumps, smears)	4	12	22	67
Overly neat	0		2	
Leaves table frequently	3	9	12	36
Restless but sits	7	21	0	
Hard to get to table	1	3	0	
Seems fearful sitting at table	0		2	6
Tantrums, cannot wait, cries	4	12	8	24
Upset if routine broken	0		1	3
Hit self while eating	0		1	3
Rocks during meals	0		0	
Eats inedibles	0		3	9
Can't chew well	0		2	6
Too slow eating	2	6	0	
Talks too much or too loudly	8	24	1	3
Gives food to sibs	1	3	0	
Total	43	1	98	3
Shows moderate to severe disturbance	5	15	16	49

[a]$p < .01.$

how lucky they are when all their children do is argue and kick each other under the table."

Food Intake and Food Tolerance Problems

Autistic children reportedly ate a smaller variety of foods than normal children (autistic, 45%; normal, 21%). While most normal children rejected certain individual foods or refused whole classes of food at some time, autistic children far more often were described as "going on food jags" for months or rejecting whole classes of foods. Similarly, more autistic than normal children restricted the amount of food they ate (autistic, 30%; normal, 9%).

At the Clinical Research Center, we put these parental observations to the test and found that the parents' views coincided with actual food intake measurement in one type of observation. Autistic children took in 30% fewer

Table 23. Food Intake and Tolerance Problems

Problem in childhood	Normal		Autistic	
	N	$\%$	N	$\%$
Restricted variety	7	21	6	18
Restricted amount	6	18	3	9
Restricted variety and amount	0		7	21
Huge appetite	0		2	6
Huge appetite and restricted variety	0		2	6
Variable appetite	0		1	3
Vomits after meals	0		2	6
Total	13	39	23	69

calories than did a group of normal children under the same experimental conditions (DeMyer, Ward, & Lintzenich, 1968). However, there were no significant differences in *kinds* of food eaten over a 3-week period. Over a 3- to 4-day-period, several autistic children "went on food jags," though they made up for these days in the rest of a 3-week-period. Their caloric intake was also more variable from day to day.

What was the significance of the "less-than-normal" amount of food intake? Of the several variables that could affect the result, the most obvious difference between autistic and normal children was in the amount of large muscle activity. Normal children rode tricycles, played on playground equipment, wrestled, and played ball more than autistic children, who despite physical restlessness seldom used their large muscles vigorously. It is possible that autistic children would have been different from normal children in variety of food intake also had we been able to make the measurements between the ages of 1 to 3 years, when most parents judged the eating problems to be most severe.

Consistent Messiness

The normal baby and toddler are fairly consistently messy eaters. As the age of 2 years approaches, the normal child is usually neat enough so that parents no longer complain. Not so for the autistic child, who in about 66% of cases compared to 12% of normal cases, was described at the time of the interview as consistently messy with food. "Messy" children played in their food, threw it, smeared it, or dumped whole platefuls on the floor. Ronnie's mother told of her son's behavior:

He grabs food from our plates or anything else within reach. We encourage him to eat with a spoon, but after one or two bites, he uses his fingers again. He pours milk all over his food and slops his fingers in it. He makes quite a puddle. He wiggles out of his chair if he sees we have moved things out of reach. He gets into the refrigerator and messes. I have to barricade the refrigerator door to keep him away because I can't teach him to stay out of it.

Autistic mothers were no more upset than normal mothers by the ordinary messing in food of the infant and toddler. This behavior seldom was a major complaint about autistic children, and yet it was something which day after day, month after month, added to the cleanup duties of autistic mothers and lessened enjoyment of mealtimes for the whole family.

Problems with Utensil Use

We did not ask specifically about delays in using eating utensils, but it was one of the most common problems mentioned by autistic parents. We asked, "How have you tried to teach your child manners at the table?" It was in response to this question that about 61% of autistic parents vs. about 18% of normal parents reported a delay in the use of utensils.

At first thought, the finding may be startling until one recalls the lack of hand-finger coordination displayed by autistic children in other activities such

Table 24. Use of Eating Utensils as Described by Mothers

Use of utensils	Normal			Autistic		
	N	%	Mean age (months)	N	%	Mean age (months)
Mother feeds mostly	0	0	—	3	9	31
Eats with fingers	1	3	(22)	13	39	52
Spoon in use mostly	4	12	39	7	21	52
Spoon and fork in use[a]	9	27	56	5	15	54
Spoon, fork and knife in use[b]	7	21	53	1	3	(76)
Not described as problem[c]	11	33	59	2	6	63

[a] Use of spoon was not described in one normal family because children were only given forks. In 2 autistic cases the use of spoons was not clearly specified.

[b] Children who used all utensils and most who used a spoon and fork were not described as having a problem with utensils.

[c] Utensil use not described.

as drawing geometric figures. All 33 of the autistic children were old enough to be expected at least to use a spoon. According to Gesell, Halverson, Thompson, Ilg, Castner, Ames, and Amatruda (1940), the normal 18-month-old uses a spoon although he is messy with it because he can't keep it straight up as he brings the food from plate to mouth. By age 2 years, the normal child uses a spoon without assistance and with little spilling. By age 2½ years, the normal child uses a fork for eating solid foods and by 3½ years consistently feeds himself using correctly all utensils and glassware except a knife, which is not used consistently until the age of 5½ to 6 years.

The failure of 48% of autistic children to use a spoon at all, even when well past the chronological age when it is expected, again seems to illustrate a neurological disability. Although some children had minimal and subtle signs of motor system damage (e.g., hyperextension of fingers on release of an object or inability to place the hand precisely on an object), most of the autistic children had sufficient motor skills to allow them to pick up and use a spoon. Their inability to use eating utensils appropriately at the expected ages might be the result of some interruption in central nervous system association areas mediating eye-hand coordination. About 21% of parents noted their autistic child had difficulty in learning to drink from a cup. Whether this difficulty represents a deficiency in mouth-tongue muscle coordination or hand coordination is not known. We can suspect that some autistic children had difficulties with mouth-tongue coordination because chewing difficulties were reported in about 12%.

Several mothers observed spontaneously that the autistic child's way of eating resembled that of infants just beginning to eat by themselves. The difference between autistic and normal children was that finger feeding and clumsy use of the spoon lasted longer in autistic children (at least several months as opposed to several weeks). About 40% of the autistic children were consistent finger feeders and about 15% could not feed themselves at all.

Wade's mother talked about his serious delay in feeding himself and his resemblance to an infant in feeding skills:

Wade (an autistic boy nearly 5 years old at interview time) always had a finicky appetite. I plan our meals around what he will eat. His eating manners are about like a small baby who is just learning to feed himself. He loves to spill soupy food over his head and rub milk in his hair. On the whole, I think he does well at the table now that he is feeding himself, which he wouldn't do until the last few months. I don't push him too hard because I recognize that he eats like the other children did before they were 2 years old. We haven't ever just outright taught table manners to any of the children. They copy what they see, but not Wade. They talk a lot and sometimes sing songs they learned in school. We haven't insisted on them leaving their elbows off the table and that sort of thing.

How did the parents respond to children's inability to learn to use utensils at the expected ages? Parents generally did not worry about it in the same way they worried about the difficulty in speaking. Not a single parent remarked on the connection between difficulties with eating utensils and with paper and pencils. Nearly every parent was aware of the far-reaching effects of not speaking, but no parent predicted later school difficulties because of serious lags in the kind of perceptual-motor coordination that is evidenced by a delay in learning to eat neatly or to draw. Parents were likely to think of these failures as somehow related to a dislike of the activity more than as an intrinsic disability.

Leaving the Table Frequently

About 36% of autistic children left the table frequently during meals in comparison to about 9% of normal children. As a result, autistic parents were often in a quandary about whether to insist that the child return to the table, often unhappily, or to let him go and miss a meal. Such restless behavior at the table would be consistent with inattentive, restless behavior in other situations. For normal children the mealtime was more than just a time for eating. They participated in the social interaction and talked to sibs and parents. Autistic children did not participate in such sociability. Once their appetites were satisfied, they had no further reason to stay at the table except to play in the food or pound on the table or scream to leave.

Problems in Emotional Reactions to Eating

Tantrums and inability to wait to be served were the most common emotional problems at the table (autistic, 24%; normal, 12%).

Jerry's parents describe this type of problem, among others:

Jerry (4 years old) has improved so much over what he used to be at the table that I hate to complain about anything. If he could talk and ask us what he wants, I think it would help with his behavior, but we're not concerned with manners right now. He's still so nervous, he's always moving, like pounding his spoon on something or pushing the chair back and getting down or grabbing at us. It used to be he would want something at the table and I would try one thing after the other because he could give us no indication of what he wanted. If I couldn't figure out right away what he wanted, he would just go to pieces. He's getting better about that now. We found ourselves yelling a lot then. Sometimes he spreads food all over the table and just generally messes. Spanking, talking, shouting—nothing did any good until I took his hand and rapped it on the table a bit; that stops him for awhile. All we can do it try talking and reserve physical punishment for times when he gets completely out of hand. His first year was a big problem, which started in the hospital right after his birth—he couldn't keep anything on his stomach. Later, any solid food brought on vomiting and diarrhea. That first year, all he ate was skimmed milk and bananas. I couldn't breast feed him because of an infection—oh, I wanted to. His older sister has always been calm at the table and eaten well. We get after her for slouching, but that is typical for her age.

One autistic child, Didi, aged 22 months, was fearful of sitting at the family table. She was viewed by her parents as alert and sociable until the end of her first year when she had a series of upper respiratory infections followed by a setback in her behavior. She lost interest in her family and became irritable and generally uninvolved with life. Her mother described her eating:

Didi used to enjoy eating at a small table near the rest of the family, and she also enjoyed the rest of us yacking away. Now, after her setback, she seems afraid of the little table, and half the time she is upset at the big dining room table even if she is sitting on my lap. Now she likes to sit on a blanket away from the family, and I feed her there. She won't even feed herself a cookie. I blamed myself for awhile and thought I didn't give her enough opportunity, but she wouldn't even pick up a spoon. I don't know anything else to try now so we go along with what she wants to eat, the way she wants it. She eats so little I worry about it.

At this point, the interviewer asked Didi's mother a question we asked of all mothers, "How have you tried to develop table manners in her?" This mother's response was, "Are you kidding?" She knew that Didi's poor hand coordination and her fear of the table precluded the teaching of good manners until later. The mother told how her other children fought to feed themselves when they were a year to 18 months of age. "Like typical kids they slopped food all over and didn't get much in, but they didn't want any help, which is more usual than Didi refusing to pick up a spoon."

Another interesting food problem reported for 9% of autistic cases in infancy and 6% during childhood was a voracious appetite. These children devoured whole jars of peanut butter or whole boxes of crackers at a sitting. A few other autistic children without huge appetites were described as getting "panicky" or physically "trembly" if mealtime was delayed.

Mimi, age 3 years at interview time, exemplified the "voracious eater" who had other mealtime problems:

Mimi can't feed herself completely yet. She is a large eater. If she doesn't get her food immediately after she gets hungry, she trembles and gets very nervous. She just *has* to eat. She is very messy and shakes food off her hands so that it goes all over the wall and table, and this does upset us. We don't spank her yet because I think it's a nervous habit she can't control. We smacked her hands a few times but quit it because it made her more nervous. She drops things a lot and has difficulty holding a spoon to eat out of it. She is beginning to learn to hold a sandwich but holds it at a peculiar angle. Mimi will take a bit of food then drop the rest of it. We don't force her to put it on her plate because it makes her so nervous. We pick it up and say "Mimi, try and keep it in your plate," very calmly. We used to bug her and holler at her but that made her worse. One of us has to sit with her at the table or she will get up and won't finish her meal. We can't take her out to eat because it excites her too much.

Parental Reactions to Feeding Problems of Autistic Children

One experienced mother with three older children in addition to her autistic child, when told that the subject of the next interview was to be feeding her autistic child, rose from her chair and said, "I'm leaving." She was not joking. She stayed for the interview but revealed the intense pain that had accrued over the 3 years of her child's life in trying to feed him. The first 2 years were marked by copious vomiting after meals followed by refeeding and by fruitless medical consultations in an effort to learn the cause of the vomiting. At the end of his first year, he began to hit himself during meals. Shortly after his second birthday, the vomiting gradually eased, but the hitting and crying continued. Mealtimes with the whole family together ceased and mother was left with a sense of frustration and futility over one of her main functions, that of supplying restful meals for her family. She felt intensely lonely, in great part from the task of feeding her son so many lonely, protracted, messy meals. The parents argued because mother felt father didn't help enough and father felt frustrated because he could not find any satisfactory solution. This case is the most extreme in our series, but mealtime for most autistic families is not a pleasant experience, stemming largely from interruptive behavior that continues meal after meal over months and years.

Parents were most upset by their child's consistent messiness (54%), getting up frequently from the table (42%), and frequent tantrums (21%). No imagination is needed to picture what it must be like to feed a family when one child throws food or spills it over his head far past the age when such behavior is expected and normal. Added to the problem of limiting such behavior was the burden of keeping a restless, inattentive child at the table long enough for him to eat enough for optimum health. Both autistic and normal mothers reported they were upset and anxious when they believed a child was not eating "enough." When parents applied their customary techniques to limit interruptive behavior, they met with indifference or with a child who screamed intensely and insistently and who never seemed to learn from their methods.

Good sense told the mothers at one level that they were not basically "bad" nourishers because other children in the family, with few exceptions, ate well enough and learned table manners as expected for their ages. But at another level, some did not quite believe that they were successful feeders because of their experiences with their autistic child. Here is a statement of a perceptive mother, "Feeding wasn't so hard in his first year. He didn't eat as much as the others did then, but at least it was peaceful and I felt no dissatisfaction with myself. But later, he ate practically nothing and there was no way I could get him to sit at the table except to let him play with the food and that upset everybody else. Any correction at all and he went to pieces. We just literally didn't know what to do, and I felt bad about myself and sorry for all of us."

Interruptive behaviors severely limited family excursions to restaurants because the autistic child was upset by the new surroundings and was even more difficult to feed and more irritable and hyperactive than at home. The usual vacations from meal preparation and cleanup thus were denied to most autistic families at least during the child's preschool years. Many parents felt this denial acutely.

Parental techniques for changing the autistic child's behavior at the table typically went through a sequence that varied with age, parental expectations, and severity of symptoms. From about one year to 18 months parents expected messiness and emotional outbursts because their other children typically behaved in the same way at those ages. As messiness continued unabated and temper tantrums got worse, parents used physical punishment. Parents of all but a few autistic children reported a worsening of behavior after physical punishment. Emotional upsets were particularly intensified. Nearly all parents then stopped punishment, but their frustration increased and one can imagine that they began to shout at one another and at the child during mealtime. A few hardy parents who were not too ashamed told the interviewers of their frustrations and of "yelling a lot then."

Eventually, as parental expectations dropped, so did frustrations, and parents began to accept more calmly the messiness, the hyperactivity, and the screaming. As the age of 4 years approached, most parents reported so much improvement in their autistic child's eating habits that they were no longer complaining or punishing at all. Raters estimated, however, that even at the ages of 4 to 5 years most autistic children continued to be messier and less calm than their normal matched counterparts.

Recommendations for Training Autistic Children at Mealtime

The parents' natural behavior cannot be criticized in most cases because in time improvement in eating seemed so substantial. Undoubtedly parents could use counselling to help institute better techniques earlier, particularly with regard to their response to an autistic child's screaming. Most parents said they frantically tried to find something or some food to stop the screaming. It would be better to note the child's favorite food and to give it to him *after* he stops screaming, thus reinforcing or rewarding quiet behavior rather than screaming.

Many parents would not try to limit interruptive behavior in their autistic child by feeding him alone or banishing him to another room until he calmed down. For one thing, the autistic child's natural tendency was to leave the table before he had eaten, and parents felt they should insist that he sit there. They were worried also about his social isolation and feared using parental isolation tactics. Raters believed that in those few cases where the autistic child was fed separately from the family for a few months mealtimes were calmer and the autistic child was happier. Gradually, as he matured intellectually, verbally, and physically, he could be more calmly integrated into eating with the family. Separate eating allowed the mother more time to wait out tantrums and to reward quiet, neat behavior while giving the rest of the family a restful and sociable family meal.

Those parents who could be calm and accepting with each other and with their child fared better than those who could not. One mother described ups and downs in family mealtime enjoyment varying with the father's moods and which child was being corrected:

Janis's father is more strict and more squeamish than I am. It's all right with our other child. She understands what he says and can shape up and I don't have the stick-to-it-iveness to make her mind all the time—my husband does. But for Janis, I think he is wrong. She doesn't understand what he says—all he does is get her all worked up. It depends on his mood. In a bad mood, he will call her a pig and leave the table and I have to feed him in his room or else we leave her, which is a sore point with me. Things go best when he is relaxed—then we see the humor in it. When we have spaghetti or noodles, she picks up a strand and shakes it just like she does her string. It really does help to let your sense of humor out at times like that. Or she gets a sly look when I put certain foods in front of her as if to say, "You must be out of your mind if you think I'm going to eat that." I can laugh about things like that and we all eat better when my husband can too. Sometimes when I am put out—like after I spend an hour and a half preparing a good meal and he is in a foul mood or I can't relax and enjoy the meal, then I am not patient either.

In the feeding situation, as in all that relates to autism, it is well to remind parents that autism is among other things a form of retardation–a strange, rare and unpredictable form, but retardation all the same. It may take the autistic child years to pass milestones that normal children pass in weeks or months, but the autistic child given help and encouragement and proper training may pass them, one after another, in his own good time.

REFERENCES

DeMyer, M. K., Ward, S. D., & Lintzenich, J. Comparison of macronutrients in the diets of psychotic and normal children. *Archives of General Psychiatry*, 1968, **18**, 584–590.

Gesell, A., Halverson, H. M., Thompson, H., Ilg, F. L., Castner, B. M., Ames, L. B., & Amatruda, C. S. *The first five years of life*. New York: Harper & Brothers, 1940.

Chapter 6

PROBLEMS WITH ELIMINATION AND TOILET TRAINING

Problems with elimination and toilet training are encountered by many parents of autistic children. But while elimination, particularly in infancy, can be a difficulty, toilet training of the preschool autistic child can become a serious struggle as the mothers find serious lags in the child's understanding of toilet training.

Regarding elimination in infancy, more mothers of autistic than of normal children reported problems with chronically hard stools or chronic constipation (autistic, 55%; normal, 33%). Incidence of diarrhea did not differ.

Attitudes of Mothers Toward Diapers and Elimination during the First Year

We asked all mothers in our survey the following question: "Some mothers like to change their babies' diapers; others don't particularly care for it. What are your feelings about this?"

Most mothers in both groups felt changing diapers was a part of being a mother that did not particularly bother them, but neither did they like it. Typical comments were, "It's something that has to be done." "I wouldn't dance a ballet over changing diapers, but I can't say I dislike it either. I think

Table 25. Mother's Feelings about Changing Baby Diapers

Expressed feeling	Autistic		Normal	
	N	%	N	%
Not bothered; necessary part of mothering	20	60	17	51
Liked infant comfortable and clean	4	12	4	12
Not bothered; BM diapers unpleasant	3	9	5	15
Liked it	3	9	2	6
Not bothered until late in first year	1	3	3	9
Didn't like it	2	6	1	3

someone who says she likes it would have to be different from most women I know."

A few mothers in both groups (12%) said that diaper changing wasn't particularly pleasant, but they really liked to know their infant was clean and comfortable. A small group (autistic; 9%; normal, 15%) added that changing a diaper with a bowel movement in it was slightly repugnant to them and a smaller group still were not bothered by diaper changing until the infant approached the end of his first year. Only a few mothers flatly stated either that they liked or that they disliked diaper changing. In this latter category was a mother who said she was fortunate enough to have a neighbor who changed many diapers for her children when they grew to toddler age.

We asked if the mothers took time to play or talk with baby during diaper changing or whether they preferred to get the job over in a hurry. About 75% of both normal and autistic mothers used the time to talk and play with the baby. The remainder preferred to make the change quickly.

Question: "What did you like most about the physical care of your infant?" Feeding and bathing were the most common responses by both mother groups. Changing diapers was not mentioned by a single mother.

Question: "What did you dislike most about physical care of your infant?" Diaper changing was mentioned more frequently than other aspects but did not differ significantly between groups (autistic, 21%; normal, 30%).

In summary, except for a greater incidence of chronic constipation, autistic infants appeared much like normal infants at the end of the first year of life, and we could detect no significant differences between their mothers in basic attitudes toward elimination and diaper changing. With the second year of life, toilet training would begin for most of our children and severe problems started for many autistic children and for a few normal children.

Factors Affecting Toilet Training

Whenever we consider the subject of toilet training, we must look at physical and neurological readiness of the child to learn control, the emotional reaction of the child to training procedures and to the mother doing the training, and the mother's attitude toward training and any difficulties she encounters along the way. A host of other variables may also affect the mother at toilet training time, including father's feelings about her and toilet training, grandparents' attitudes, her experience as a mother of older children, and other problems she must deal with at the same time. To expect retrospective data from one source to definitively point out the preeminence of any one factor is to expect too much. However, mothers' reports of how they went about toilet training and how they responded to difficulties were illuminating and strongly suggest why most autistic children fail to learn toilet training at the usual time. First, autistic children took longer than normal children to understand the connection between sitting on the potty and what they are supposed to do there. Language difficulties were involved, but so too was intellectual failure. Second, autistic children had more cases of chronic constipation than did normal children. This physiological problem when moderately severe or severe tended to interfere with acquisition of elimination control in both groups of children. Other problems, while they tended to be greater in autistic than normal children, did not seem to interfere so much with the training process. Strong negativism, for example, was not reported significantly more often for autistic children than for normal children. There was no indication that autistic mothers either approached toilet training differently or responded differently to accidents than did normal mothers. Similarly, normal parents were about as upset as autistic parents when a child exhibited long-standing problems in toilet training. In short, intellectual deficits and physiological difficulties seemed to account for most instances of serious delay in acquiring elimination control in the autistic group. Let us examine the data that led to these conclusions.

Ages at Beginning and Completion of Toilet Training

Question: "When did you begin toilet training?" Most mothers started bowel and bladder training within a few weeks of each other in any given child, and estimated at what age they began. There were no significant differences between normal and autistic children in the age at which toilet training was started (see Table 26).

Question: "Is toilet training complete now? If so, when was it completed?" There were significant group differences in the status of toilet training at interview time. Normal children were far more likely to be trained than autistic children. About 60% of normal children were fully bowel and bladder

Table 26. Chronological Age at Beginning of Toilet Training[a]

Chronological age	Autistic		Normal	
	N	*%*	*N*	*%*
About 1 year or before	8	25	12	38
About 1½ years	10	30	9	28
About 2 years	10	30	8	25
About 2½–3 years	2	6	2	6
Not started	3	9	1	3

[a]Bowel and bladder combined.

trained (with no accidents) as compared with only 27% autistic children. In contrast, 48% of autistic children were not trained at all. The relation between chronological age and toilet training is shown in Table 27. There is a positive relationship between chronological age and completion of toilet training in both groups, but autistic were much slower to train then normal children.

About 63% of normal children were nearly or fully trained by the age of 2½ years if we take the whole group into account and collapse the "fully

Table 27. Status of Toilet Training at Interview Time[a]

Chronological age	Fully trained		Fully trained and accidents		Partly trained		Not trained	
	Autis-tic	Nor-mal	Autis-tic	Nor-mal	Autis-tic	Nor-mal	Autis-tic	Nor-mal
Below 2½ years								
N	0	0	0	0	0	0	2	2
%							100	100
2½–4 years								
N	0	7	0	3	3	2	8	0
%		58		25	27	18	73	
Over 4 years								
N	9	13	2	6	3	0	6	0
%	45	68	10	32	15		30	
Whole group[a]								
N	9	20	2	9	6	2	16	2
%	27	60	6	27	18	6	48	6

[a]33 autistic and 33 normal children; $p < .01$.

Table 28. Age of Complete Toilet Training

Status	Autistic[a]		Normal	
	N	%	N	%
Not trained or partly-trained	22	67	5	16
Fully trained or fully-trained with accidents				
About 1 year	1	3	3	9
About 1–2½ years		12		54
About 2½–3½ years		6		18
About 3½–4½ years		12		3

[a]$p < .01.$

trained" and "fully trained plus accidents" categories. Only 15% of autistic children were trained by the age 2½.

The problems of toilet training still lay ahead for 67% of the mothers of autistic children who participated in these interviews. It was not only the mothers of the younger autistic children who had yet to train their children but also 45% of the 20 autistic children over 4 years of age. Of these 20, 6 were not trained at all and 3 were only partially trained; i.e., the mother had to take most of the responsibility or else only one function was under control. No normal control child over 4 years had failed to learn both bowel and bladder control, although about 6 normal children were still having some accidents in one function or the other.

General Training Process

Question: "How did you go about training your child?" As they began to train their child, nearly all mothers looked for a regular pattern of bowel movements, then tried to catch the bowel movement in a pot. If in early infancy the baby was regular and agreeable to sitting on a potty chair, mothers would try catching at that time. Nearly all the mothers who started in the first year said infants below 12 months didn't understand the process but that since they were regular in their habits, the mother caught the stool. Most infants and young children evacuated bowels immediately after breakfast or during naptime. For urine, most mothers watched the clock and put the child on the pot at intervals. Every mother stated that she seldom kept the child on for longer than 15 to 20 minutes. Every mother but three (2 normal and 1 autistic) told us she did not believe in punishing the child as part of the regular procedure of toilet training. Nearly every mother tried to make sitting on the potty a pleasant experience. Mothers of both groups regularly talked, read to, or played with the child and provided favorite toys or cookies for the child as he sat on the pot as his first toilet training began.

This vastly simplified description of the general way that mothers of both groups proceeded does not give a picture of the great variety of training styles the mothers used, but it does show that the mothers were remarkably uniform in the way they began the procedure and that most felt at the beginning of the process that they knew what to do and when to start. The individual differences in methods, attitudes, and self-doubts were highlighted when the children failed to respond to training or had relapses in training after some initial success.

Mothers' Usual Response to Accidents and Negativism

As stated previously, all but 3 mothers of the 66 in the two interview groups did not start toilet training with a deliberate policy of punishing the child as a routine part of toilet training procedure. The three "different" mothers were firm and consistent and spanked or scolded as the child tried to get off the pot, and they felt little or no guilt about such punishment. One normal mother said, "I know he understood what I was talking about, but he didn't want to cooperate. I got irritated and smacked him on the rear end. A couple of times of that and it worked. That goes against anything you read in child training books, but it worked." Another normal mother said, "I knew he was ready and he knew he had to learn. I spanked him immediately as he got off the pot, and he quickly learned to sit there until he was through. Oh, I didn't believe in letting him sit very long." Both mother and father of this normal child spanked for accidents in the same way. However, most mothers (92%) initially proceeded with a policy of positive reinforcement for the child's sitting on the pot: cookies, stories, praise, toys, books. Most mothers who spanked or scolded professed guilt and a sense of failure that they did so.

Individual styles of toilet training began to emerge when the children failed to learn toilet training or had accidents. We asked the question: "What did you usually do when your child had accidents after some response to training? Did you punish? Scold? Spank?" (see Table 29). The most common description for both groups was a matter-of-fact or even sympathetic response (autistic, 45%; normal, 33%). This maternal reaction is typified by the following normal mother's statement: "I hardly ever scolded or punished unless I was just super tired or irritable. Generally, I would say to him, 'That's too bad, Honey' and then just clean him up."

There was a behavior to which every mother quickly and definitely reacted by punishing the child or showing strong disgust. That behavior was smearing feces, playing in them, or eating them. Even mothers who ordinarily did not

Table 29. Mothers' Reactions to Training

Reaction	Autistic		Normal	
	N	%	N	%
Nothing—accepted matter-of-factly until child did something extreme like smearing or eating stool.	15	45	11	33
Nothing until child became "older" or became "deliberately defiant" or "too lazy" or "knew better".	8	24	10	30
Changed from scolding or spanking to being non-punishing.	4	12	1	3
Scolded or spanked or showed definite disapproval for accidents since the child first began to have some response to training.	2	6	9	27
Serious training not started or completely discontinued; considers child's failure to train acceptable behavior ("not ready" or "does not understand").	4	12	2	6

punish and usually were relaxed about accidents were upset about fecal smearing and through a combination of punishment and close supervision tried to prevent reoccurrences. One accepting and relaxed mother of an autistic child said, "I know Jane can't learn to toilet train yet; she just doesn't get the idea. I really accept this state for now, and I don't punish except for something extreme like smearing. Since she doesn't learn from punishment, I really have to watch her close and get in there immediately after her nap, or everything is covered. That's a cleanup job I hate."

A normal mother said, "He smeared his BM twice all over his bed and himself. I don't remember spanking him, but he got a big reaction from me. I whisked him out of bed and yelled, 'Oh, you dirty child'—no cuddling or anything, and just deposited him in the tub and scrubbed him none too gently. The BM was caked all over."

The second most common response was to be accepting of toileting accidents until the child became "older" or appeared to the mother to be deliberately thwarting her efforts to train him. These reactions were not more commonly expressed by one group than the other (autistic, 24%; normal, 30%). As long as the child appeared "not to get the hang of it," many mothers refrained from punishment or shaming.

Once a child seemed to understand what he was supposed to do, then mothers who reported difficulties in training were likely to punish for accidents. One autistic mother said, "For a long time, he didn't seem to understand at all what I wanted him to do. He began to scream when I brought out the potty. I never thought of punishing him because then he couldn't help it. But then he started sneaking off to have his BMs behind the chair, and I knew he knew it was wrong. I have started to spank him and make him sit there and now we are making some headway."

If the child did not understand and was strongly negative to the whole procedure, mothers seldom punished until another factor emerged, that of increasing age. This combination of factors did not occur with any normal children because these children quickly came to understand what was expected, even though negativism might persist. The normal child reportedly understood what was expected of him at no later than 2 years of age.

The relationship between chronological age of the untrained or partly trained autistic child and the degree of upsetness in the household is shown in the following schema (Table 30):

Table 30. Parental Reactions to Autistic Childrens' Lack of Toilet Training[a]

Degree of parental distress	N below 3½ years	N above 3½ years[b]
Minimally upset	9	1
Moderately upset	1	8
Severely upset	1	3

[a]Or partial training as well.
[b]Not shown for normal parents because children were nearly all trained by 3½ years of age.

If the normal child was being indifferent or negativistic even after he understood, his mother was prone to punish and to feel anguish over the child's failure and the resulting family pressure. Here is one normal mother's account of her reaction to a late training normal boy.

I was completely frustrated. My family didn't understand or sympathize. The pressure from grandparents from having a child 3 years old and not trained was tremendous. I tried not to put it on him, but I'm sure I did at times. There were some awful times for him and me. My mother told me she would not take a boy with her that wet his pants. He was 3½ and she refused to have anything to do with him until he kept dry pants.

There were 27% of normal children described as having a strongly negative reaction to toilet training compared with 39% of autistic children. This difference is not significant.

Some autistic children older than 3½ years still escaped punishment because their parents detected signs that they still did not understand the the connection between sitting on the pot and eliminating. The mother of a 6-year-old autistic boy who was still untrained and a confirmed fecal smearer describes her reactions: "I feel he can't help it, and I never punish. He hasn't been able to learn toilet training as my other children did. Sometimes I think, 'Oh dear, all day long all I have been doing is changing him.' But that doesn't happen too often."

Other mothers of autistic children who still were not trained after 3½ years began to punish even though they believed the child had little understanding. Ezra's mother said,

> I'm sorry to say that Ezra's difficulties have caused me much grief. At first, at about age 2, I didn't punish because he was a different child and I excused him. In the last year or two (Ezra was 5 years 8 months at interview time), it's gotten to be a big deal for me—I overreact. He smears his stools also and it's just about gotten me. I've spanked and scolded, but I know I am beating my brains against a brick wall. My husband also thinks since Ezra's older that I'm not going about it right. He thinks he could toilet train him, but he's had no more luck than I have. If I sit down and bawl real hard after Ezra has smeared all over, I feel better and don't punish him.

The third most common response to toilet training lapses among normal mothers (27%) was to scold or punish but this was so of only 6% of autistic mothers. The difference here seems to be again that normal mothers do not excuse early lapses because most normal children understood early in life what they were supposed to do and autistic children do not. In over half the normal cases the punishment seemed mild, and in nearly all cases it was short-lived because of the child's quick response.

Austistic mothers in 12% of the cases and normal mothers in 3% changed their tactics drastically in the face of toilet training difficulties by virtually ceasing to punish. An autistic child of 3½ years at interview time had responded well to toilet training at age 15 months. She then had a severe social and language regression beginning at 18 months. Her mother described her own response: "Well, she had been potty trained and then went backwards and was so irritable. It was very upsetting to have her go backwards, and she smeared too. I reacted by spanking her. Now, I think that was wrong, but at the time I didn't understand what was happening to her. I just don't spank anymore."

A mother of a normal boy of 3½ who had problems with too frequent stools since infancy and who was difficult to train told of the about-face she and her husband made:

> We punished Martin too much too early for messing his pants. I've read so much about toilet training methods and about college-trained parents having more trouble than other people who just matter-of-factly expect their children to do it. My husband goes so long without punishing Martin; then "Whammo!" he'll get disgusted, and he'll make such awful faces and noises when he changes Martin. But I've read a book called *New Methods of Discipline* which we are following. We have said to Martin, "Mommy and Daddy were wrong for spanking you for messing your pants," and we are encouraging him to express his anger over our punishment. It seems to be working, and I hardly ever spank him now.

The last maternal response to difficulties in toilet training was to stop trying to train altogether until the child appeared to be ready (autistic, 12%; normal, 6%). Many autistic mothers let up in intensity of training at some points, but few stopped altogether. These mothers did not punish because they believed the child was far from ready for training.

We counted the number of mothers in both groups who indicated they spanked for lapses and found that about 18% of autistic mothers and 21% of normal mothers spanked more than occasionally over toilet training difficulties. The difference is not significant.

Difficulties in Training

Question: "What types of difficulties did you meet?" There were decided group differences in the number of difficulties met in the training process. Autistic children had more than two training difficulties per child while the normal children had less than one per child. Seven types of problems were described for both groups of children. The autistic children tended to exhibit more of each of them, but autistic and normal groups differed most in "catching on" to the meaning of the training process (autistics, 58%; normals, 9%). The problem was commonly spoken of in terms of a lack of verbal comprehension. Mothers of normal children could explain what was expected of the normal child while autistic mothers thought their explanations were not understood. Praise for accomplishment was used successfully as a reward for normal children, but not so for autistic children, partly because of a general indifference to the whole process and partly because the autistic children did not understand the praise.

Table 31. Difficulties in Toilet Training

Type of difficulty	Autistic[a]		Normal[b]	
	N	%	N	%
Couldn't learn or understand	19	58	3	9
Physical problem such as moderately severe to severe chronic constipation or diarrhea	14	42	6	18
Strong negative reaction	13	39	9	27
Smearing stools	12	36	6	18
Wouldn't sit still even a few minutes	6	18	3	9
Indifferent	6	18	2	6
Never indicated need to go	5	15	2	6

[a] Index = 2.3 children.
[b] Index = 0.94 child.

Physical Problems with Elimination

Question: "Did your child have any problems with constipation? Diarrhea? When?" Austistic children had more physiological problems connected with elimination than did normal children. About 75% of all autistic cases compared with 33% of all normal ones had either chronic constipation or diarrhea. For about 48% of autistic cases in comparison to 23% of normal ones, the physiological problems were moderately severe to severe and were judged to have affected toilet training to some degree.

During the first year of life the differences in physiological problems between normal infants and autistic infants, while significant (autistic infants, 55%; normal, 33%), were not quite as great as during childhood (autistic children, 73%; normal, 24%). Furthermore, while normal children tended to have a smaller incidence of physiological problems in childhood than in infancy (normal infants, 33%; normal children, 24%), autistic children tended to have more problems in childhood (autistic infants, 55%; autistic child, 73%). In most cases the problems were most severe in the first two years of life and tended to improve or even disappear as the children grew older. However, a few autistic children of 4, 5, and 6 years of age still had problems with either chronic constipation or diarrhea.

Table 32. Incidence of Diarrhea and Chronic Constipation in Infancy and Childhood

Group	Infancy[a]		Childhood[b]	
	Diarrhea	Chronic constipation	Diarrhea	Chronic constipation[e]
Autistic[c]	8	10	10	14
Normal[d]	7	4	4	4

[a] $p < 0.1$.
[b] $p < .01$.
[c] $N = 42$; 25 autistic = 75%.
[d] $N = 19$; 13 normal = 39%.
[e] 13 autistic judged severe in comparison to 4 normal cases.

Effect of Chronic Constipation and Diarrhea on Toilet Training

If the physiological problems were severe, they tended to have an effect on toilet training. Those children who had chronically hard, infrequent stools sometimes showed pain on evacuation which acted as a negative reinforcer in toilet training. A mother of an autistic boy said, "He has always had hard BMs and sometimes goes 3 or 4 days without having one. He can't talk but sometimes he acts as if it hurts him to go on the potty. He'll go out in the yard and wander down by the fence all alone, and I can see him straining. I think he is more comfortable that way."

In contrast to small hard stools, some chronically constipated autistic children had "huge" infrequent stools. Robbie's mother described the effect of this problem:

> His constipation began before he started to walk and one reason I didn't start early with training because he was so irregular. When he wouldn't go for 3 or 4 days, the doctor gave him a laxative because if we waited too long it would be painful for him. It upset him so for us to try to train him that we let it go until he was nearly 4. It was one of the worst problems we faced—the irregularity and his pain and unhappiness about toilet training. I got so I didn't know what to do. I guess I'm not good at it. His constipation is much better now (at age 5).

Another autistic child of 5 still became impacted in the absence of consistent efforts of the parents to ensure evacuation about every 3 or 4 days.

Chronic diarrhea also had a negative effect on toilet training because the child had a more difficult time controlling the movements. The frequent messy pants also in some cases affected parents' feelings towards the child. This adverse feeling was more often reported for fathers than mothers. Short-lasting, acute diarrhea in several cases gave way to chronic diarrhea. In three autistic and two normal cases, a severe acute infectious diarrhea was accompanied by dehydration and subsequent hospitalization for successful treatment. In one autistic child the offending organism in chronic diarrhea was identified as *Giardia lamblia*, but whether it was the original source of the infection is not known.

A mother of a normal boy tells how a chronic diarrhea upset toilet training and disturbed his father and herself:

> Toilet training with Kim was complicated because he had diarrhea about every other month. During his first months of diarrhea (about 15 to 22 months), I wouldn't spank or insist or get angry. Later on, I did get angry because he would balk so at sitting on the toilet. Just after I let him up, he would fill his pants. Now I insist that he sits there, and I spank him if he doesn't. His father's attitude has become a problem. I think he is too hard on him and he's trying to add his own training method to mine and it's confusing. He demands Kim do it immediately and yells at him. He never interfered with training the other children and everything worked out fine. It's only the BMs we have trouble with.

Strong Negative Reactions to Training

Although strong resistance to toilet training tended to be more frequent in autistic (39%) than in normal children (27%), it was only the third most common toilet training problem for autistic children while it was the most common for normal ones. One normal boy was described as having a "very possessive" attitude towards his stools; he objected vociferously to having them flushed away. Three normal children, otherwise easy to train, initially cried hard when put on the pot and could be placated only with difficulty. Of the 12 autistic children with strong negative reactions, there were 3 whose response was described as "hysterical" or "completely unstrung." Myra's mother said, "The first day I put her on the pot she cried wildly. If she even sees the potty now she just goes to pieces. I can't understand it as no one has ever punished her about toileting. Besides, she is indifferent to punishment." An interesting question which cannot be answered by these interviews was whether resistance was more common in children who were physiologically or intellectually unready to be trained than in those who were.

Smearing of Stools

Twice as many autistic children (about 36%) as normal children (about 18%) smeared or played in their stools. Nearly every mother strongly punished or showed strong disgust over these activities. When a normal child smeared, it was for only one or two times. The normal child learned quickly that the behavior was taboo. Not so the autistic child. Of the 12 (36%) autistic children who smeared, three quarters of them did so on many occasions although parental disapproval and punishment at least in beginning stages seemed little different than that given by normal parents. In some cases it took months for autistic children to learn to curb this activity, while in other cases they seemed to tire of doing it. For 9% of the sample this behavior continued for several years. The same proportion of autistic children also occasionally ate their stools.

The three remaining toilet training problems—not sitting still, indifference, and not indicating need to go—were two to three times more common in autistic than in normal children, but reported for only 15 to 18% of autistic cases.

Ease of Toilet Training

These interviews made it clear that normal children as a group were much easier to train than autistic children as a group. The raters defined the categories of child response shown in Table 33, which includes fully trained and partly trained children.

Only about half of autistic children could be rated for ease of toilet training because so many remained untrained, while about 94% of normal children could be so rated. About 12% of normal children were described as training themselves. These children are typified by the following normal

Table 33. Ease of Complete and Partial Toilet Training

Degree	Autistic[a]		Normal[b]	
	N	%	N	%
Easy—child virtually trained self	0		4	12
Easy—almost no problems	4	25	11	35
Moderate problems	3	37	12	39
Severe problems	9	37	4	13

[a]$N = 16; p < .01.$
[b]$N = 31.$

mother's statement, "I was embroiled with his older sister who was 2½ at the time. She was very balky about training. Then I noticed that Trevor was going by himself. No one suggested it to him. Maybe he heard me talking to her, but that didn't faze him in other ways." Another normal mother said, "She saw us going and at one year of age she climbed by herself on the big toilet stool. I wouldn't have dreamed of starting her that early. The baby books say not to." No autistic child was described as a self-learner.

Those children rated as "easily trained" included 12% of the entire autistic group and 33% of the normal group. These children required only a few trials and exhibited only mild problems, if any. Children moderately difficult to train included those with problems lasting several weeks to a few months (autistic, 9%; normal, 36%). Severely difficult trainers took over 8 months to attain a trained or partially trained status (autistic, 27%; normal, 12%). All but one of the normal children in this last named group had a chronic diarrhea interfering with training.

Degree of Upset in Parents Over Toilet Training Problems

We have already seen how a mother will accept difficulties in training with relative equanimity as long as she perceives that the child has not caught on to the meaning of sitting on the pot, that the child is not deliberately thwarting her, or that the child is relatively young. For many normal mothers the dividing age was about 2½ years while for autistic mothers it was about 3½ years.

The farther beyond these ages the child became if he remained untrained, the more likely the mother was to be upset and the more likely father was to be upset both with the child and with mother. Father became critical of mother and began to participate in the training, generally not ensuring a successful outcome. There were about 42% of autistic households and 15% of normal households where toilet training problems were severely upsetting to one or both parents.

A mother of an autistic child described the development of rising household tension over toileting problems:

> At first, I was very relaxed. My experience with my older child who took a good long time about it prepared me to be relaxed. Everyone eventually learns. I thought, "There's no point in persecuting any child over toilet training, especially one who hates it as much as Janis. I'll come back to it when she's ready." This is the way I've proceeded until this day. Unfortunately, this is not my husband's way. He wants to lock her in a potty chair and let her sit indefinitely, which I don't go for at all. If I leave on an errand, he does this so that now I seldom leave if she is awake. He didn't do

this until he thought she should be at an age of understanding—about 3 years old. We have argued about this—I get very vociferous at times, but there is nothing gained. He doesn't see my point that it will make her hate the potty even more.

It was the rare father who participated more than marginally in routine toilet training in either normal or autistic households. However, several normal mothers mentioned that they thought it helped when the little boys saw their father standing to urinate. "Balky" 2-year-old boys were eager to imitate their fathers in this regard. Such imitation was mentioned only by normal mothers at that age.

Recommended Methods for Training

The question raised by many autistic mothers concerning toilet training, often indirectly and occasionally explicitly was this: "If I had proceeded in some other way, could I have successfully trained my child earlier?" I think the findings suggest that about 80 to 90% of autistic children will probably not be verbally, intellectually, and physiologically ready to train before the age of 4 years no matter how skillful the training. However, there are some autistic children ready to be trained at 2 or 3 years of age and the advantages of training at that time are real. Successful training gives the child a feeling of accomplishment, adds to his physical comfort, and makes him more socially acceptable. Not having to change and wash diapers gives the mother more time to attend to others aspects of child care and family living. The question is how to tell if an autistic child younger than 4 years is ready. The basic guideline is that most children should have a physical and verbal age of about 18 months to 2½ years. Azrin and Foxx (1974) give a set of requirements that normal children should successfully pass before training should begin. These can be used to test the autistic child's readiness.

We can also use some clues from behavior that the mothers in our interviews said they used to tell them their normal children were ready: The child should be capable of understanding the connection between sitting on the pot and eliminating there. He should be able to sit for 5 to 10 minutes at some activity, understand some speech, be aware he is urinating (which he can indicate by facial expression or bodily attitude), be uncomfortable when wet, or at least interested in the procedure.

If the autistic child is mute, as he frequently is, mothers may find it difficult to tell how much he understands of cause and effect. There are some nonverbal skills, however, that the mother can use as guides.

The following test will indicate if the child has the nonverbal understanding of an 18-month-old toddler (Cattell, 1940).

From a druggist, purchase a 2 oz. glass bottle with an opening small enough that the child cannot get his finger in it, but large enough that it will admit a small piece of candy or sugared cereal that your child likes. Give your child the bottle with the sweet inside. Do not say anything to the child or try to explain or help him. An 18-month-old with average intelligence will turn the bottle upside down to get the sweet with no help. He will waste little or no time in trying to get out the sweet with his finger. He will solve the problem quickly in his head.

Another simple response shows the mother that her child's nonverbal understanding is like that of the average child at about 2 years, 3 months (Gesell, Halverson, Thompson, Ilg, Castner, Ames, & Amatruda, 1940).

As the child is watching, put a piece of candy or other highly desired object on a shelf or piece of furniture that is out of reach of the child. He should not be able to climb on the furniture or the shelves directly to reach the desired object. Place an ordinary, adult size, kitchen chair about 4 feet away from the furniture on which the desired object is placed. If the child pushes the chair toward the object, stands on the chair, and reaches the object without help and without coaching, he has the understanding and physical control of the average child at 2 years 3 months. That child should be ready for toilet training barring extreme negativism or fear.

When a child has a mental age of about 18 months as determined above, his mother should start looking for other signs of readiness and begin training once the other signs appear. If the child has a mental age of about 2 years, then he should be more easily trained than the child with a mental age of 18 months. Barriers such as negativism and fear should be eliminated by positive rewards for any cooperative behavior. Physical punishment and harsh scolding should not be used, but neither should the parents give way because of tantrums once the initial extreme negativism is cleared away.

During the actual training process, rewards should be used for success and disapproval expressed for accidents. No physical punishment should be used, but expressions of affection should be given frequently. Simple explicit verbal explanations accompanied by physical guidance and gestures should help the child understand what he is to do.

This process of explanation, showing the child what is expected, and then rewarding with candy, kisses, hugs, and praise is excellently presented by Azrin and Foxx in their books and journal articles listed at the end of this chapter. They are recommended reading for anyone who is going to toilet train an autistic child. A modification of the method is used in a day school program by Hazel Watson, an experienced teacher of preschool autistic children. She finds that the best age to start most of them is somewhere between 4 and 5 years and the process takes one to several days with parents participating at home.

She prefers that the child be able to respond successfully to a two-part request such as: "Take off your pants and put them in the hamper" which signifies the child has a verbal receptive age of about 2 years. A good sign of readiness to Mrs. Watson is the child's discomfort on wearing wet diapers. If the child is very fearful or negativistic, she works to reduce these attitudes before beginning. "Once I start, I'm extremely lavish with praise for any partial performance and quite firm in expressing disapproval for accidents." She does not punish physically but shows disapproval in words and tone of voice.

Before starting to train, Mrs. Watson has already accustomed the autistic child to sitting in a chair during class for other activities such as language training. She thus has little problem with tantrums or refusal to sit on the potty. If a tantrum occurs, she goes ahead with the procedure and insists that the child does as she asks.

To be avoided at all costs is pushing strongly for training before the child is intellectually and physically ready because both mother and child become frustrated and angry and any tendency of the child to be negativistic is accented. A battle of wills ensues and toilet training is postponed needlessly. The child who is ready in mental and physical age and not too negative will learn in a few hours to a few days provided skill is used by the mother. On the other hand, waiting too far beyond the time the child is ready causes the mother needless work and deprives the child of a skill that would make him more socially acceptable.

Above all, parents should realize that nothing worthwhile is accomplished by making critical and harsh judgments of each other. Mothers of autistic children need all the moral and practical support they can get, especially from their husbands. Toilet training of any child should proceed from relaxed enlightenment. If a mother and father are at war over it, expert professional advice should be sought from someone well grounded in the laws and milestones of child development. If the child is physically and mentally ready to train, operant conditioning methods used by sensible behavioral psychologists such as Azrin (Azrin & Foxx, 1971, 1974; Azrin, Sneed, & Foxx, 1973) and Foxx (Foxx & Azrin, 1973a, 1973b) are practically guaranteed to work.

Mothers who have previously started to train their autistic children and have met with problems might consider getting outside help before starting again. In such cases, both mother and child may have such a desperate sense of failure about toilet training that achieving the necessary optimistic firm attitude can be nearly impossible to attain. This help should come from someone familiar with the Azrin and Foxx methods. Those parents who have difficulties in continuing with an activity if their autistic child has tantrums need counselling to help them stand firm.

REFERENCES

Azrin, N. H., & Foxx, R. M. A rapid method of toilet training the institutionalized retarded. *Journal of Applied Behavior Analysis*, 1971, 4, 89–99.

Azrin, N. H., & Foxx, R. M. *Toilet training in less than a day.* New York: Simon & Schuster, 1974.

Azrin, N. H., Sneed, T. J., & Foxx, R. M. Dry bed: A rapid method of eliminating bedwetting (enuresis) of the retarded. *Behaviour Research and Therapy*, 1973, 11, 427–434.

Cattell, P. *The measurement of infants and young children.* New York: The Psychological Corp., 1940.

Foxx, R. M., & Arzin, N. H. Dry pants: A rapid method of toilet training children. *Behaviour Research and Therapy*, 1973, 11, 435–442. (a)

Foxx, R. M., & Azrin, N. H. *Toilet training the retarded: A rapid program for day and nighttime independent toileting.* Champaign, Ill.: Research Press Company, 1973. (b)

Gesell, A., Halverson, H. M., Thompson, H., Ilg, F. L., Castner, B. M., Ames, L. B., & Amatruda, C. S. *The first five years of life.* New York: Harper & Brothers, 1940.

Chapter 7

SLEEPING PROBLEMS

Nearly all of the autistic children evaluated at the Clinical Research Center had sleeping problems at some point in their young lives and about half of the cases were rated as severe. Autistic children had difficulties in falling asleep, sometimes far into the evening. They also had periods of wakefulness in the middle of the night when they sometimes played quietly in their beds but more often roamed the house or cried uncontrollably. Parents of autistic children, particularly mothers, found little time for their self-fulfilling evening activities and were often sleepy and cranky themselves after a sleepless night. Infancy was the time sleep was reported at its best and in the year between the ages of 2 and 3 it was at its worst. Parents thought the autistic child's inability to relax caused him to have trouble going to sleep. After going to sleep, the autistic child was often restless and easily awakened. As parents learned ways to keep him in bed and devised strategies to promote relaxation, then sleep problems generally improved slowly over time.

Differences Between Normal and Autistic Children

Even though sleep problems were common in normal children, they were significantly less severe and less common than in autistic children (autistic,

Table 34. Sleeping Problems of Children[a]

Problem	Autistic[b]		Normal	
	N	%	N	%
Severity of sleep problem				
Severe	16	49	1	3
Moderate	11	33	5	15
Mild	6	18	12	36
No problem	0		15	46
Type of sleep problem				
Resist going to sleep	32	97	12	36
Wakes in middle of night or	24	73	10	30
early morning			11	33
Night terrors	9	27	0	
Night fear (verbal expression)	1	3	4	12
Hysterical laughing	2	6		
Wakes early	3	9	1	3
Upset with change of routine	1	3	0	
Behavior on awakening at night				
Cries	16	49	4	12
Roams house	7	21	1	3
Plays or rocks in bed	6	18	1	3
Up for definite purpose	4	12	6	18
Change in sleep problem at interview				
Better now	20	61	7	21
About same	5	24	9	27
Questionable	3	9	1	3
Worse	2	9	1	3

[a]N with sleeping problem = 32 autistic (100%) and 18 normal (55%); N with no current problem = 4 autistic (12%) and 15 normal (46%).
[b]$p < .01$.

100%; normal, 55%). Every autistic child demonstrated sleep problems at some time before initial evaluation. In about 49% of cases, the autistic child's sleeping difficulty was rated as "severe" in contrast to only 3% normal children so rated. A severe sleeping problem was defined as one that occurred at least several times a month over 6 months. When a normal child had troubled sleep, the problem was most often (35%) rated as "mild"; i.e., occurred not more than 4 or 5 times or was extremely mildly expressed if it occurred more often.

One mother cried as she described her autistic daughter's long-time sleeping difficulty. Question: "What upsets you the most about your child's sleeping habits?"

> The fact that she has been getting up in the middle of the night—since a long time age. When she wakes up, sometimes I think she is thirsty or hungry, but mostly I don't know exactly what is troubling her. I wish she would sleep through 'til morning. It does distress me. All of us need our rest. She won't settle down until late in the evening. She's always had sleeping problems. She never slept through the night as a baby. We've also had troubles with her afternoon nap. If she doesn't take one, she gets tired and very cross. She seems to require more sleep than other children her age, but she can't go to sleep!

Differences in Sleeping Patterns

Resistance going to sleep was the most common problem in both groups, but significantly more prevalent and strongly expressed in the autistic group (autistic, about 97%; normal, about 36%). When a normal child resisted going to bed, he could be talked out of staying up or successfully led by the hand to bed. Once in bed, after the customary ploys of asking for a drink of water or going to the bathroom, the normal child quickly went to sleep. The autistic child's resistance was more likely to be hours long and unresponsive to any parental blandishments, threats, punishment, rocking, or soothing. The autistic child was likely to "go until he dropped." Sheer exhaustion was often the only condition that would bring on sleep.

Meg's mother said, "Generally we don't have any trouble with her, but sometimes she won't go to sleep all night, and sometimes she wakes in the middle of the night and there is nothing in the world you can do about it. She doesn't want a drink or to be patted or rocked or anything. She just cries until finally she goes back to sleep."

Gino's parents described extreme problems in getting him settled for the night:

> Gino (aged 4 years and 3 months) gets hyperexcited. We try to calm him, but once he is in bed he starts laughing hysterically. His big problem is getting too wound up. He just can't let go like a normal child. He almost explodes with laughter. Sometimes he will wake in the middle of the night and be awake for 2 or 3 hours. He likes to come out and run and play and eat. He doesn't want to go back to bed, and he doesn't want to be held. It didn't do a bit of good to spank and we were getting completely worn out. He would fight

sleep. Finally, we tried tying him in bed during the worst period and gradually he would relax and go off to sleep. He is better now, but it has been a problem for a long time. At times we give him medicine for sleep. The medicine works for a short while and then loses its effectiveness, and so we save it for his worst periods.

The second most common sleep problem was waking in the middle of the night (autistic, about 72%; normal, about 33%). Here again the quality of the behavior on awakening differentiated autistic children from normal. Normal children seldom cried upon awaking but awoke for a purpose, getting a drink or going to the bathroom. If the normal child awoke fearful or from a "bad dream," he could be soothed and would shortly return to sleep. Autistic children often cried (about 48% of cases), and in many instances the parents could not ascertain the cause or soothe the child except with great difficulty.

> One thing that bothers me is that Mindy will wake up crying without even opening her eyes. She may cry for an hour—sobbing in her sleep. I've wondered if she was in pain. Last time I thought her legs hurt because she kept drawing them up and stretching them out. I put a heating pad on her and held her and finally she stopped.

An autistic child with mild sleeping problems was described thus: "Once in a while he wakes up and cries out. I never know what's wrong, but I cover him up in case he is cold. Sometimes he doesn't seem to be awake when he cries out, but he quits on his own. I go to see what is the matter and pick him up and talk to him if he is awake."

Several autistic mothers thought their autistic children were restless, light sleepers: "Once I could not go into Robbie's room, even on tip-toe. He would wake up and not get back to sleep for hours. He would cry for hours. Now (at age 5 years) I can even cover him up. If it wakes him, he smiles and goes back to sleep." One autistic child screamed hysterically if he lost his blanket while sleeping, and another habitually woke screaming when her string fell out of her hand.

Roaming the house in the middle of the night was reported for about 20% of autistic and only 3% of normal. Following are two mothers' accounts:

> Terrie has always been an irregular sleeper. At one time I thought I ought to get her on a schedule like the rest of us, but it turned into a hassle and she never got onto a schedule. Then we had the bright idea just to let her sleep whenever it suited her. When I was making her sleep a certain time, she would wake about 3 a.m., and I'd hear a noise and she'd be downstairs. She might be in the ice box or perched high up on a cabinet. I have gotten to be a very light sleeper myself. I have to be.

Howard gets in our bed and wants to cuddle. This is all right except he gets to wiggling and kicking and then he gets up and wanders around the house. Of course, I have to get up with him. My husband and I try lying down with him or sitting on the floor beside the crib and holding an arm down, but he requires less sleep than the rest of the kids. He won't sleep the night through but is still going strong early in the next morning.

About 18% of autistic children played or rocked in bed when they awoke in the middle of the night.

Sometimes at about 2 a.m., she'd start this violent crib rocking, and I would have to do something to stop it or she would rock for hours making a fearsome racket.

Some autistic children rocked themselves to sleep as did Benjie: "When he was in his baby bed, he would grasp it by the arms and rock it—not just easily, I mean violently. He wasn't mad. He just rocked himself to sleep."

Course of Sleep Problems in Autistic Children

As previously noted, sleep problems were least severe during infancy. While about 36% of sleep difficulties began then, few mothers reported difficulties to be at their worst then. Most mothers (about 48%) thought the autistic child slept worst between 2 to 3 years of age. The worst sleep period for 24% was over 3 and for 9% between 1 and 2.

Infancy was picked by about 66% of autistic mothers as being the period when their autistic child's sleep was best. In about 11 cases, some ratings could not be made because of unclear descriptions or because the mothers could not be sure themselves. For several infants, mothers reported sleep times that seemed somewhat longer than they recalled for their other children, but no autistic infant slept for such a long time that parents were alarmed.

Improvement by evaluation time was reported for about 60% of autistic cases and for the normal children whose sleep problems had been rated as moderately severe or severe (18%).

Parents' Responses to Sleep Problems

Those parents who reported being awakened frequently at night were most distraught. The pattern in most families was that mothers took frontline responsibility in going to the child, mainly because they took this responsibility in nearly every aspect of child care. Fathers and older sibs helped when mothers got too tired or were sick. The main effect on mothers

Table 35. Development of Sleep Problems in Autistic Children

Pattern	Chronological age	N	%
Sleep problem commences	Infancy (0–12 mos.)	12	36
	Toddler (1–2 yrs.)	15	46
	Early childhood (2–3 yrs.)	3	9
	Questionable	3	9
Sleep problem at worst	Infancy (0–12 mos.)	0	
	Toddler (1–2 yrs.)	3	9
	Early childhood (2–3 yrs.)	16	49
	Early childhood (over 3 yrs.)	8	24
	Questionable	6	18
Sleep at best	Never a good sleeper	3	9
	Infancy (0–12 mos.)	22	67
	Toddler (1–2 yrs.)	0	
	Early childhood (2–3 yrs.)	1	3
	Early childhood (over 3 yrs.)	2	6
	Questionable	5	15

who lost considerable sleep was to make them irritable. As one mother said, "I get downright angry sometimes about having my sleep interrupted so many nights."

Children who played quietly in their beds caused little difficulty, but those who roamed the house in the middle of the night forced their mothers to become light sleepers. The house roamers were described as fearless in climbing and fearless about the dark. Several were unintentionally destructive in their play, but one autistic boy derived pleasure from throwing screens and other household objects from the upstairs windows. Parents were concerned for the children's safety and that of the household. That these parental concerns were justified is illustrated by what happened to one child at 9 years of age when he played with matches at a private residential school: He set a blaze in his room and sustained fatal burns before the school staff could reach him. In a home, these children could do the same unless the mother developed a ready ear for her child waking during the middle of the night.

While most parents did not argue about mother's methods of putting the autistic child to bed, tensions were increased between the couple by worry and frustrations over not knowing what to do to improve the child's sleep patterns as well as by loss of sleep. The reason parents did not fight was the realization that sleep was something they could not force on any child. At first, most parents tried to handle the situation by a combination of spanking and scolding. As with eating problems, these tactics merely increased the tension in the child and all but three sets of parents said they soon stopped spanking altogether for sleep problems. Then came the search for other methods for helping the autistic child sleep.

Parents reported some defeating problems in using the method of letting the autistic child "cry it out." About 65% said they had used this method successfully with their other normal children and expected initially that they would likewise be successful with the autistic child. There were two common snags: Most autistic children when sleepless climbed repeatedly out of bed far into the night and parents had extreme difficulties in keeping them in bed. They found that repeatedly putting an autistic child back into bed merely increased tension and crying and further delayed the onset of sleep. If they left him strictly alone during the crying-it-out period, he frequently became "hysterical" and cried until exhausted. This problem existed for most sleepless, crying autistic children, whether they stayed in bed or whether they got out of bed repeatedly.

Through observation and a trial-and-error process, mothers usually could ease the autistic child's path into sleep by doing two things: finding a way to keep him in bed and finding a way to help him stop crying. Repeatedly, parents observed that their autistic child was physically and psychologically more tense than their normal children and that they must help him relax so that sleep would be possible. While most autistic children did not want to be held, a few were quieted at times by mother's rocking. Patting, talking, massaging the child's body, singing, sitting beside or lying down with him were the most commonly used successful methods. A few parents locked the bedroom door and let the child play undisturbed until he fell asleep on the floor or on his bed. Afterwards, they could put him comfortably in bed or cover him. This method worked only with children whose crying did not increase their tension. A few parents set a relatively early bedtime for everyone. As one mother said, "Merrill goes to sleep with the least fuss when every light in the house is off, the TV is quiet, and the rest of use are in bed too."

Medicines were tried for about half of all the children, with disappointing results in every case but one in which the medicine was only partially successful. The types of medicines used were either not known or forgotten by most parents, and most were ambivalent about using medicine. Parents worried about harmful side effects, but they also wanted some relief from sleep-interrupted nights. Because of the lack of positive effect, most parents did not want to try other medicines, and thus no systematic efforts were made by physicians to locate more efficacious sedatives.

Several parents said they coped with sleeping problems by trying "everything reasonable" to help the child relax than "tough out" the nights when "nothing worked." Eventually the passage of time and increasing parental know-how eased but often had not entirely erased the sleep problems by interview time.

Fathers' Participation in Sleep Activities

Only a few fathers in both groups routinely helped at bedtime, but nearly all helped out if mother was overtired, away, or ill. Fathers also stepped in to settle down the normal children if there was an uproar at bedtime, but most parents agreed that it was the mothers who were the most successful in handling the problems of the sleepless autistic child. In one case, the parents took turns. While one put the autistic child to bed, the other put the normal children to bed. The next night they shifted responsibilities to facilitate as much good humor as possible and to relieve the mother's burden. Likewise, fathers did not routinely go to the child at night, the rationale being that they had to get up to work the next day. However, many mothers said they were often tired from lack of sleep and could not usually make up for sleep loss during the day because autistic children did not as a rule nap and could not be left safely to their own devices.

Sleep Studies at the Research Center

As with eating problems, we were interested to see whether parents' observations would correlate with our own observations while the child was in the hospital. Most children who slept poorly at home also slept poorly at the hospital. For 6 weeks, averaging 4 to 5 nights per week, sleep records were kept on 14 interview-study autistic children. A member of the nursing staff made a bed check each 15 minutes after the child fell asleep. Time of going to sleep, awaking in the morning, and wakeful periods during the night were logged and the total time of sleep computed for each night. Each mother's description of the child's current sleep problems in the home was rated for severity.

Displayed in Table 36 are the results. Using a sleep disability score, we see that the group of children who had virtually no current sleep problems at home achieved the lowest average sleep disability score. Generally speaking, the worse the problems at home, the higher the score. No formal statistical analysis was done because of the small samples.

Sleep studies using electrophysiological methods revealed no differences between autistic and normal children in amount of time spent in dreaming sleep. Dreaming sleep is the period with rapid eye movement (REM) (Onheiber, White, DeMyer, & Ottinger, 1964; Roffwarg, Dement, & Fisher, 1964). Sleep deprivation studies of two autistic children (Sage & DeMyer, 1966) revealed essentially the same kinds of findings associated with sleep

Table 36. Hospital Observations of Sleep Problems

Severity of home problems at time of interview	% of nights slept < 7 hrs.	% of nights awakened	Total hospital sleep disability score	Average hrs. of sleep per night
None				
Victor	0	2	2	9
Candace	0	10	10	9.5
Maurice	0	6	6	9
Terrie	5	26	31	9
Mild				
Sheri	4	10	14	9
Isaac	0	31	31	9
Louis	8	31	39	8
Moderate				
Larry	12	14	26	9
Susanne	8	41	49	8.75
Severe				
Horace	8	10	18	9
Sarah	3	44	47	9
Andy	9	48	57	8
Nathan	14	40	54	8
Ian	28	32	60	7.5

deprivation in normal adults. On subsequent recovery nights, both children made up for lost sleep by having increased amounts of stage-I REM time and decreased body movement during REM periods.

One other item of interest concerns the relation of EEG abnormalities to sleep. We found that the one best period to see spikes and spike-wave abnormalities in the EEGs of autistic children was to obtain a light sleep recording (Small, Milstein, DeMyer, & Moore, 1977). Whether there is a relationship between this finding and the sleep problems of autistic children is unknown. Light sleep is the one best condition to see abnormal EEG records in all types of children since sleep is a general activator of brain waves.

Handling of Sleep Problems in the Hospital Setting

The nursing staff of the Clinical Research Center handled the children at bedtime for undressing, bathing, snacking, and cuddling much as the parents said they did. Although bedtimes varied at home, all the autistic children were put to bed at about the same time because they were fairly close together in age. Not all of them went to sleep at the same time, and some were highly variable in when they went to sleep. One child took from 17 minutes to almost 5 hours, as measured in the sleep laboratory. To encourage more consistent behavior, the staff allowed the wakeful children to play alone in their beds or in the day room with the lights low. During wakeful periods, the ward staff paid no obvious attention to the children. The children were not played with or cuddled or fed. Wakeful periods in the night were handled in much the same way except that initially the child was soothed, made physically comfortable, and offered a drink of water. During this period everything was low-key, and there were no reinforcers for disruptive behavior or continued wakefulness. This program reduced sleep problems but did not eliminate them entirely.

The ward staff contrived several conditions that could not be set up by parents in the usual home. There were no breakable items about. These were shut in rooms that could be locked during the night. If a child wandered around the day room, he couldn't hurt himself easily, and there were no harmful substances within reach. He couldn't open the door and run outside. The ward staff on duty at night didn't have to worry about their own lost sleep as their working period lasted from 11 p.m. until 7 a.m., and they were required to be awake all night. Thus each wakeful child could be managed with equanimity for as many hours as he was awake. A separate shift handled the evening program for the children and put them to bed. Again, there was no hurry or push to save a little free time for the adults as would happen at the parental home. Putting the children to bed thus was a relaxed, unhurried affair every night.

In the parental home, one person, the mother, had to be mainly responsible for all three shifts, so to speak. If mothers were to have any time for themselves or with their husbands, they had to get the children to bed at a reasonable hour. Many parents seldom managed these moments together. Following is an account of how one autistic child's sleepless evenings and nights affected a marriage:

> About one out of every three nights, Jerry gets up in the middle of the night. It's a curious thing; he will have very active periods and won't rest in the afternoon at all and he won't sleep at night, which wearies me terribly because I have to watch him constantly when he is awake. His naps and evening sleep time are my times to be an individual human. Just about the time I think I can't stand it any more and I'm in tears, then his sleep gets better for a week or two. But about the worst thing of all is his getting up in the middle of the night, because if he gets up repeatedly my husband will go in and spank. In some respects at those times, my husband is more effective than I am—he is very firm. He'll yell at Jerry quite loudly, which probably sounds pretty terrible to you, but Jerry can be quite tiring.

I can see how a lot of men would just walk out and never come back.

But the whole thing is just a vicious circle—Jerry wakes up and wakes us all and my husband gets annoyed and upset and Jerry gets more upset. A man has a right to his sleep, and a man and a woman have a right from a certain point in the evening, say 9 o'clock, to be together uninterrupted. Some nights are just an all around mess and a three-ring circus. We may end up in a big argument for half the night, and I do get very tired.

The most severe case of sleeping disability was that of Ian, age 5 years 10 months at interview time. Here is the account his mother gave in response to the question: "Let's talk about Ian's sleeping habits. How does bedtime go at your house?"

With all the other children—fine, but with Ian, it's horrible. It's him getting up then our putting him back to bed, then him getting up and our chasing him upstairs, him getting up and our getting him out of messing in things. With him it's a riot, but with the others—they're ready for bedtime. Usually his bedtime is quite late, but we can't get him in bed at all until he is very tired.

Question: "What upsets you the most about Ian's sleeping habits?"

Oh! This middle of the night business. When you hear him hit the floor about 2 a.m., you know he's generally up for the rest of the night. I try to put him in bed with me, but he would rather get in the food or his toys. He will turn all the lights in the house on, everything from the bathroom to the living room to the kitchen—all of them. It used to be even more of a riot than it is now—he is quieter now.

Question: "What do you do about this?"

When his sleep problems first started (about 2 years of age), I got up and stayed up with him, but it was too tiring. I'm now to the point where I sleep in a light doze or try to keep him in our bed. Unfortunately, he will slip out. We tried several tranquilizers which made him worse and the doctor took him off altogether. On some types he became too tranquil during the day when he should have been alert, but never did any medicine make him sleepy at night. The nights we can get him to stay in bed he generally goes to sleep. Sometimes we give up. Oh, we tried having him sleep with his brother, but it just kept his brother awake. The doctor suggested we tie him to the bed by winding him in sheets which we tried to do in whatever way would be most comfortable for him—but he'd just chew his way through the sheets. All of our other children went to bed without even rocking and we never did anything to help until we got desperate over Ian's sleep.

It's hard for me to remember all the things we did because it seems like the problems have been going on forever. But it's getting better now—down from several nights a week to about one. The last 6 to 8 months he has been better. I think you forget what you would like to forget but things never got just real terrible for us. I used to get real upset with him and end up with a spanking that maybe I'd been better off not to have administered. It would depend on how many long nights I had been up as to how desperate I would get.

When Ian was in the hospital, he was wakeful for short periods about one night out of every three and had several hours of wakefulness about one night a week. The ward staff estimated over a 6 week period that he averaged about 7½ hours per night of sleep. If this pattern was in effect at his home, then his parents could expect to be awakened for several short periods about two nights and up all night for an additional night each week.

REFERENCES

Onheiber, P., White, P. T., DeMyer, M. K., & Ottinger, D. R. Sleep and dream patterns of child schizophrenics. *Archives of General Psychiatry*, 1964, 12, 568–571.

Roffwarg, H. P., Dement, W. C., & Fisher, C. Preliminary observations of the sleep-dream pattern in neonates, infants, children and adults. In E. Harms (Ed.), *Monographs on child psychiatry, No. II, problems of sleep and dream in children.* New York: Pergamon Press, 1964.

Sage, J. A., & DeMyer, M. K. *Sleep deprivation in two autistic children.* Research Report No. 12. Indianapolis: Clinical Research Center for Early Childhood Schizophrenia, 1966.

Small, J. G., Milstein, V., DeMyer, M. K., & Moore, J. E. Electroencephalographic (EEG) and clinical studies of early infantile autism. *Clinical Electroencephalography*, 1977, 8(1), 27–35.

Chapter 8

PROBLEMS WITH SOCIAL BEHAVIOR, EMOTIONAL EXPRESSION, AND DISCIPLINE

Some of the parents' most painful reactions and some of their most difficult decisions involved their autistic child's reactions to people. One of the primary symptoms of autism has been called social distance or, as several parents phrased it, the autistic child "lives in his own world." We learned from parents and our own experiences that the withdrawal was seldom total, and that it varied depending upon the situation the child was in, on his age, and on the identity of the people trying to relate to him. In general, parents described the most severe social distance as occurring between the ages of about 15 months and 2½ or 3 years. By the time the child was 4 to 5, parents described him as beginning to relate not only to people in the family but also to others. Unfortunately, despite diminution in degree of social distance, the autistic children remained severely handicapped in this sphere and their budding attempts to relate to people brought new problems. The children often ignored visitors to the home, but they also might crawl over them and do other acts that made both visitors and parents uncomfortable.

Disorders in emotional expression, such as intense anger and fear and prolonged screaming put family members on edge. Such behaviors coupled with other activities the parents wanted to eliminate or change resisted their efforts at discipline. Parents found the primary problem was that the autistic child failed to understand the meaning of any kind of punishment, explanation, or reward for "good" behavior. Consequently, parents remained uncertain about the adequacy of their methods and the children's social/emotional inadequacies and destructive behaviors continued.

Let us look in detail at parents' responses to interview questions concerning disorders in social skills and emotional expression and the uncertainties of parents in their efforts to change some of the more disturbing behaviors, such as destructive acts, intense fears, anger, screaming, messing, and running away.

Social Responsivity during the First Year of Life

Questions: "How did your (index) child respond to you as a tiny baby?" How did he let you know he was responding to you as people? How much attention from you did the infant want? How did he differ from sibs in the amount of cuddling and attention needed and wanted?" (See Table 37).

Autistic infants on the whole were described as less socially responsive than the normal matched control group and less responsive than their siblings. However, only about 21% seemed definitely and worryingly unrelating from the earliest months of life, and only about 9% regularly rejected cuddling and attention. A mother described such extreme social nonresponsiveness: "Jerry didn't want any attention from us even in the first year and he didn't mimic anything we did. He was so different from the others. He didn't smile much or play pat-a-cake or raise his arms to be picked up." Another infant was perceived by his mother this way: "When any of the family picked him up,

Table 37. Scale of Social Responsivity and Withdrawal in Infancy

Scale	Autistic[a]		Normal	
	N	%	N	%
Extremely responsive/demanding of attention	6	18	13	39
Responsive but often content alone (no less responsive than sibs)	5	15	16	48
Less responsive than sibs, or liked being in crib better than being with people	12	36	4	12
Definitely socially withdrawn	10[b]	30	0	0

[a]$p < .01$.

[b]Three infants had exhibited adequate social responses for several months during their first year of life.

his attitude was 'Well, I don't care one way or the other whether you play with me or leave me alone.' "

The social distance for about 36% of autistic infants was more subtly expressed. They used most of the social mechanisms of the normal infant but to a lesser degree. They smiled and acted excited at the approach of an adult or sibling and they might lift their arms to be picked up, but they were remembered as being less sociable than their siblings at the same age. Many of these infants were more content to be in bed or in a baby chair than to be with people, and yet they generally accepted attention in a positive way when it was offered. A description of this type of infant was given by Janis's mother:

> Janis was alert and interested in people. She looked at us and smiled, but she accepted rather than demanded attention. When she was old enough to sit, she would rather sit and bounce in her teeter-babe than be held. She was less sociable than her brothers.

About 33% of autistic infants seemed much like normal infants in both amount and type of social responsiveness. There were two essential types of social response found in normal infants: (a) the infant who wanted and "demanded" much attention and social interaction and was more oriented toward human interaction than occupying himself with toys or activities (autistic, 18%; normal, 39%); and (b) the infant who liked and sought attention but also was often content to play alone (autistic, 15%; normal, 48%).

The following descriptions by mothers typify these two normal infant types:

> Leonard was a very cuddly baby, much more so than our other children. He smiled a lot at us, fussed to be held, and was very affectionate. As a first child, he got an awful lot of attention.
>
> Jarvis was a cuddly baby. He enjoyed the attention we gave him, but he never demanded much more than we gave. He could be happy for a long stretch playing alone in his playpen.

A variant of the normal social response was a lessening in desire for and acceptance of holding and cuddling that occurred when the infant learned to crawl or walk. At this point, many normal infants preferred actively to explore their environment over passively sitting in their parents' laps. The normal infant did not, however, lose social contact with the parents. As Eva's mother said, "Eva fought to get off my lap and onto the floor when she learned to crawl, but she was always following after me."

In contrast, when autistic infants learned to crawl or walk, some parents noted a diminution in sociability. On hindsight, Candy's mother recalled, "When she started walking at 10 months, she never stopped running, and I think she paid less attention to us from that time on. We weren't alarmed about it, but comparing her with our other child, Candy was less sociable at that age."

Normal Infants with Unusual Social Responses

About 12% of the normal infants appeared somewhat withdrawn socially. "Ronnie didn't want a lot of attention. He was very content to lie or play in his crib all alone. My other children weren't like that." Brad's mother said, "He was a wiggly baby who was stiff and hard to hold and didn't seem to enjoy it. Oh, he looked at us and smiled and put his arms up when he was unhappy, but he wasn't what you would call a cuddly baby." The phenomenon of the stiff and hard-to-hold baby was uncommon in both groups. Only 9% of autistic and 3% of normal infants were so described.

Emotional Expression in the First Year of Life

The baby who is "too good" has been called typical of autism. There were 33% of the autistic sample who appeared to be overly passive and placid infants. Felix's mother said, "He was a fat, pokey baby who didn't move around much. He was a good, happy baby." One autistic infant was so "good" that he never cried, not even when he was hungry. On the whole, raters had difficulty in distinguishing parental descriptions of the normally "good, happy baby" from those of the "too good, too passive baby." Such distinctions would have to be made with on-the-spot observations. Some autistic infants appeared to be relatively inactive physically and parents' perceptions of their emotional expression were colored by the amount of physical activity they showed in some cases.

About 15% of autistic infants were "too irritable" or characterized as "sad and unhappy." Sherry cried frequently. Her mother said, "She was a crabby baby. For a long while I thought I wasn't doing things right with her, but after the other kids came along, I realized she was different. The only things that soothed her at that time were holding and rocking."

Edward's mother described a combination of irritability and passivity:

> Eddie cried easily, especially if we changed anything around or if he heard a sudden sound. We couldn't go anywhere when he was a baby because he would cry so hard that he couldn't quit; but he was a quiet baby a lot of the time and didn't smile much. He looked bored and unhappy.

Mimi also showed a combination of under- and overreaction. She cried frequently at night but during the day was "sedate, tranquil, and placid—a very good baby."

In summary, about 66% of autistic infants were rated as less responsive socially than their siblings or more withdrawn than the normal control infants. However, only 30% were largely indifferent to or rejecting of attention. About 33% of autistic infants, even on hindsight, seemed to their parents to be in normal social contact. In emotional expression or temperament, about 15% of autistic infants were rated as too irritable and unhappy and about 9% were rated as a combination of too irritable and too placid. In many cases, the raters could not distinguish the normal "good, happy baby" from the abnormal "too good" baby, but the too-placid autistic infant probably did exist in 30 to 35% of cases.

Social Withdrawal Symptoms after the First Year

Those 30% of cases who were withdrawn in the first year of life remained that way during the second year. For the rest, unless there was a definite, sudden change in the character of the toddler's manner of relating to people, parents had difficulty in recalling the exact time when social withdrawal began. For most autistic children, the withdrawal began somewhere in the second year of life or "around 2 years of age" (54%). In only 12% did the withdrawal begin between 2 and 3. The latest development of the phenomenon was at around 4 in one child. In some of these later developing cases, the parents seemed to deny the presence of earlier withdrawal symptoms, or else the autistic child was their only child and they had no comparison to make with other children. To establish the date at which social withdrawal first began, it may be useful to look with parents at the albums of family photographs, which in hindsight often reveal the beginning of an increase in social distance even though no one in the family noticed it at the time. While we asked parents to bring photos of their children to help establish dates of symptom onset, in practice many families had taken few pictures or saved only the best pictures.

Because the onset was gradual in well over half the cases, the factors synchronous with the onset of withdrawal were often unclear. They included illness in three cases, family moves in two, learning to crawl or walk in four, a sibling's birth in two, people visiting in the house in one, and an accident in one. About half of the mothers partially blamed themselves in a nonspecific way. All but three of these mothers stated they had neither neglected the child nor were less warm than with their other children. The mothers who blamed themselves generally were unclear in their own minds about their specific deficiencies. Their statements can be typified by the following: "I

Table 38. Development of Social Withdrawal in Autistic Children after First Year of Life

Commencement of withdrawal	N	%	Development of withdrawal	N	%
First year	10	33	First-year symptoms continued	10	33
Second year	15	45	Sudden onset	5	15
About 2 years	3	9	Gradual onset	18	52
Between 2 and 3 years	1	3			
About 3 years	3	9			
Between 3 and 4 years	1	3			

don't know the cause of it, but I wonder if I did something wrong. Maybe I left him alone too much, but I don't think so. I treated him just like his sister and she's all right." Another mother, sorrowing over the death of an older sibling, felt she might have been withdrawn from her child. Yet another said she treated her son as if he "lived in a white room." However, there were only three mothers who unequivocally claimed they were to blame for the social withdrawal.

Fathers in all but two cases did not agree that the mothers could have been even partially at fault, citing the mothers' attention to and affection for the infants as ranging from adequate to superb. One father said, "Neither of us particularly wanted another baby; but after Jana was born, that tremendous mother instinct that my wife has just took over. That child got excellent care."

Character of Social Withdrawal Within the Family

The hallmark of the autistic child, social distance, was evident in every child and yet was variously expressed in each one. Rarely was the social isolation complete in the family. For example, most parents felt close to their autistic child and at least partially able to read his moods and emotions. Reactions of anger and fear seemed adequately described and differentiated by most parents. Many times parents couldn't relieve a distressful emotion but neither did they feel emotionally separate, which was a surprise to the raters. Most parents described the social distance in terms of people outside of the immediate family. Autistic children looked to the mother for some things such as feeding, protection from sibs, bedtime comfort, and to the father for other things such as wrestling and chasing. Clearly most of the autistic children differentiated their parents from each other and other people. A minority of parents thought they were used only as conveniences and that their child had no feeling for them. Mothers and fathers expressed these feelings in a sad and poignant way. As Matt's mother said, "He can do without most anybody. He won't respond to our love. My husband misses his companionship and he is a good father. I miss being able to cuddle and comfort him." One mother described her own intense sorrow when her daughter, between 15 months and 3 years of age, was unable to respond affectionately to her. "I got so unhappy over this that I just didn't think life was worth living. For a while, my hair fell out in patches and I cried all the time."

Despite many parents not feeling emotionally isolated from their autistic children, nearly all the children were described as less affectionate to the parents than were their siblings and this undoubtedly in some cases led parents to approach the child with affectionate gestures less often than their siblings. As one mother said, "When cute little Mary throws her arms around you and says, 'I love you', it's impossible not to be responsive, but Merrill never does this." However, 90% of mothers said they were frequently affectionate toward their autistic child and seldom missed an opportunity to demonstrate their affection physically and verbally. Only a few fathers (about 12%) characterized themselves as "reserved" in their expressions of affection, seldom kissing and hugging the autistic child or his siblings. Several autistic children learned to "give a kiss" when asked, but these were characterized as automatic gestures and rarely spontaneously offered. One 3-year-old boy patted and kissed his parents when they drove by a McDonald's restaurant and they rewarded him with a treat.

We asked, "In the immediate family, whom does the autistic child get along with best?" The mother was picked in 43% of the cases, both mother and father in 21%, and in the remaining cases it was either a sibling or the father or various combinations of family members. We asked for the reason why the parents thought the child got along best with this particular person. The mothers developed a special knowledge of the autistic child based on close contact all his life. Through observation and trial and error, mothers learned to read the autistic child's wishes and to respond so that he was more comfortable physically and psychologically. Mothers were best able to reduce screaming and induce smiling at least part of the time. We learned from responses to these questions that most mothers did not feel at interview time as if the child were emotionally distant from them. In the past, most had felt, at one time or another, that the child was emotionally withdrawn from them, but in only a few cases at interview time did a mother complain that this child seemed not to know her from anybody else or to be truly withdrawn from her. The autistic mother did not describe a "normal" relationship in the sense that she felt she was treated by the autistic child as her normal children treated her, but neither did she feel as if the autistic child isolated himself from her emotionally.

When the father was the favored person, it was because he often took the time to play or do something pleasant with the child. Sometimes he understood the social withdrawal of the child because he tended not to be as outgoing as the mother and thus could understand the child's social isolation better. When a sibling was favored, it was because this sibling developed maternal qualities and could take over the mother's special understanding when she was fatigued or busy with other duties. Some siblings developed a special quality even superior in some respects to those of the parents.

Here is how one father responded to the question, "In the family, who would you say that Jerry gets along with best?"

> I'd say that it's probably a toss-up between my wife and myself and our oldest daughter. I have found this a bit hard to understand, but a couple of weeks ago I realized I'd never seen Anita mad at Jerry. She can be unhappy if he's torn up something of hers, but she seems capable of being unhappy at Jerry's act without being unhappy with him as a person, and this is very different from any of the other children. I think I don't do as good a job in this regard as Anita does. She spends a great deal of time with Jerry after school when her mother is busy getting supper.

Visitors to the Home

The parents described four main types of response to people who came into the home for visits. The most common response was indifference (72%), meaning that the child paid little attention and continued his autistic pursuits. However, about 58% of this indifferent group showed some social response to visitors, such as occasionally accepting affectionate gestures or sitting on the davenport next to the visitor and bouncing or playing some trick for attention. About 21% actively avoided visitors by going to another room or to a corner and about 6% were fearful of visitors and clung to parents or a sib for comfort.

All but 30% of autistic children showed favor toward visitors in some fashion. Tim's mother said:

> When Tim was very little (about his second year of life), he was fearful of all visitors, even his grandmother and aunt. They visited several times a week. I felt bad for them. They wanted him to like them so much. We decided they should just keep visiting and this year he smiles when they come and likes them to pick him up for a little while. He doesn't accept this from other visitors.

Felix's mother:

> There are some people he dislikes more than others. I can tell because he gets agitated when they come in, but I don't always know why. One man upsets him when he speaks—he has a booming voice.

In one extreme case, a 2½-year-old autistic boy apparently ignored everybody who came into the house and showed little feeling one way or the other when visitors would try to interact with him. However, his worst setback occurred after the parents had a large group of people in one evening. The day after this occurrence the boy intensified his crying and self-hitting to the point that he had to be hospitalized in order to save him from serious injury.

Over half the autistic children did something that was annoying to visitors. A few behaviors such as rummaging in their purses, could be managed without much trouble, but others caused acute embarassment to both visitor and parents. One couple described the reaction of other people to their 4-year-old autistic boy:

> People are puzzled by him. On the one hand, he seems in his own world, but on the other hand, he has no special discipline. He will climb on their backs, crawl over their heads even. This is different from when he was younger and he totally ignored them.

The mother described her reaction as follows:

> I don't encourage people to come and see me now. I am too embarrassed. He pays no attention to my telling him not to climb on them and he is too strong for me to hold back. Visitors act embarrassed and upset.

The father described his reaction this way:

> I'm not so embarrassed; particularly since other men with children of their own don't mind him climbing over them.

Janis' parents said:

> She's generally in a world of her own, but when people come to the house now she throws herself on them. She puts her hands in their mouths and screams loud and long if something happens that she doesn't like which could be almost anything.

Another child, a 4-year-old boy, was calm until visitors paid any attention to him. Then:

> He cries, and he cries loud and long. In fact, he cries at a lot of things. If people don't pay any attention to him he will jabber at them in his own particular language, but then, if they respond to him, he cries and runs out of the room.

We asked the parents what they liked least about the index child's response to other people. As in language problems, many parents had a larger worry and a smaller worry. The larger worry concerned the future—what would happen to the child if he didn't get on better with outsiders. They also indicated, in most cases that this larger worry was tied to the communication difficulty which most parents saw as the basic problem underlying the social distance. A few parents made statements such as, "I think his relations to people are the whole thing."

The "smaller" worries concerned the annoying things the children did around other people. Cheri's father said:

> She will not pay attention to things people say, and she used to totally ignore them. Now she may crawl on people's laps to look at a book, which is fine, but she also rubs fingers over people's legs. She especially likes to feel women's stockings and you have to pull her away to get her to stop. This can happen anywhere. We have definitely cut down our social life because of this.

The raters believed that many parents, in contrast to Cheri's father, tended to hide from themselves just how upset they really were over these so-called smaller worries. Some children screeched when visitors came, or pulled down their pants and urinated, or grabbed eye-glasses, or screamed when spoken to, or became more active so that the visits were marred by incessant running. One child leaped on visitors to "kiss" them but in his excitement often bit them instead.

Ambivalence was another reaction voiced by several mothers over these inappropriate behaviors. The mothers had been so worried about a child's previous total ignoring of visitors that they welcomed any evidence that he was bringing other people into his "own little world." Kim's mother said, "I hate it when he crawls all over visitors, but I also hate to discourage the first signs that he is taking notice of other people. I'm not sure what to do about it."

In over half of the families, there were at least one or two consistent visitors who made special efforts to relate to the autistic child. These people were generally grandparents, aunts, uncles, close friends, or neighbors. Parents were grateful to those who took the trouble to visit routinely and gradually form one of the first positive links the child made in his socialization outside the immediate family.

Visiting in Homes of Others and Community Excursions

Question: "How does your autistic child react when he goes places outside the home, especially unfamiliar places?" Parents reported all gradations of acceptance of these activities. A few of the children were not upset at all, but most parents could not take their autistic child to certain places in the community. Restaurants were a prime example. Eating out generated all of the child's most difficult behaviors: screaming, hyperactivity, hitting, biting. (It helps to get a table in the corner of the room and seat the child so he faces the corner.) Many could not take the autistic child to drive-in movies or to any movie at all because he was not interested and became impatient over having to sit too long.

Those parents who took the children on shopping trips or to a friend's house had many painful feelings as their child dismantled grocery displays or went to the friend's basement and spilled soap powder over the floor in "the twinkling of an eye." Parents differed on how much embarrassment they could stand and how much criticism they could take over not "properly controlling" their child in public. Many parents freely acknowledged that they limited their excursions into the community because they could find no satisfactory way to alter these disturbing behaviors. In contrast, some parents made heroic efforts to acclimate the child to a few new places. Larry's parents took him week after week to Sunday school along with his favorite chair. Gradually, crying and agitation were replaced by stoic tolerance and then by glimmers of enjoyment. This improvement was a great relief to the parents. Merrill's mother said, "I remember how cooped up I felt when Merrill was little. We couldn't go anywhere and have fun. He was always running. Once he got clear away and a policeman finally found him playing in an alley. I was frantic."

One child, age 4 years 3 months, had not improved, and her father said,

I think both of us (parents) are at our wit's end. We haven't had a vacation in 4 years. A month ago we said that no matter what, we were going to visit some people we had known in school. We planned to stay a weekend. We took Sue's bed and everything we could think of to make her feel at home. After a terrible night (she screamed a day and a night), we packed up at 5 in the morning and left. Everybody was wrung out. How much can one family take!

Behavior with other Children Outside the Family

The autistic children were almost universally described as not getting along well with children outside the family. By interview time, about 25% of them were showing some interest in other children, mainly looking and hovering at the edge of the group. While most were passive and noninteractive with regard to other children, a few would bite, hit, shove, or scream if their wishes were thwarted in any way. One mother noted this about other children:

> Shanan is absolutely unable to adapt to anybody else. Everybody else has to adapt to her. Older children and adults consistently try to make her more comfortable. Children almost never do. They try to pull her into activities. When she won't do what they want or try to play with them, they ignore her, and she, of course, ignores them. However, she may run up to another child and for no reason at all just shove him over or hit him, and this goes over like a lead balloon.

In general, there was a gradation of response depending on how much the outsider tried to go along with the autistic child's wishes. Adults and older children in general tried to make the autistic child as comfortable as possible. If the autistic child wanted to be alone, the older child and other adults generally let him alone. Younger children and agemates seldom attempted to make him comfortable, and thus relationships were thwarted.

Problems with Emotional Expression

The autistic children characteristically, in periods of calm, had a flat, uninterested manner interrupted by periods of irritability. At times parents had difficulty in deciding whether the irritable behavior manifested by screaming or temper tantrums meant that the child was angry or that he was easily frustrated. In any event and no matter what the cause, about 85% of the children screamed excessively, sometimes because they were angry and sometimes because they were frustrated or fearful and sometimes for no outwardly discernible reason.

About 30% of parents said extreme shows of anger made life difficult. If Jana lost her string or was thwarted from destroying something, such as a bedspread, "to make a string," she screamed at the top of her lungs, sometimes for hours. Robin, a 5-year-old autistic boy, was described by his mother as "going through periods where he just seems to have to work his aggression out of his system. We have had a great problem with shows of temper which just recently have got better." One 3½-year-old boy kicked, bit, scratched, or urinated on the floor if his parents did something different from what he preferred. Another young child, Mickey, screamed and hit out "over simple things that the other children would overlook." In contrast, about 12% of autistic children were seen as being unusual because they so seldom expressed any anger at all. Sanford's mother said, "He is not a difficult child to care for. He doesn't get angry much at all. Mostly he wanders around the house carrying something." What caused anger most frequently was thwarting of desires. In this respect, autistic children were little different from normal ones. It was the extreme manifestations that differentiated autistic anger.

Fear responses caused serious problems in relatively few instances (about 12%). One 5-year-old boy, between the ages of 18 months and about 4 years was fearful of strangers, the outside, car rides, new situations. Sometimes he had inexplicable fears which consumed him and which could be soothed away only with difficulty. About 21% of children had strong fears that made an aspect of life a problem. Didi's mother said:

> Her fears of new places are quite strong. If we took her all the places a normal 4-year-old child would go, she would be fearful a lot, but we don't. For 2 years now, I have been doing my grocery shopping in one store, and it's just in the last few months that she is at ease there. I just decided she had to get used to at least one place outside of home and my parents' house.

One boy was terrified and uncontrollable around doctors and dentists. Two children were terrified of toilet training. In general, those who were extremely fearful of strangers and of new places caused the most difficulties as parents could not protect them from these fears without great curtailment of pleasurable and even necessary activities.

There were about 12% of children who were fearless, and of the remainder, about 55% had some fears that either were weakly expressed or concerned objects or activities that could be avoided without serious consequence to the family's life style. Examples of these fears were certain things on TV, elevators or escalators, thunderstorms, animals, and wading too deep in the water. Some feared objects were unusual, e.g., watermelons, a certain water tower, moving windshield wipers, strange toilets, holes in the street, light fixtures.

By far, the most common type of fear, found in about 42% of autistic cases, was the fear of certain noises and high pitched sounds such as vacuum cleaners, factory whistles, and sirens. Mimi "went wild" when her mother turned on the vacuum cleaner. Lenny's parents disposed of their food mixer because of his terror when they ran it. Scratchy sounds, radio static, and loud or high-pitched music caused fear in some. Several parents thought the children also felt pain on hearing the feared sounds.

Reactions of parents were to hold and soothe the fearful child and say reassuring words. If these measures did not work, they avoided the fear-arousing events or objects as much as possible, in some cases curtailing the life style of the family. Like many other symptoms, fears tended to get better at about the age of 4 to 6 years.

A lack of fear of common dangers was reported for about 30%, meaning that the parents had to watch for the child's safety constantly. These children could not understand the dangers of the street, and panic reigned in the family if they escaped the parents' sight. They played with controls on stoves and with hot pans. Neither burns nor bruises nor punishment kept some children from common dangers. One family sold their gas stove for an electric one to solve a major problem. Constant vigilance and making the house as safe as possible were the only resources for most parents as the children were impervious to learning to protect themselves.

Normal children differed from autistic children in that there were none whose fears were so intense that they curtailed the lifestyle of child or parents. Most normal children were more easily soothed by words and physical comfort. The types of fears were different; few had fear of strangers or of new places or odd things. Normal children quickly became alert to and protected themselves from common dangers. Normal children also feared "things that went bump in the night," but they could be soothed and recognized their parents' presence. Those 15% of autistic children with night terrors were less soothable and seemed out of contact with the parents during the terrors. Normal children, of course, verbalized their fears and were more amenable to explanation.

Discipline Problems

Before approaching a discussion of parental methods of discipline, we asked, "What sorts of things does your autistic child do when he is naughty?" The most common behavior considered naughty by parents was "messiness" (36%), e.g., spilling household chemicals, playing in toilet or excretory products; and the next most common was destructive behavior (21%). The rest were miscellaneous behaviors such as running off, striking sibs, not minding, and temper tantrums. About one-third of the parents refused to answer the question as posed because they believed the autistic child had no concept of being naughty. A few parents gave a list of naughty behaviors but added that since the child had no concept of right and wrong, the parents would not call them naughty. Mimi's mother answered this way:

> She plays in the toilet, throws things, runs in the street, but I must add, I don't think she realizes she is naughty. I realize this now. At one time, I might have called it naughty, but not now.

Table 39. Types of Autistic Behavior Particularly Irritating to Parents

Behavior[a]	N	%
Hyperirritable[b]	26	78
Messing	23	69
Hyperactive	14	42
Destructive	13	39
Runs away	6	18

[a]Cases with 1 behavior—21%; with 2 or 3—54%; with 4—21%; with 5 behaviors—3%.
[b]Excessive crying, temper tantrums, screaming, anger.

Isaac's mother said:

> He will scold himself, using my exact words and tone, but goes right ahead doing the things I've told him not to do. He's not advanced enough to know right from wrong and has no sense of shame.

Unfortunately, we did not inquire specifically about the children's concept of right and wrong or about guilt and feelings of shame, but only about 15% of the parents indicated their autistic children showed such reactions. In each case, the reaction was rudimentary. "He will hang his head if I scold, but he still does the same things over again."

Despite so many parents refusing to enumerate "naughty" behavior, there were major behaviors that parents found irritating or wished to change. These major "unwanted" behaviors are listed in Table 39. The most common were excessive irritability in about 78% and messing behavior in about 69%. Next most common were hyperactivity and destructive activities (including self-injury, injuring of others, and destruction of household possessions) in 42% and 39%, respectively, and frequent running away in 18%. Making family life difficult was the fact that about 78% of the autistic children had two or more such behaviors. About 24% possessed four of five. It was clear that nearly every parent implicitly or explicitly wished to change some irritating, destructive, messing behaviors that got on the nerves of all family members.

Parental Methods of Discipline

We asked about the commonly used methods of discipline: scolding, spanking, setting on a chair, isolation, deprivation, explanation, rewards, and praise. If there is one statement that describes the most common types of discipline used by parents of autistic children and the problems met in using any method, it would be the following:

> When he first started acting the way he does—messing in everything he can reach, pulling down the drapes, I thought it was just a phase. I scolded but didn't spank too much. He kept getting into things and began to bite and pinch and hit himself. Then people—my mother, the doctor—said he was spoiled and we weren't being firm enough. We started spanking him a lot but it didn't do any good. He just ignored it. Sometimes his father spanked too hard, which was a bone of contention between us. You couldn't set him on a chair—he either jumped off right away or seemed to enjoy it, twiddling his hands. I don't want to send him to his room—he's too withdrawn anyhow. The big thing is he doesn't seem to understand what punishment means—he goes right ahead doing the same thing over and over. You just can't reach him. He doesn't understand praise. We finally realized that spanking doesn't do any good and we have stopped completely except when he's doing something downright dangerous like getting into the street or pushing the baby downstairs. We really don't know what to do. I don't know whether we are too strict or not strict enough. I wish we knew!

Nearly every autistic child's failure to learn from discipline was to some extent seen by the parents to be the result of a failure to understand what punishment meant. These remarks were spontaneous. We asked no question about the child's understanding of punishment, making the nearly 100% rate a remarkable phenomenon. Following are some illustrative quotes:

> He doesn't understand deprivation of things or sitting in a chair. When I try to explain, it's like talking to a blank wall.
> I don't feel like spanking or scolding Ian. It's like punishing a child without arms for not feeding himself. He doesn't understand and I think his behavior is something he can't help.
> I can say that George doesn't understand any kind of punishment. I used to spank him more when I didn't realize that he does not understand and thought he was just being uncooperative.
> If you don't catch him immediately after he has done something, then you haven't even a small chance of getting him to see the connection between the punishment and the act. I wonder if he gets the connection even then.
> There's no point in getting severe because I don't think he understands what you are doing.

Only the rare autistic child was seen as even partially understanding rewards or praise. As Kitty's mother said:

Even before the age of 2 years, the other children knew about give and take. They would bring me some toy on the floor and I would praise and they would bring me more toys. Kitty (age 5) has never reached that stage. She's never brought me anything and never responded to praise. The only thing that works, maybe, is a spank on the bottom.

In the second and third years of life, most parents thought that discipline should begin. Scolding was used by all parents. Spanking was used by all but about 10 to 15% at one time or another. Most parents (about 75%) reported spanking the autistic child less than they spanked siblings. Sheri's father said, "She doesn't get it near as often as the other two because it doesn't do much good to spank her. She'll just do the same thing again, time after time. We've never spanked her much." Sheri's mother added, "She will go for weeks without a spanking. Then I do it only because I'm aggravated with her, not because I think it will do any good."

We asked the parents to compare the autistic child's achieving good behavior with that of the siblings. Most parents thought the autistic child's behavior was so different from that of the siblings that comparisons were meaningless. Merrill's father said:

His behavior is so different from theirs that you can't compare it. It seems inappropriate to label his behavior as either bad or good. You can't call it naughty either. Without getting into a discussion of free will, nonetheless the other children have more of a choice in how they will behave than Merrill does. When you do punish him, it's more because you are aggravated, because punishment is meaningless to him.

His mother added:

Some of the things he does when he gets carried away in excitement or anger I don't punish because he doesn't have the good judgment that I expect from the others. They would get punished right away if they pitched the screens from the windows as Merrill does.

The normal control parents also punished when angry and like autistic parents felt guilty about losing control. Normal parents' guilt seemed almost always to be evanescent in contrast to autistic parents whose guilt nagged at them for they had a "mentally disturbed child."

Comparison of Punishment Used by Autistic and Normal Parents

The raters picked out the principal punishment used by parents with a given autistic child (see Table 40). Spanking and scolding were the two most common methods (48% and 30% of cases, respectively). In contrast, about 64% of normal parents used no one major method of punishment. Instead, they found that in certain situations their normal child responded to different types of punishments and they typically could use a variety of them (scolding, deprivation of privileges, isolation, and spanking).

Autistic children, on the other hand, did not have the vaguest idea what deprivation of a privilege meant, and therefore autistic parents did not use the technique. Isolation techniques were largely not understood either, or autistic parents were reluctant to try them because of the fear that they might accentuate even further the child's self-isolation. Autistic children, if they responded at all, tended to show some behavior change only if they felt an immediate pain or a change in tone or sharpness of voice.

We asked the parents how effective they thought punishment was in effecting behavior change. Normal parents thought punishment generally effective in about 60% of cases and somewhat effective in 40%. As a consequence, 100% of normal parents used punishment with the normal index children. In contrast, only one set of autistic parents reported punishment generally effective and 60% reported it to be ineffective. Punishment was at best effective in changing behavior for a few minutes and then in only 37% of autistic children (see Table 41).

Then why did parents continue to use punishment with their autistic children if it was so ineffective? We looked at all of the interview responses on discipline to find the answer to this question and found that lack of response caused a considerable modification of parents' actions. At the onset of the autistic child's screaming, messing, and destructive behavior, parents reported treating it as a passing phase and punished an autistic child much as

Table 40. Punishment of Autistic and Normal Children

Principal punishment	Autistic		Normal	
	N	%	N	%
None	7	21	0	0
Scolding	10	30	2	6
Deprived of privileges	1	3	5	20
Isolation	1	3	2	6
Spanking	12	48	6	18
Several of above	2	6	16	64

Table 41. Response to Punishment

Factor	Autistic		Normal	
	N	%	N	%
Emotional Response[a]				
Feelings hurt	7	21	30	91
Angry	2	6	3	9
"Falls apart", extreme crying, shaking	3	9	0	0
Indifferent; may smile	10	30	0	0
Not spanked enough to know	6	18	0	0
Effectiveness of punishment[a]				
Generally effective	1	3	20	60
Effective for a few minutes	12	37	13	40
Not effective	20	60	0	0
Hardest punisher in the family				
Father	16	49	16	49
Mother	8	24	10	30
No difference between father and mother	9	27	7	21
Other person	0	0	0	0

[a]$p < .01$.

they would punish their other children at the same age. Since the troublesome behavior continued unabated or worsened, most parents tried to be "firmer," punished more severely and frequently. Such a course did not bring about the desired change in the child but did cause the parents to feel guilty and inadequate.

In addition to punishment being ineffective, there were strange and puzzling responses to spanking in about 39% of autistic children. They were either indifferent to the punishment, not crying or sometimes smiling (30%), or they "fell to pieces" (9%). One mother said, "She acted if a catastrophe befell her with a light spanking." Another mother said, "Jerry just acted as if nothing had happened." Ian's parents gave his school teacher permission to slap his hands when he started to tear pages out of books. His mother said:

> We were happy to cooperate in anything within reason, and I knew she wasn't mean. Well, the teacher didn't have any success because Ian would smile when she slapped him and got so he would happily put out his hands for a spank.

About 43% of autistic parents then cut down on the amount of spanking (see Table 42) and consciously planned to use it only in extreme situations,

Table 42. Spanking of Autistic Children

Pattern	N	%
Child never spanked	3	9
Spanking has always been rare	9	27
Spanked in past more than currently	14	43
Systematic spanking	5	15
Currently spanking more severe	2	6

generally when the child endangered himself or others. Parents used the theory that if they seldom spanked, the child would surely learn from a smart slap when it was imperative that he learn. While parents cut down on the amount of spanking, they generally did not reach their goal of spanking only in emergencies. They reported spanking at times when they were extra tired, out of sorts, or "driven up the wall" by one of the autistic child's repetitive, irritating behaviors. Some parents felt guilt, as Isaac's mother did: "I think punishment does no good but at times he just gets too much and I spank and feel very badly afterward." Kitty's mother said, "There are days when she irritates me to no end. Her screaming goes on so long that I scream back and spank her. I know I shouldn't but I can't help myself and then I feel awful."

Other mothers were more philosophical. Ordinarily Jerry's mother spanked only if he urinated on the floor (about once every two weeks), but he liked to "stomp all the water out of the bathtub. Usually I go along with this unless I'm very tired then I may yell and spank. I know this inconsistency isn't good, but I do the best I can in the face of things. I try to accept my imperfections."

Did relaxed discipline accomplish the desired goals? The results were somewhat mixed and the children's behavior was largely unchanged, but in most cases parents felt a bit better about themselves. Merrill's father said:

> When I used to punish, I'd always end up worrying that I might be blocking a relationship with Merrill because it made him so mad. Maybe his behavior has improved under conditions of relaxed discipline. (Pause) Well, at least it hasn't gotten any worse.

Despite feeling some lessening of guilt after lessening punishment, parents of autistic children continued to be plagued with feelings of uncertainty over discipline. There were only three sets of parents who expressed satisfaction with the way they were currently managing discipline, and these were parents who were just beginning to use professional advice. They believed they were learning when to be more strict and felt strengthened by professional sanctions to be firm about prohibiting some of the more irritating behaviors.

In the past, there have been disputes among professionals (Goldfarb, 1961; Pitfield & Oppenheim, 1964) about whether these "parental perplexities" represent an extreme character deviation in autistic parents. All of our evidence supports the idea that the problem begins with the failure of autistic children to understand the meaning of punishment or praise as practiced in the "average" home so that the children do not respond to punishment in ways the parents expect. The end result is the parents' perplexity over the best way to discipline the autistic child.

Professional Methods of Changing Emotional and Social Responses

In the past, the basic tenet of most therapy with autistic children was first to change the social and emotional responses of the child to the therapist, i.e., to encourage the child to lessen social distance and feel comfortable with him. Hand in hand, the parents were also expected to change their personal and social deficiencies to encourage better social response and less negativism in the child. The basic idea was that the autistic child's developmental failure and social isolation were consequences of a failure to develop a basic trust in his parents during the earliest months of life. The flaw in this procedure was that social distance could be lessened with considerable regularity in the treatment situation, but the accelerated improvement in speech and intellectual skills frequently failed to follow.

On the ward of the Clinical Research Center, we developed some direct methods of encouraging more adequate social responses by direct behavior modification methods (DeMyer & Ferster, 1962). Using a procedure of pleasurable social rewards (e.g., roughhousing, cuddling, rocking), professionally untrained child care workers were able to improve social responses of eight autistic children.

> An example was Pete, an extremely isolated boy, 6 years of age. Before behavior modification he responded to his individual therapist, but only in the therapy room. If he met the therapist in the halls he paid no attention to her social overtures. Left to himself, he flipped and spun objects endlessly. He amused himself by sitting on his knees, feet tucked under his buttocks, and laughing uproariously as he looked at one of his feet as he slowly moved it from under a buttock. He screamed at changes in routine or thwarting of a wish, slept and ate poorly, and bit and kicked when taken to music and art activities.
>
> The behavior modification procedure began with the child care worker standing beside him and talking while Pete engaged in his

repetitive activities. When Pete no longer moved away, the child care worker carried Pete on his shoulder. Then he used the same type of reward when Pete made any response to the worker, calling his name after Pete made eye contact with him. Tricycle riding, other appropriate use of toys and eating utensils, and toilet training were taught in the same way. After 11 months in this operant conditioning program, Pete regularly engaged in specific new behaviors shaped by free operant conditioning methods, e.g., kissed and looked at adults, and signaled to them when he wished to be picked up, rode a tricycle and rocking horse, spent less total time in flipping objects, and participated willingly in music and art. In addition, five of the children showed some behaviors that generalized to other situations and to other people, e.g., happier affects, more affectionate gestures towards family members, and decreased repetitive behaviors. Nevertheless, without consistent stimulation, especially in appropriate use of objects, these autistic children would revert to previous levels of meaningless, repetitive routine, and they seldom enlarged any activity that had been taught to them.

Later, Churchill (1971) conducted an experiment using 12 autistic children in which he showed that avoidance, self-stimulation, and frustration all increased significantly when the child failed to do something that he tried to do. The longer the child failed, the more avoidance and self-stimulation occurred. Excited pleasure and absorbed concentration in tasks that could be successfully completed were noted in most of the children. In general, in both of these studies, pleasant, positive relationships developed between the autistic children and the staff person teaching purely perceptual-motor or verbal tasks, even when no thought was given to the social relationships per se. In helping an autistic child be successful at doing something, anything, the adult was avoided less and the child happier.

Such studies gradually taught us that no longer would we spend months developing trusting relationships between the staff members and an autistic child. Instead, we taught them simple, everyday tasks within their level of competence, and the relationships grew automatically out of such interactions.

Punishment or aversive methods (Lovaas, Schaeffer, & Simmons, 1965) played a small part in our procedures. Time-out, letting the child's temper tantrums recede before giving reinforcers, was the only one consistently used. We never spanked, not only because it was prohibited by state law in institutions, but also because our experience had shown it was not helpful. Painful procedures did not help the children. With one boy whose self-injury was severe, we used Lovaas' electric shock method only to find after a short period of betterment that the boy hit himself more frequently than before. When we were sure that a behavior was within a child's grasp by knowing his mental and adaptive ages, we insisted on attempts at performance no matter how angry the child got or how long he screamed. Reinforcers were given for partial performance, then gradually for more exact performances until the task was mastered. Smiles and emotional equanimity were the final accompaniment of mastery.

What Can the Parents Do at Home

To decrease social distance, parents should continue their natural and spontaneous affectionate gestures. To increase mastery of everyday environmental tasks, the parents need to know what sorts of things the child is ready to do. For example, before the child is given the task of buttoning his coat, the parents should be sure this is possible; i.e., the child's perceptual fine-motor development should be equal to that of a normal 3½-year-old. Most parents need expert professional help to know the developmental levels for everyday tasks and should probably get help before any vigorous home-training program is instituted. However, books on child development (Gesell & Amatruda, 1965; Gesell, Halverson, Thompson, Ilg, Castner, Ames, & Amatruda, 1940) can be read with profit by most parents and can help them appreciate better the level of development of their autistic child. The guiding rule is to present a new task graded just a few months above a lately mastered task, and then insist on performance no matter what avoidance behavior the child uses. In my experience, most parents find difficulty both in picking appropriate tasks and in following through without an experienced counsellor guiding them.

To reduce screaming, parents should avoid rewarding the child while he is screaming. Do pleasant things with the child before screaming starts. After the onset of screaming, ignore the child until it ceases. Then grant the child's wish or do something pleasant. In other words, reinforce (reward) the child for not screaming.

Self-mutilative behaviors can be very difficult to control even by experts in a controlled environment. Parents report that holding the child to reduce his tensions works at times. We found self-hitting was reduced in several children when increased mastery of simple tasks also brought about a happier disposition. Tranquilizing medication can help if prescribed by a physician experienced in medicating children. When all these measures fail, protective measures can be used. One mother made a head covering of double thickness quilting material for her son who beat his head against a wall and thus reduced amount of bruising. Light arm splints or a man's shirt put on backwards and shirt arms tied firmly behind the child's back reduced the number of times Mandy hit herself. Severe self-mutilation can be one of the most difficult symptoms for the parents to control and they should not hesitate to seek professional advice for this distressing symptom. There is evidence that some children mutilate themselves because they enjoy having their hands tied. For such children, the behavior is reduced if their hands are tied only when they have *not* been hurting themselves.

Lastly, our parents advised other parents to keep spanking to a minimum and use it only when the behavior is dangerous to the child or others. Several parents thought they said "no" too much to their autistic child. Rather than scolding and prohibitions, some parents "child-proofed" their homes to reduce messing and destruction. They advised accentuating positive behaviors by acclimating the child gradually to stores and the homes of friends. If the child had regular periods of irritability, parents would try to abort them by car rides or walks.

We were impressed that parents who conquered their feelings of embarrassment finally managed community excursions to at least a few places and to have a few regular visitors to their homes. These social contacts somewhat lightened their lives and those of their children.

REFERENCES

Churchill, D. W. Effects of success and failure in psychotic children. *Archives of General Psychiatry*, 1971, **25**, 208–214.

DeMyer, M. K., & Ferster, C. B. Teaching new social behavior to schizophrenic children. *Journal of the American Academy of Child Psychiatry*, 1962, **1**(3), 443–461.

Gesell, A., & Amatruda, C. S. *Developmental diagnosis.* New York: Harper & Row, 1965.

Gesell, A., Halverson, H. M., Thompson, H., Ilg, F. L., Castner, B. M., Ames, L. B., & Amatruda, C. S. *The first five years of life.* New York: Harper & Brothers, 1940.

Goldfarb, W. The mutual impact of mother and child in childhood schizophrenia. *American Journal of Orthopsychiatry*, 1961, **31**, 738–747.

Lovaas, O. I., Schaeffer, B., & Simmons, J. Q. Building social behavior in autistic children by use of electric shock. *Journal of Experimental Research in Personality*, 1965, **1**, 99–109.

Pitfield, M., & Oppenheim, A. N. Child rearing attitudes of mothers of psychotic children. *Journal of Child Psychology and Psychiatry*, 1964, **5**, 51–57.

Chapter 9

INTELLIGENCE PERCEPTUAL-MOTOR AND MUSICAL SKILLS

To know the general intelligence of autistic children is important clinically and, as we have found, prognostically. The measured IQs of the autistic child while he is still in his preschool years provide one of the best predictors of outcome (DeMyer, Barton, DeMyer, Norton, Allen, & Steele, 1973). Historically, Leo Kanner, in his early observations of the syndrome, speculated that infantile autism is not the same as mental retardation (Kanner & Lesser, 1958). Since that time, many workers have assumed that most autistic children have a basically normal intelligence locked within the socially withdrawn child. A common early idea was that if mental retardation or neurological disfunction was diagnosed in a child, then that child *ipso facto* could not be autistic no matter how profound the social withdrawal or how defective the communication skills. The idea that most autistic children were basically normal in intelligence was widely held before good research on intelligence in autistic children was conducted. Intelligence testing was considered invalid by many people because autistic children refused to try to perform. When people did report IQs derived from systematic testing (Pollack, 1958), those IQs were generally in the retarded range, but such results were largely ignored or discounted.

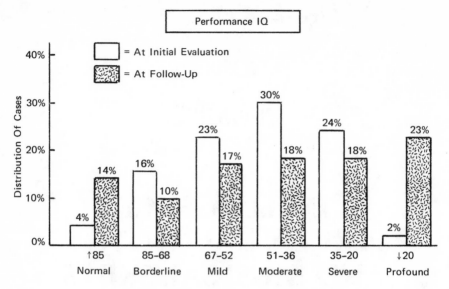

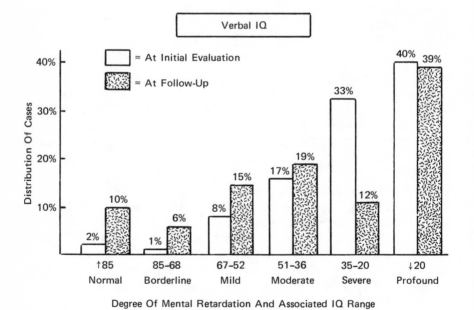

Fig. 1. Percentage distribution of performance and verbal IQs for autistic cases at initial evaluation and follow-up.

About midway in our studies, we decided that intelligence should be considered as one dimension of infantile autism just as it is considered a separate dimension in every other type of mental illness. People suffering from an adult mental illness, schizophrenia, have differing levels of intelligence. They have IQ levels as widely varied as in the general population—from the near genius (IQ above 150) to the retarded range (IQ below 68). Our clinical observations revealed that some autistic children were more intelligent than others. We decided that if we were smart enough ourselves, we ought to be able to measure the differences in intelligence reliably and compare the intelligence of autistic children to that of normal children and other diagnostic groups.

In a survey (DeMyer, Barton, Alpern, Kimberlin, Allen, Yang, & Steele, 1974) of the measured intelligence of 115 autistic children at the mean chronological age of 5 years 6 months, we found that the overwhelming number (97%) had verbal IQs in the retarded range (67 and below). On follow up of 69 children, mean age 12 years, about 84% tested verbally in the retarded range (DeMyer, Barton, DeMyer, Norton, Allan, & Steele, 1973). Verbal IQs were generally lower than those estimated from the performance of perceptual-motor test items, which nevertheless were mainly (80% initial evaluation; 76% follow-up) in the retarded range. In our studies (Alpern, 1967), we found that every autistic child was "testable," even in verbal modalities, when infant testing items were used in combination with infant testing procedures. However, we learned also that we had to use a wide range of items graded in mental age from infancy into school age because of the wide scatter in the abilities of many autistic children.

While the overall IQ of most autistic children is in the retarded range, about 60% of them have some kind of splinter ability, a skill that stands above the individual child's general IQ level. For example, if a child has a general IQ of 50 and the ability to do fitting-and-assembly tasks such as puzzles and formboards and color matching at an IQ level above mentally retarded levels (about 68 or above), then this fitting-and-assembly skill would count as a splinter skill.[1] These splinter skills have been interpreted by many people as a sign that the autistic child has good overall intelligence. However, in our research, we found that a splinter skill was usually not a reflection of equal potential in other dimensions of intelligence. The general IQ was a more powerful predictor of later general intellectual skill and overall outcome of illness.

We also found in our IQ survey that autistic children's IQs, like those of normal children, were quite stable over short and long periods of time. For example, if an autistic child had an IQ of 50 at age 4 years, then he was likely to have approximately the same IQ 1 year later and also 6 years later. Autistic children were about the same as normal children in this regard.

However, about 20% of autistic children had significant increases in their IQs over time and about another 15% had significant decreases.

In the minds of many professional people and parents, all autistic children are viewed as having the capacity for accelerating in intellectual progress and finally becoming normal or nearly so if the right treatment key can be found. Autistic children who make this accelerated progress are sometimes given wide publicity, and it is claimed that a certain type of treatment was responsible for the progress and that most autistic children would make similar progress if such a treatment program were used universally. Such claims have been made for megavitamin and megamineral therapy, the so-called motor patterning techniques, behavior modification, and other environmental modifications such as unlimited love.

Unfortunately, experience has shown that out of large samples of autistic children, only about 11% at later ages have a general (combined verbal and perceptual-motor) IQ in the normal range, about 11% achieve borderline normal general intellectual skills, and the remainder (78%) must live forever dependent on others in parental homes and institutions because they can learn only simple intellectual and perceptual-motor skills (DeMyer et al., 1973; Rutter & Lockyer, 1967). Even the children whose general IQs were in the normal and borderline ranges generally had a splinter disability that compromised their ability to achieve at average levels later in life.

The percentage distributions of general IQ levels at follow-up remained roughly the same whether the child had received therapy or not, with the exception, perhaps, of one group of autistic children, those whose tested IQ in preschool years was above 70 (Rutter, 1970) or 50 (DeMyer et al., 1975). Psychotherapy and a special educational program seemed to enhance but not guarantee the chances for a fair to good outcome in this one group of children. In children whose preschool IQs were below 40, the outcome was universally poor no matter what the treatment or how good or special the education.

Given this importance of the IQ, we were interested to know the parents' observations of their children's intelligence. We had several important questions about when signs of intellectual and perceptual-motor difficulties first appeared. Were the intellectual limitations associated with any important events, such as childhood diseases? Even though parents could not often be expected to be expert, unbiased reporters of such an intellectual history, they were practically the only observers of development during infancy and toddler years that we had. We had also one measure of mothers' skill as estimators of developmental level. Schopler and Reichler (1972) asked a series of parents to estimate what chronological age level their autistic child most nearly approximated in overall functioning. Correlations were high between parents' estimates and those based on formal tests. Therefore the investigators concluded that parents were in general good estimators of the intelligence of their autistic children. However, as we shall see, parents of autistic children tended to overestimate the probable intellectual *potential* of their offspring. They tended to read too much into a splinter skill. They liked to believe that if a child could stack blocks or draw with exceptional skill then he ought to be able to do everything else with equal skill. They also tended to see signs of high intelligence in certain of their children's activities that in reality revealed only some degree of retardation.

Parents' Estimation of General Intelligence

To see how parents in our structured interview viewed their children's general intelligence, we asked the following question: "If you were to estimate the general intelligence level of your child at this time, how would you rate him/her?" If the reply did not contain a general estimate that could be rated as above average, average, or below average, then the parents were asked to pick one. Autistic parents overwhelmingly (about 72%) said their autistic child was below average while not a single normal parent gave this reply. Normal parents (about 88%) felt that their normal child was somewhat to very much above average in general intelligence while only about 15% of autistic parents thought their autistic child was above average.

During the first year of life, about 40% of autistic parents felt their autistic infant was below his siblings or other infants in general alertness, as compared to 12% of normal parents (DeMyer, Pontius, Norton, Barton, Allen, & Steele, 1972). In the transition between the first year of life and the time serious symptoms appeared, some autistic children were viewed by their parents as having a decided setback in development. Whether this was an intellectual setback was difficult to tell in some cases, but raters judged that it occurred in about 34% of the cases. Another 36% seemingly failed to keep up during the second year of life with the normal developmental timetable, and the remaining 30% continued in the general slow development which was evident in the first year.

Such data, being retrospective from parents largely untrained in child development, can be viewed at best as rough, but it does suggest that the typically low intellectual function of autistic children can develop out of a background of seeming normality during the first year of life or can appear in a child or infant who has had some developmental delay or abnormality since the earliest days of life. Causes of setback were unclear, though some parents wanted to blame an emotionally traumatic event such as the advent of a sibling or a parental vacation. In about 12% of cases, the setback coincided with an infectious illness such as measles or severe dehydrating diarrhea. In most cases, no obvious physical or psychological cause could be recalled.

Parental Views of Intellectual Potential

Whenever someone gets a low score on an intelligence test or acts unintelligent, the question arises as to whether the intellectual lack stems from a malfunctioning brain or from adverse psychological factors. Many parents who noted that their autistic child functioned far below average in intelligence nevertheless said they believed that the child potentially had normal intelligence. The most frequently mentioned reason (about 33%) was that the child either currently or in the past had had some speech. Even if the child had only a word or two in his vocabulary, the parents thought those two words were indicative that the child had "good" intelligence and could "catch up" with other children.

Other reasons parents gave for believing their autistic child had potentially normal intelligence were: any recent improvement the child had made in intellectual skills or perceptual-motor skills; the presence of any splinter skill; the presence of an "alert" infancy; no specific, hopeful sign—parents just believed the child was "not going to be retarded forever."

Progress in Mental Age

Most parents (about 80%) of high and middle functioning autistic children pointed to some progress in intellectual or perceptual-motor development in the months previous to evaluation at the Clinical Research Center. Some examples of progress were the ability to carry out a one-step verbal request whereas previously the child failed to do so; the ability to unhook a screen door with an out-of-reach hook by using a tool such as broom handle; making a mental association between sitting on the potty and eliminating there; learning how to turn a door knob whereas previously the child had stood before the door and screamed to be let out; and the acquisition of a few more words in vocabulary.

Parents of 3½- to 7-year-old children used these actions as signs of good intelligence though they were activities that are routinely learned by normal toddlers about 18 months to 2 years of age. All of us must remember that such activity in a child 3½ to 7 years of chronological age is not a sign of good intelligence. It is a sign that autistic children can learn things, but at a much slower rate than the normal child. It is a sign that the autistic child's brain is maturing anatomically and physiologically as he increases in chronological age. Such brain maturation is accompanied in the retarded child as well as the normal child by a corresponding increase in the mental age level of the child's activities. In order for intellectual progress to be predictive of intellectual capacity in the normal range, this progress must be accelerated. To do better than nature, any successful treatment or education procedures must enable the autistic child to accelerate the intellectual progress that occurs naturally as the brain matures anatomically.[2]

When autistic children were treated, we saw this accelerated intellectual progress in only about 20% of children and much of the progress occurred in children in the range of about 4 to 6 years, and the accelerated progress generally stopped short of average levels. As previously noted, few (11%) of the autistic children demonstrated average combined verbal and perceptual-motor IQs at follow up. Even fewer still (8%) tested at average levels in both principal modalities of intelligence. The remainder of those who had made accelerated intellectual progress continued to perform in the borderline normal or retarded ranges.

A word of caution is in order here. We were never convinced that our treatment procedures or those of any other professionals brought about this accelerated intellectual progress. I strongly suspect, as do Bartak and Rutter (1976), that the autistic child with the higher IQ potential may differ in some important way from those with lower IQs. Good teaching techniques, such as behavior modification intelligently and creatively applied, make it possible for the autistic child to make the best use of his endowment, but no current therapy can replace brain cells that have been destroyed or hasten biological maturation of the brain if the matrix for this accelerated maturation is not within the child's brain. All we can do is provide good therapeutic practices that can ameliorate some of the psychological problems that may have arisen through a less than optimum environment and through the autistic child's consistent failure to master it. Such therapy coupled with good education techniques help the child to make the best use of a less than optimum central nervous system.

Autistic Children Who Regressed Intellectually

About 15% of 70 autistic children regressed significantly in intellectual abilities during a 6 year follow-up period despite continuing efforts of parents and schools in many cases to supply effective stimulation and education. The reasons for the intellectual regression remain an interesting question, but the answers must be speculative. In about half of the regressed sample, the failure appeared mainly due to lack of motivation in the child himself. No matter how creative and enthusiastic the teaching, the child remained apathetic. A second reason was that the child received too little environmental stimulation from parents or schools or both. Either type of child may have kept his innate ability intact but could not keep up with intelligence tests because he learned little, and intelligence tests during school years, especially verbal sections, depend on learning as well as on innate ability. A third type of child, generally hyperirritable in temperament, appeared to regress in actual ability.

Mattie was able to recognize and spell a few printed words at age 4 years, a skill she picked up without teaching. By the age of 5 years, she ceased adding to her sight vocabulary despite expert and patient teaching. By age 7, she had lost all ability to recognize printed words. Her speaking vocabulary, mainly echolalic, contained over 500 words at age 4 years and she sang songs in good tune. On occasion, she communicated verbally. Over the years, expressive speech and singing faded away until at age 20 she was mute. Therapeutic efforts began with Mattie at age 3½, and included psychotherapy, educational therapy, behavior modification, and finally psychoactive medication which was necessary to control cyclic aggressive and regressive behavior. The parents and siblings were active, interested, perceptive participants in therapy throughout the 17 years that elapsed between the diagnosis of autism at 3 years of age and Mattie's admission to a chronic care institution at age 20. Formal tests of intelligence mirrored the downhill course with decreasing IQ scores at ages 5, 7, and 10.

Another child, Amanda, began her intellectual downhill course even earlier. At age 2½ years, her IQ was about 83, by age 5 about 70, and by age 8 about 65. She showed the same cyclic irritability with self-mutilative behavior, striking other people, and intense sadness which occasionally reached suicidal proportions. Her intellectual regression stopped at about 8 years, but the cyclic increase in irritability remained a severe problem and was only partially controlled by behavior modification techniques and psychoactive drugs. Amanda's parents, like those of Mattie, were intelligently committed to treatment and good education for their daughter.

A third example is that of Buddy, who in preschool years was lower functioning than the previous examples. He became unbelievably destructive of household furnishings and, on hospitalization, of the ward furnishings. All environmental alterations and ordinary psychoactive medications were ineffective. An experimental medication given at age 15 years ameliorated the destructive behavior to the point it virtually ceased. Buddy then responded mutely but positively to social overtures of the ward staff. Unfortunately, the drug (clozapine) caused a diminution of white blood cells in him and in other patients and was withdrawn from further clinical testing. Buddy's behavior rapidly deteriorated after clozapine withdrawal and his ward psychiatrist went back to retrying previously ineffective therapies.

All three of these individuals were studied by pediatric neurologists for neurologically destructive conditions. EEG records were abnormal but had been since early childhood and were essentially unchanged on follow-up studies. Investigation of the thyroid system, serotonin levels, and numerous measurements of other moieties which might reflect a metabolic or structural abnormality were unfruitful. After participating in the psychiatric care and research study of these patients at intervals over the years, I still suspect that a metabolic defect of unknown nature might be affecting (principally) the central nervous system. However, decreasing effectiveness of neuronal inhibitory systems typical of the neurologically disfunctional brain is an equally plausible explanation given by many neurologists.

These three children are not typical of the autistic population as a whole, and it may reasonably be asked if they were truly autistic in the classic, Kannerian sense. However, all three showed the classic signs of severe social isolation, noncommunicative speech, and nonfunctional repetitive use of objects, becoming manifest in the second year of life. Many autistic children are hyperirritable, screaming easily, restless, and inclined to self-abusive behavior and destruction of objects. In our sample, many parents reported decreases in severity of this behavior over the years, but for a certain percentage (about 5 to 10%), it continued unabated or worsened or was cyclic. In one child, the aggression, self-abuse, and screaming varied with the season of the year. In my experience, severe hyperirritability is a sign of a guarded prognosis, no matter how good the general intelligence.

Such children, whether classically autistic or not, deserve intense study, since any hypothesized metabolic or neurological defect is likely to be severe and more easily detected in them. These hyperirritable autistic children closely resemble in behavior a known neurological condition, Cornelia DeLange Syndrome, in which the hyperirritability often increases over the years and in which a serotonin defect may be involved (Greenberg & Coleman, 1973). These children also have many behavioral features in common with Lesch-Nyan syndrome.

Parental Reaction to Mental Retardation in their Autistic Children

During preschool years, only a few professional people will make a firm diagnosis of mental retardation in an autistic child. The reasons are several: few clinicians, even psychologists, are familiar with the techniques of reliably estimating the intelligence of an autistic child. The methods are available (DeMyer, Barton, & Norton, 1972).[3] Most clinicians know that a small percentage of both autistic and nonautistic retarded children will accelerate significantly in intellectual skills. The wise clinician will withhold an unequivocal diagnosis of mental retardation in a young socially withdrawn child until the child has at least reached 6 years. The intellectual spurt, if it comes, usually does so between the ages of 4 and 6 years. Many clinicians, despite the studies of Lockyer and Rutter (1969) and DeMyer et al. (1974), still operate with the myth that most autistic children have a good intelligence that the behavioral symptoms mask. Thus they would not believe any intelligence test valid and would not usually make a diagnosis of mental retardation.

For these reasons, during preschool years many parents are led to believe that their autistic child is basically of at least average intelligence. This attitude blunts the early parental fears arising from their own observation that the child is probably intellectually retarded. Then at some time or another the possibility of mental retardation is broached to the parents, who often react with feelings of panic. They deny that their child is retarded and cling to the diagnosis of autism even though most parents have been told its outcome is not hopeful. The parents reject the diagnosis of mental retardation because they believe the outlook is bleak for retarded people. Since mental retardation is so common, parents have at least had hearsay experience with its devastating effects.

In contrast, autism is a relatively rare condition and parents generally know very few families with an autistic child. The things they do hear about autism are often distorted. For example, most TV programs and newspaper articles stress the cases that have had a relatively good outcome, insinuating that some new treatment technique gives high promise of "curing" autism in many children. These sources fail to state that for every 2 or 3 autistic children with a good outcome, there are about 97 who never make more than a marginal social adjustment no matter what the treatment. These sources fail to reveal the subsequent history of "new and promising" therapeutic techniques for autism. First, there is hyperbolic fanfare over one or two cases, then the "new cure" drifts into oblivion because succeeding cases did poorly. From such distorted reporting, parents get the message that if their child is autistic, he can probably be cured. Even if some realistic, experienced clinician points out the low recovery rate for autism, parents will cling to the hope, "My child will be among the fortunate few if he has autism." The diagnosis of "mental retardation" promises no similar hope to many parents.

When parents are at last faced with the knowledge that their autistic child is always going to be "slow" or "delayed in development," their grief can be considerable, prolonged, and painful. In my experience as a clinician, there is no more dreaded and hated "nonfatal" diagnosis than mental retardation. This label activates all of the parents' childhood memories of the "dumb kid in the neighborhood" who was scorned, teased, feared, and ostracized. Most parents will reject the diagnosis for variable periods of time until they can assimilate the initial shocking effects. Parents need to know that a wise clinician has used reliable diagnostic methods in a skillful way before they can begin to think the diagnosis may be correct. Parents need to feel their grief and work it through or it will needlessly complicate their lives. One of the most common responses of parents is to deny their own perceptions and endlessly seek a "better" treatment.

During the mourning period, parents need continuing emotional support and enlightenment from the physician, psychologist, teacher, and other parents. They need adequate schooling for their child. If the parents are angry about the diagnosis, they need professional people who will understand and not react with anger themselves. If parents' "realism" about accepting the diagnosis seems faulty, they need continued and patient education, not censure. Sooner or later nearly every "difficult" parent will respond with a more cooperative and realistic spirit to the clinician who understands the devastating effect of being told that a child may be not only autistic but also mentally retarded.

Perceptual-Motor and Motor Difficulties

The autistic child has often been described as singularly free of motor deficiencies. Like so many other early observations, these have to be modified considerably. We found from our extensive studies of motor and perceptual-motor development that the autistic child is likely to be overrated in both motor and perceptual-motor performance. The detailed findings can be studied in the original papers (DeMyer & Barton, 1972; DeMyer, 1975). Summarized here are some conclusions:

(1) The autistic child is generally at his best in gross motor function of legs and feet, as in walking and climbing stairs. Even so, most autistic children do not perform as well as normal age-matched children.

(2) While the motor system *per se* seems relatively intact, most perceptual-motor skills are performed at below average levels by most autistic children. Examples of these deficiencies are in drawing geometric figures, imitating hand and finger gestures, tying shoes, and buttoning buttons.

(3) Autistic children are also deficient in skills demanding that the body be coordinated with vision, e.g., playing ball and riding a tricycle.

(4) Nevertheless, one type of perceptual-motor activity is commonly performed nearly as well or as well as average: fitting-and-assembly tasks such as putting puzzles together, matching block designs, building block towers, and matching colors and shapes.[4]

We asked the following questions of the parents concerning motor development: (1) When did your child first sit alone? Walk alone? (2) How did your child compare with his brothers and sisters in reaching these milestones? If an only child, with his cousins or neighbor children?

Typically, parents could remember only an approximate age of sitting and walking alone and seldom remembered any of the subtleties of motor development. They typically were fairly certain which children in the family were relatively slow or fast. Their observations revealed that, in general,

Table 43. Commencement of Sitting and Walking Alone

Chronological age (months)	Sitting[a]				Chronological age (months)	Walking alone			
	Autistic		Normal			Autistic		Normal	
	N	%	N	%		N	%	N	%
6−8	105	58	46	98	Before 15	97	63	46	98
8−9	19	10	1	2	15−17	19	12	1	2
9−10	11	6	0		17−19	15	10	0	
Over 10	17	9	0		Over 19	23	15	0	

[a]$p < .001.$

autistic children were slower than normal in sitting and walking. More autistic children than normal children were judged to be slower than their siblings in motor development (see Table 43).

Paper-Pencil Activities in the Home

Early in our testing of autistic children, we noted that most preschool autistic children could do no more than scribble if given paper and pencil, an activity that is average for an 18-month-old normal toddler. Sometimes autistic children just chewed up crayons or mouthed the pencil, usual activities of the normal 9-month-old infant when given a writing tool. We wondered if we were obtaining the autistic child's highest level of performance in the testing situation and asked the parents for their observations. Parents reported that over half of the autistic children had never progressed beyond a scribble even though they were old enough to begin to draw. Only 6% of autistic children approached their chronological age level with respect to graphic activities in the home. Thus, inability to draw straight lines, circles, squares, and other geometric figures at expected ages is nearly as common in autistic children as is their verbal disability. Visual-fine motor deficiency constitutes a severe disability which we found on follow-up still handicapped most autistic children in their school work.

The two autistic children of this group who were most talented with a pencil could print many words from memory but did nothing creative. They drew no faces or other pictures. On follow-up at age 14, one child, though placed in a classroom with normal junior high students, largely was able to complete only work that could be memorized by rote. His ability to think symbolically and use abstractions was considerably below that expected for his age. In writing, he mostly copied his school texts word for word.

About 90% of normal control children during preschool years were judged to be at least average in drawing and writing and often drew pictures of people, favorite activities and objects as a routine part of their play activities.

Use of Books

Most autistic children were reported to be unenthusiastic about books. Only about 12% of autistic children liked to hear stories read to them, in contrast to 90% of the normal children. An autistic child, if interested at all in books, was more likely to flip the pages or destroy them than to be interested in what was printed or pictured on the pages. However, about half of this group would look at pictures occasionally and attempt to identify some.

In contrast to most autistic children who are little interested in books, there were about 15% whose chief interest was books. Three of these children early learned (about age 3) to identify printed words without being able to understand reading content. Parents had mixed feelings about these apparently precocious skills. First, they didn't understand why the children were so exclusively interested in books or why they could learn this one skill and be so behind in others. None of the autistic parents had purposely taught their child to read. They were torn between seeing the skill as a sign of superior intelligence and seeing it as an abnormal facet of their child's behavior. They met criticism from some quarters as having pushed their child too hard and were naturally resentful of such remarks. One father told of a business associate who visited in the home and observed Stanton reading and filling whole tablets full of printing that he had memorized while ignoring all the people around him. The visitor told the parents, "If that child were mine, I wouldn't let him have a book or a piece of paper or anything to write with. I wouldn't let him even see any printing of any kind." The father's response was anger and wonderment that any person would want to deprive Stanton of his only joy in life. The mother said, "We've tried everything to interest him in other things, but there's no way you could take away the one thing he likes."

Curiosity

High curiosity is generally correlated with high intelligence in children (Terman, 1960). In 96% of the cases, autistic children were described as extremely uncurious when compared to others their age. The usual response to the question; "What kinds of things is your child curious about," was typified by these mothers' statements:

Ian has almost no interests like my other children. The only things he is curious about are what is in paper sacks or in people's purses. If he sees us put something up out of his reach on a shelf, he may yell bloody murder to get it. When he gets these things, he just twiddles them or immediately loses interest.

Charlene will look at something to see if it has a string or cord that can be pulled off and jiggled. If she goes somewhere she looks for lamp cords. The only other thing that interests her is food and that is just to eat it.

We found that the bulk of autistic children were interested in or "curious" about the things they could jiggle, spin, twirl, or use in some simple, repetitive way. If they saw a sack or a purse or a box, they investigated what was inside it to use in their idiosyncratic, repetitive fashion. The second most common items of curiosity were mechanical objects such as record turntables, fans, lawn mowers, and things that can be taken apart. Noticing animals and touching them was reported for a few autistic children. The strongly echolalic children were curious about TV commercials and stopped to listen and look when their favorites were aired. Curiosity about books was found in about 18% of the children, but for some this was only to see how the pages could be flipped or torn out.

Parents tried a number of strategies to expand the interests of their autistic children. They tried to divert attention from their repetitive activities by hiding the flippable objects and giving them toys, tried to read to them or point out pictures when they flipped the pages of books. On outings in the neighborhood, most autistic children found flippable objects. Parents would try pointing out animals, cars, and other objects that interest most children but generally to no avail. Parents realized the autistic child's lack of joy over exploring the environment and felt sorrow that one of their children would be so restricted. Jon's mother expressed her reaction to her son's lack of curiosity about Christmas presents:

When Jon had his second Christmas, we knew beforehand that he just didn't care about much of anything, but we were not prepared for his complete lack of interest in the Christmas packages. Finally, my husband and I opened them for him, and then he wouldn't play with the toys. Was that ever a gloomy Christmas. The same thing happened every year until he was 5, and then he opened the packages and smiled at some of his presents. I tell you I cried my heart out when he couldn't even enjoy Christmas.

The one thing Jon was consistently curious about were TV commercials, and typically the mother blamed herself for letting him watch too much TV.

About 12% of autistic parents said their autistic child was curious about "nothing."

Normal children, in contrast, were described as moderately to highly curious. About 33% of normal parents responded with the word "everything" when they were asked to describe the types of things the normal index child was curious about. In case after case, normal parents said the normal children were interested in the whole range of the living and inanimate world around them. Normal children actively explored use of tools, clocks, cooking, art, and music. Normal children 4 years of age and older continuously expanded their knowledge of nature and people by asking "why" questions. Their subsequent questions showed they had learned from answers to previous questions. Only 6% of autistic children asked "why" questions, and these were monotonously repetitive. Despite patient and careful parental explanations, these children did not learn from the parents' answers. Only the younger normal children were primarily curious about objects in sacks or about the mere identification of animals. The older normal children, ages 5 to 6 and over, were curious about definition of words and other abstract topics and complex aspects of nature, such as "why the sun set."

The Brightest Thing the Child Has Done

A discussion with parents of autistic children about intelligence of their children usually elicited the following statement: "I know he seems unintelligent about some things, but he seems so smart about others." We tried to learn more about autistic splinter skills from the parents by asking, "What is the brightest thing you have ever seen your child do?" We required a specific description of the act and the age at which it occurred. The raters then assigned an approximate mental age level to the "brightest" acts and compared this estimated mental age with the chronological age of the child. The raters found that mental age levels of 57 of the 58 "brightest" acts of normal children were about equal to or above the chronological ages of the children. Only about half of the total 47 "brightest" acts of autistic children were rated in mental age as equal to or above the child's chronological age. In other words, for half the autistic children, the brightest thing the parents ever saw the autistic child do could have been accomplished by a younger normal child.

There were striking group differences between the kinds of brightest acts mentioned. About half the normal children engaged in high-level abstractions of a verbal nature, e.g., understanding and rephrasing a scientific concept explained by the parent, making an original verbal observation that showed appreciation of a general physical law, understanding what they read if they recognized the printed word. In the 15% of preschool autistic children who could "read," none understood what they read. Understanding written texts occurred later in life for about 9% of this sample. Normal children were frequently quoted as making witty remarks. No autistic child was so described. Normal children frequently wove language skills into perceptual-motor activities, such as in imaginative play. Autistic children never did so. Creative drawing was common in normal children and rare in autistic children.

A case of a striking splinter skill in drawing is reported by Selfe (1978). This autistic child, Nadia, let her skill lapse after slight improvement in speech and social ability. We have seen in our own sample this same dropping of splinter skills. The reasons for ceasing to practice these normal or supernormal skills vary from child to child. In some cases, newly developing skills, even if of a lower order of complexity, take precedence in the child's interests. Some observers have taken this event as a sign that therapists have stamped out valuable creativity while helping the child develop some "less valuable" social skills (Dennis, 1978).

The more likely explanation is that Nadia's verbal skill in abstraction was of such a low order that her incredible skill in drawing at the level of a gifted adult artist could not develop into the creative pictorial statements of the mature, verbally normal artist. Nadia's drawing skill might be likened to a pleasant play activity that could not be integrated into her thinking life because her verbal abstractive skills were those of a 2- or 3-year-old child. She could have little concept of the social statements she could make with her art or of the financial and personal rewards she could receive. Having no concept of the wider uses of her skill, she tired of using it, just as a normal person would tire of some diversionary activity. If Nadia's verbal brain had not been damaged by some unidentified traumatic event, it is possible she could have woven her drawing into the warp and woof of her thinking and become a mature artist; but without a verbal abstractive brain to match her intact parietal lobe, there was no chance for true artistic development. Similarly, such a dropping out of precocious "reading" ability occurred in some of our sample of children when verbal abstractive capacities failed to develop at the ages of 4 to 6 years.

The most frequently mentioned high mental age activity for autistic children was doing fitting-and-assembly tasks (23%). These activities were done in a stereotyped way and consisted of puzzle assembly, stacking blocks, and lining up objects in rows. These are visual-motor activities that we found also on formal testing of autistic children to be the top performance items of many autistic children (DeMyer, Barton, & Norton, 1972).

About 15% of both normal and autistic children learned to recognize the printed word at an early age, i.e., about 3 years of age. A few children between ages 2 to 4 of both groups differentiated other types of symbols, such as trademarks, chiefly from seeing TV commercials and magazine ads.

Only one mother taught her normal 3-year-old son how to recognize words from flash cards. As the normal children approached the age of 5, most learned to recognize words from the printed text as their parents read to them. A few additional autistic children also learned this way, but only the normal children understood the substance of what was read to them or of what they read themselves.

About twice as many normal youngsters as autistic were described as having well-developed auditory skills in reciting whole pages or complete stories their parents read to them. Interestingly, twice as many normal younsters as autistic youngsters learned many TV commercials. This was a favorite activity in normal children between 2½ and 3½ years of age and was cited by both normal and autistic parents as being a sign of high intelligence.

Sadly, far too many "brightest acts" recalled by autistic parents were that the autistic children could remember the location of various objects in the home or on car rides. The ability to remember where an object is located begins at about 15 months of age in normal children and is well developed by 24 months of age. In a child of 3 to 6 years of age, the ability to do an act a 15- to 24-month-old toddler can do well is not a sign of good intelligence if it is the brightest act ever observed.

Parental Reports of Musical Interests and Abilities of Autistic Children

Observations have been made that autistic children may have some normal or supernormal music abilities. Rimland (1964) has stated that special musical abilities are "nearly universal" in autistic children. Cain (1969) has also indicated that a considerable number of autistic children are good at music and deplores the fact that so little has been written or studied about this talent.

In our structured interviews, we asked the parents about music:

> What is your child's response to music? (a) Does your child sing songs by him/herself? (b) Carry a tune? (c) Know the words? (d) Where and how did your child learn this music?
> Does your child have any special gifts?

In essence, the normal children were more enthusiastic and responsive to music, and their music sense and performance were more highly developed in every way than those of the autistic children. About 60% of normal children were described as loving music, listening frequently, and singing alone and with others. They were more likely than autistic children to make up their own songs and dance interpretively to music. Many normal children talked about playing or tried to play a musical instrument. Only 18% of autistic children were described as highly enthusiastic about music, and to be so rated, they didn't have to talk about music. However, about 76% of autistic children were said to like music and to listen to it, but they didn't go out of their way to seek out music sources such as by turning on the radio or running a record player. Only 3% showed no interest at all, and only 6% actively rejected music. Thus, it is remarkable that one aspect of living experience elicited some interest and response in about 90% of an autistic population which is noted for its lack of positive response to the environment.

Listening to Music

Parents described seven different types of listening to music. The autistic children differed from the normal children in the following ways:

(1) More normal children listened to classical music (33% normal vs. 3% autistic).

(2) More normal children "loved" several varieties of music as opposed to one type (52% normal vs. 18% autistic).

(3) More autistic children listened to only one or two types of music (30% autistic vs. 15% normal).

The following descriptions were reported only for autistic children:

(4) About 27% liked and listened to music but showed signs that high tones or loudness, such as cymbals crashing, made them uncomfortable; i.e., they cried or put their hands over their ears.

(5) About 6% rejected most music and showed signs that music made them uncomfortable.

(6) About 6% were described as being soothed by music, but they made no efforts to seek music sources.

(7) About 3% showed no signs of listening.

Music Performance

In this age group, about 2 years to 7 years, few children would be expected to play a musical instrument, but singing songs could be expected in about 88% (Alpern & Boll, 1972). About 79% of normal children could sing all or nearly all the correct words and carry a correct or nearly correct tune of several or many types of songs. Only some 16% of autistic children could sing this well. Roughly 47% of autistic children never even hummed tunefully or put words to a tune. The remainder (36%) at least attempted to be tuneful or put a few words to an approximate tune.

Rhythmic Responses to Music

In rhythmic activities, normal children were described as more able than autistic children. We did not ask a question about rhythm, but most parents included a description of rhythm at some point in describing their child's response to music. About 51% of normal children were said to have "good rhythm," including dancing, marching, beating time with their hands, or showing good rhythm in their singing. Only about 15% of autistic children had "good" rhythmic response including real dancing. Autistic children's dancing was described, in 24% of cases, as "jiggling up and down," whirling or rocking in approximate time to the music.

If this group of autistic children is so far behind their normal counterparts in music listening and expression, then why has it been said that "most" autistic children have special music abilities? I can only guess at the answer, but one possible reason is that if 90% have a positive response, even if it is only listening or rocking or being soothed by music, this is a notable phenomenon. In low-performing, generally uninterested children such positive signs are likely to be overemphasized, especially by people who know little about developmental levels of music skills in normal children. A second reason is that in my experience, when a few autistic children have a highly developed skill, we have been likely to overgeneralize the phenomenon to include all or most autistic children, partly because of the myth of locked-in normality and partly because all of us want so much that these children should be capable of greater things. In short, we indulge in wishful thinking before the subject has been well studied.

There were several autistic children in this sample who really had developed some one aspect of music. There was only one child in the sample of 33 who, upon first being evaluated, seemed from parental report to be at chronological age level in all aspects of music listening and performance. In the larger sample of 115 that we followed for an average of 6 years, there was only one who exhibited above-average music performance and could dance. Both of these children were normally functioning children at follow-up in intellectual and social skills, but they were exceptions. Even those 15% who had good rhythmic sense were poor at carrying a tune, and those 15% who could carry a tune were not described as having rhythm. In other words, it was not uncommon for an autistic child to have one aspect of music "normally" developed, but it was uncommon for the autistic child to be able to integrate words, music and rhythm or to perform for an audience musically.

Let us look at two autistic children who probably had superior partial talents in music. Both were boys about 4 years of age when first evaluated, and both were described by their musical parents as having "perfect pitch." Sean's parents described him thus:

He has an unusual talent to pick up music by ear and remember tunes. He's uncannily musical. If he hears something, he can pick it out on the piano. He doesn't remember the whole pieces or long tunes, but he can pick out some chords on the piano. When he was just 2 years old and could barely see over the keys, he would pick out short melodic lines on the piano. He never banged on it.

At interview time, Sean could pick out some chords and locate octaves on the piano. If his siblings made a mistake in their piano practice, Sean would sometimes run to the piano and play the correct note. However, he never developed good rhythm nor could he ever learn to read music. His lack of fine motor coordination probably also hindered him from learning scales and arpeggios. When he was seen at follow-up at 9 years of age, his rhythm was still poor. He could perform some simple duets with his brother on the piano, and his ear was still excellent.

The second autistic boy with perfect pitch also learned snatches of poetry, but his music and literary performances were partial, and his fine motor skills and low general intelligence made it impossible for him to do more than learn to sing songs by rote. He also seemed to lack a well-developed rhythmic sense. On follow-up at age 11, this child spent most of his time listening to music.

O'Connell (1974) reported the case of Joseph, an 8-year-old autistic child with "extraordinary capabilities" in music memory, pitch, and harmonic perception, and "extraordinary handicaps" in rhythm and concentration. Joseph "could play or sing the correct pitches immediately but only haltingly, one note at a time, and seemed to have no concept of how to put them together to flow as a melody." With ingenuity and skill, O'Connell engaged in a 3-year program of teaching Joseph to play a piano and read music. Joseph made much progress, but all of his musicality was "marred by a serious lack of rhythmic feeling . . . ; it is doubtful that his rhythmic attainments will ever match his grasp of harmonic concepts and the tonal aspects of music." Improvement in musical performance was accompanied by improvement in social skills and speech.

These cases of partial musical aptitude illustrate an important aspect of the neuropsychological handicaps of autism: Even if an autistic person is gifted with normal or supernormal ability in some one modality, other related modalities necessary for the development of superior total performance are generally below average levels. Thus it is that the superior splinter abilities of most autistic children, like those of the *idiot savant*, are destined to remain minimally useful for want of even average attention, perceptual-motor, abstract language, social and emotional skills.

Where the Children Learned Their Music

Both autistic and normal children learned much of their music from their mothers, from records, and from TV. Normal children also learned from other children, a source that autistic children seldom used. It appears both from parental observation and from my observations that the TV commercial is especially suited to the teaching of the autistic child, as it is for the young normal child. First, the TV commercial is played in the familiar atmosphere of the home. Going to unfamiliar settings was upsetting to most autistic children, and they could not concentrate on material presented to them in unfamiliar settings. Second, the TV commercial is highly repetitive. The same words and the same simple tunes are used over and over again. This constant repetition of simple material met the autistic child's need. In these young autistic children, as was discussed in the language chapter, speech skills were heavily concentrated in rote repetition of what they heard. They understood only simple speech, and their expressive speech was uncreative since they could not master syntactic rules or deal in abstractions (Churchill, 1972; DeMyer, 1975). A simple TV commercial, which abounds in repetition and which is also repeated several times a day over a period of several weeks, set up the conditions for the autistic child to learn.

TV commercials are also especially suitable as an instructional medium for the young normal child. Normal children between 2 and 3½ years of age were reported as being fond of learning and repeating the words and songs of many TV commercials, and this was one of the principal ways these young normal children learned music expression other than from their mothers. By the age of 4, most normal youngsters were no longer intrigued by the commercials, but were interested in learning other songs at nursery school or from their sibs. Time and again normal parents described their normal children as picking up music wherever they heard it, whereas the autistic children needed a highly repetitive, simple presentation of music in a nondistractive atmosphere such as their mothers and the TV commercial could provide in the familiar atmosphere of the home.

Relationship of Speech to Competence in Carrying a Tune

Raters compared the relationship of the ability to carry a tune well to the presence of speech. All the autistic children who could carry a good tune and sang correct words to tunes used echolalic speech fairly often in everyday life, but not all echolalic children could carry a tune well. With two exceptions, those children who were largely mute or who had only a few words of expressive speech could not carry a tune. One of these exceptions was Sean, age 4 years, described by his parents as singing more words than he ever said.

His words were pronounced more clearly when he sang them than when he spoke them. For awhile, the father communicated with the child by singing, but even with this approach the child's deficits in communication and verbal abstraction were profound, and over the years little speech developed. The other mute child hummed tunes on correct pitch. In both of these cases, at least one of the parents was a talented musician.

I would like to report the comparison of music skills in autistic children with those of parents and sibs, but unfortunately we did not routinely ask that question, although some parents volunteered such information as we talked about their child's music skills.

Summary of Music Skills

While most autistic children like music and have a positive response to it, only about 3 to 6% of this sample showed overall performance that approximated that shown by normal children of their own age. Some of the autistic children had normal or even supernormal abilities in one facet of music; i.e., about 15% were described as carrying tunes unusually well for their age, and another 15% were described as having unusually well-developed rhythmic response to music. However, only 15% of the children were able to sing songs in the sense that they could learn most of the words and carry a reasonably good tune to several different songs. In contrast, the normal children were more intent listeners and better performers. About 79% of the normal children were described as being like or better than other children their own age in music performance. Fifty-one percent of them danced to music in an interpretative way or showed a decided and adequate rhythmic response to music.

About half of the autistic children showing decided rhythmic response to music did so in a primitive way by rocking or whirling. Even those 6% described as having "perfect pitch" had abstract language and symbolic difficulties and also perceptual-motor difficulties that prevented them from making full use of their advanced tonal skills. All the children with well-developed rhythmic sense, with the exception of two, lacked other musical abilities that would have allowed them to perform up to age level.

Some research work should be done with autistic children of all three levels, high, middle, and low functioning, to confirm or deny these parental observations. For many preschool autistic children it will be necessary to invent ways of testing children who cannot hum a tune or beat out any simple rhythms. This suggests that school-age autistic children should be studied first.

Notes

[1] Actually there is no precise definition of a splinter skill. If a child has a general IQ of 35, for example, and has some skill at an IQ or development quotient of 60, that

higher skill will appear quite good in contrast to the child's overall ability and might be called by some people a splinter skill.

[2]A hypothetical example would be as follows: If a child who is retarded in his development is tested at age 3 years and performs like a normal child of 1½ years, he has a resultant IQ of 50. Given an average environment and no special training, we would expect this child automatically to increase in mental age as time passed because his brain matures. If we test this same child again at age 5 years, we would expect his mental age to be higher than at age 3. In fact, we would expect a one year increase, so that by age 5 years his IQ would remain around 50, the same level as at age 3 years. If, however, we enrolled our hypothetical retarded child at age 3 in a special education program, we would hope this program would enable the child to progress in mental age faster than could be expected merely as a result of the passage of time. We would hope that his mental age at age 5 would test at, say, 3½ years rather than 2½ years, which would raise his IQ to about 70, a substantial increase over 50.

[3]The author will send free to any clinician the manual, test directions, test material list, and scoring sheets of one reliable and valid method for testing preschool and primary school-age autistic and nonautistic children.

[4]In these tasks, the motor component is relatively noncomplex, consisting of picking up and voluntarily releasing an object, which is easily done by a normal infant 12 months of age. The visual cues remain within the child's field of vision as he accomplished the fitting-and-assembly task. While studies concerning adequacy of visual memory in autistic children are contradictory, it does appear from our studies that the preschool autistic child's performance deteriorates if he has to remember a visual cue or if the motor component needs a skill level much above 15 months in developmental age.

REFERENCES

Alpern, G. D. Measurement of "untestable" autistic children. *Journal of Abnormal Psychology*, 1967, **72**, 478–486.

Alpern, G. D., & Boll, T. J. *Development profile manual*. Indianapolis: Psychological Development Publications, 1972.

Bartak, L., & Rutter, M. Differences between mentally retarded and normally intelligent autistic children. *Journal of Autism and Childhood Schizophrenia*, 1976, **6**, 109–120.

Cain, A. Special isolated abilities in psychotic children. *Psychiatry*, 1969, **32**(2), 137–149.

Churchill, D. W. The relation of infantile autism and early childhood schizophrenia to developmental language disorders of childhood. *Journal of Autism and Childhood Schizophrenia*, 1972, **2**(2), 182–197.

DeMyer, M. K. The nature of the neuropsychological disability in autistic children. *Journal of Autism and Childhood Schizophrenia*, 1975, **5**(2), 109–128.

DeMyer, M. K., Barton, S., Alpern, G. D., Kimberlin, C., Allen, J., Yang, E., & Steele, R. The measured intelligence of autistic children. *Journal of Autism and Childhood Schizophrenia*, 1974, **4**(1), 42–60.

DeMyer, M. K., Barton, S., & Norton, J. A. A comparison of adaptive, verbal, and motor profiles of psychotic and nonpsychotic subnormal children. *Journal of Autism and Childhood Schizophrenia*, 1972, **2**(4), 359–377.

DeMyer, M. K., Pontius, W., Norton, J. A., Barton, S., Allen, J., & Steele, R. Parental practices and innate activity in normal, autistic, and brain-damaged infants. *Journal of Autism and Childhood Schizophrenia*, 1972, 2(1), 49–66.

Dennis, N. Portrait of the artist. *The New York Review of Books*, May 1978, 25(7), 8–15.

Greenberg, A., & Coleman, M. Depressed whole blood serotonin levels associated with behavioral abnormalities in the DeLang syndrome. *Pediatrics*, 1973, **52**, 720–723.

Kanner, L., & Lesser, L. Early infantile autism. *Pediatric Clinics of North America*, 1958, **5**(3), 711–730.

Lockyer, L., & Rutter, M. A five to fifteen year follow-up study of infantile psychosis: III. Psychological aspects. *British Journal of Psychiatry*, 1969, **115**, 865–882.

O'Connell, T. S. The musical life of an autistic boy. *Journal of Autism and Childhood Schizophrenia*, 1974, 4(3), 223–229.

Pollack, M. Brain damage, mental retardation and childhood schizophrenia. *American Journal of Psychiatry*, 1958, **115**, 422–428.

Rimland, B. *Infantile autism*. New York: Appleton, Century, Crofts, 1964.

Rutter, M. Autistic children: Infancy to adulthood. *Seminars in Psychiatry*, 1970, 2, 435–450.

Rutter, M., & Lockyer, L. A five to fifteen year follow-up study of infantile psychosis: II. Social and behavioral outcome. *British Journal of Psychiatry*, 1967, **113**, 1183–1199.

Schopler, E., & Reichler, R. How well do parents understand their own psychotic child? *Journal of Autism and Childhood Schizophrenia*, 1972, 4, 387–400.

Selfe, L. *Nadia: A case of extraordinary drawing ability in an autistic child*. New York: Academic Press, 1978.

Terman, L. M. *A Stanford-Binet intelligence scale, manual for the third revision form L-M*. Boston: Houghton-Mifflin, 1960.

Chapter 10

EFFECT OF EARLY
SYMPTOMS ON THE FAMILY

During two decades of working with autistic and other intellectually disabled children, I have become aware of the enormous difficulties and pressures parents face in rearing them. Participating as an interviewer in the interviews made me increasingly aware of these parents as people with all the usual failings and usual strengths of the human condition in a stressful situation, and decreasingly inclined to hold them responsible for infantile autism. In the foregoing chapters, I have described one large source of the stress, the inability of the autistic child to understand what is expected of him or to master the usual developmental tasks of childhood. Autistic parents, far from being aloof and akin to disinterested spectators, were intensely affected by the developmental failure of their autistic child. Just as the child was meeting many daily frustrations, the parents were facing similar impasses because, as Ray's mother said, "I've tried and tried to do things right with him, but I think I must have failed. My oldest daughter seems to do things better than I do."

A later chapter will deal with specific problems parents faced in finding professional help for their child, but it must be stated here that the process was nearly always stressful. While many members of the extended family tried to be helpful in childrearing, the parents, already beleaguered and supersensitive, sometimes felt more stress than help from the family. Remarks from neighbors, friends, and utter strangers, made generally in a spirit of helpfulness, were nevertheless often critical in substance and contributed to the stress. As Maria's mother said, "Nearly all my family and neighbors have said they could teach her to talk and some of them have tried—the same things we have tried—but they can't either. They just don't know how old all those comments get." Another mother said, "Everyone who comes to our house is a self-appointed psychiatrist. I've gotten so I don't want visitors."

Such multiple stresses, continuing over months or years, had effects on the parents as individuals and marriage partners and eventually on the other children in the family. We asked a direct question about the effect the child's symptoms had on the family and on the parents. Responses to this question were often meager or contained a denial of any serious effect. Gino's mother blandly replied: "I don't think it's had any effect. We do just like we always did." Yet contained in replies to other questions scattered throughout the interviews were descriptions of great upheavals in the lives of the families and of the sadness and inadequacy felt by many mothers. Thus it seemed that many parents had not pulled together their thoughts about how the child's problems had affected them.

The raters were asked to examine the interviews for such scattered statements as well as for answers to specific questions. They found many expressions of parental guilt, anger, feelings of sadness and failure, "nervousness," and a general diminution of joy in life. While a few parents were innately somewhat joyless or nervous people, many reported a turnabout following years of struggle to help their autistic children. Many fathers were especially sensitive to these changes in their wives.

Because mothers took so much larger a share than fathers in the day-to-day care of the children, the effects on mothers were more direct. This is not to say that fathers weren't touched deeply by the autistic child's problems; but they had their work and not only could derive self-esteem from it but would also gain a legitimate escape hatch. Most mothers had few outlets outside the house. Mothering was their main job and having a child that failed was a serious assault to their self-esteem.

The raters could see that the mothers shared all the effects in common and yet each experienced the problems in a unique way: Some were overcome with guilt while others felt it briefly and lightly—or said they did. Some mothers reported they had lost all joy in life while others managed to find good times for themselves. Some mothers seemed swallowed by one particular feeling while a host of painful feelings assaulted others. The raters picked the painful reactions that were mentioned by the mothers. In Table 44 is listed the incidence of these reported reactions.

Table 44. Effect of Autistic Child's Symptoms on Mothers

Expressed feelings	N	%
Physical and psychological tension	33	100
Guilt	22	66
Unsure of mothering ability	11	33
Anger at some symptom or feature of illness	10	30
Hurt because of child's lack of emotional response	6	18
Tired physically; feels old	6	18
Extreme worry and anxiety over symptom; demoralized	6	18
Restricted; trapped	6	18
Enjoyment of life seriously curtailed	5	15
Frustrated; can't find help	4	12
Unsure of genetic adequacy	3	9
Fearful of next pregnancy	3	9
Retreat into alcohol	1	3

Guilt

Guilt was a common feeling. At some level, at some time, probably each mother felt guilty about something she had or had not done and about 66% mentioned such guilt. In only about 15% of cases was it clearly expressed. For example, one mother had sustained a family tragedy that put her into a mourning state during her autistic child's first year, and she "always felt" that she was "the cause." Judy's mother had elevated her socioeconomic status through her marriage. She said, "I think she was sent as punishment for me being too haughty." Alvin's mother felt her failure to break her childish tie to her own mother led her to infantilize her child to the point he became autistic. In the case of Ronnie's mother, her preoccupation with another family problem was seen as "the cause." The guilt of the very few mothers who had never wanted the baby and felt little motherly feeling during his first year was great: "I lay awake nights realizing how I didn't want him, and how I didn't do extra things for him as a baby—not like my other one." To her husband, Jeremy's mother voiced the fear that her failure to "feel close" to her autistic infant might have caused his problems. She told of her pain:

> Oh, I have suffered this last year until I just—oh, it is terrible. I think the guilt that mothers go through when they find out something is wrong and that it is probably our fault is terrible. I have spent nights crying and walking the floor and thinking "What did I do and why did I do it?"

Most mothers tempered their guilt with observations such as the following: "I often find myself feeling guilty about my child's condition even though I say to myself, 'Why, I know I've done nothing to hurt my child.' " In the case of Terrence, the parents allowed him to spend much time in a jumper chair after he learned to sit up because he preferred to be there. His mother recalled that period:

> Maybe I could have done better—I don't know. He certainly wasn't neglected—I wouldn't want anyone to think that. But maybe I have a sense of guilt because of that chair—but at the time I didn't. He certainly was happy there and all the family was around him and paying attention.

The father thought he should have worked harder with Terrence to teach him to walk sooner and then observed that their other children never had to be "taught such things."

Doubts about Mothering Ability

Guilt and inability to help the autistic child "become normal" led about 33% of the mothers to express serious doubts about their capacity as mothers. As Rupert's mother said, "I feel like I'm really not (long pause) ah, maybe I'm not a very successful mother (laughs). There's not much to say about my success as a mother." Cheri's mother said about her good points as a mother, "Now that I'm thinking about it, I don't think there's anything I handle real well now." When Dale's mother was asked about her best points as a mother she said, "I used to think I was made to be a mother—had lots of patience, but I've lost it." Marvin's mother said, "This experience—I get to the point where I'm not adequate—am I inadequate to raise him? Am I—am I—I have felt a little inadequate." Caroline's mother: "I don't know if I have any best points at all. No. I don't believe so."

Anger

Several mothers expressed anger at some symptom or feature of the condition. Rarely did a mother say she felt direct anger toward the child. Perhaps most mothers felt so either consciously or unconsciously but could not make the admission either to themselves or to the interviewer. One of the mothers who was especially frank in discussing her faults as both she and her husband saw them said this:

> Well, my attitude is bad and my husband tries to take things in his stride, but it's increasingly difficult for him, probably because of me.

I feel bitter because I wanted to feel proud of my child. Well, my husband says I'm mad all the time and this bothers him—he says I go around like I'm mad at the whole world for our problems. I'm tense and don't laugh and smile as much as I used to when we were first married.

A few mothers were angry at the messes they had to clean up constantly or the fact they had so many sleepless nights or had to curtail so many activities. Of course, most mothers felt guilty about their anger, which in turn added to their general feeling of inadequacy. Cora's mother however was handling her child's screaming better since she became angry. She said, "Lately Cora has been bringing out feelings of anger in me. My ears must be getting frayed. When she screams—as only she can do—I don't have the patience I used to have. I used to try to find out what was wrong. Now I say 'All right, go to your room,' and she knows—she marches right to it."

Increased Physical and Psychological Tension

At some point in the series of interviews, one or both parents described increased physical and psychological tension. The statements exemplifying the tension were as follows: "I think we both live under a lot of tension—there is so much uncertainty about what is causing the trouble, what we should do, and the messes Donnie makes can be awful." Shelly's mother said, "I feel on tenterhooks all the time—whether I'm saying the right thing to her, how I should act. The other day I just yelled out something—we were riding in the car. She shrank back in the seat and was quiet. I didn't want to frighten her, but it was good to have her quiet." Daniel's mother said, "I feel nervous because of his behavior." Many mothers mentioned the "added pressures" of always having to watch the autistic child to prevent injury, getting into the street, or running away. Other mothers mentioned the "nerve-wracking" effects of constant restlessness and screaming.

A poignant daydream was described by Elaine's mother in response to the question, "Is there anything you can't get out of your thoughts?"

> Mother: I have this urge to take the children, and in my thoughts I'm almost on the beach where it's very relaxed and they're running up and down the beach—I think about this quite a bit.
> *Interviewer*: You sort of daydream?
> Mother: Yes, oh yes. We're just—like at a beach in Hawaii or someplace very beautiful and the children playing very happily—it's just a feeling that I have—I guess I want to be removed from all the tension.
> *Interviewer*: Does it give you relief?
> Mother: Yes.

Effect on Fathers as Individuals

It was apparent to the raters and interviewers that fathers were not as deeply engrossed in child care as were mothers. This condition was as true for normal fathers as for autistic fathers. The mothers referred to their children more frequently in the interviews and remembered developmental milestones better. When the parents were interviewed together, the mothers took the lead in answering questions about the child. Fathers, as a group, were less expressive of their emotions than were mothers, though a father might blurt out one or two emotional statements. Nevertheless, fathers' lives were affected seriously by the experience of having an autistic child. They too experienced feelings of guilt about what their role might have been in producing the symptoms as well as anger over some of them. Like some mothers, they felt hurt over lack of affection from the child. We suspected that fathers had the same troubling feelings of guilt, inadequacy, frustration, and anger as the mothers but that most did not, or could not, express them. Gary's father, who was thought by his wife to have little interest in his child, said in confidence to the interviewer: "You know I have a lot of feeling for him, but I can't express it. My wife doesn't know how strongly I feel. I think I put other things first but I feel strongly." A few fathers felt a sense of outrage that they had been singled out by fate. "Why me!" said Jane's father. "I've been hard-working and law-abiding."

An important effect on many fathers was their reaction to the mother's pain and preoccupation over the autistic child's problem. About 45% of the fathers appeared to be affected chiefly in this way. George's father: "I think my wife worries too much. It gets me down. Of course, I know she has a lot to worry about." Ronnie's father: "I really get upset when she gets depressed. She seems to be better now, but there are periods where this deep pessimism over Ronnie's condition just gets to me." Dana's father, with obvious anguish, told the interviewer how his wife's deep worry over Dana "just breaks me up—just tears me up. I don't want my wife to know how I feel—she cries at the mention of it." This same father, in one more emotional statement, told of his feelings for Dana: "I pity her—I just want to pick her up and hold her, you know."

Several fathers mentioned that the mothers' preoccupation with her child and the need to be at home with the child cut down on their pleasure in life because they could not go out much as a couple.

Several fathers worried about their wives' emotional health or about their loss of joy, not so much through its reflection on father but through its direct effect on mother. Albert's father said, "Before Albie's problems, my wife was a buoyant person with lots of energy. She joked and laughed a lot. Now I really worry about her if we don't do something soon about him. We took a month's vacation and I became aware of its tremendous effect on her. She was enjoying things again. When we got back she began to go backward. She tries so hard to get her optimism going, but it's no go." Another father said, "I don't think my wife can take it much longer. She is constantly searching for some answers to our child's problems and never finds them. It's frustrating. It's an unnatural way to live."

Psychiatric Conditions in Parents

Parents of autistic children differed from those of normal ones in only one psychiatric condition: About one-third of the autistic mothers had troublesome depressive symptoms in reaction to their stressful living situations. However, overall function was not reported to be reduced in any

Table 45. Incidence of Psychiatric Problems in Parents of Autistic and Normal Children[a]

Psychiatric disorder	Autistic (N = 66)		Normal (N = 66)	
	Mother	Father	Mother	Father
Alcoholism[b]	1	4	1	3
Depression				
Functioning not seriously impaired[b]	10			
Functioning impaired[c]	3	3	7	
Psychotic reactions				1
Anxiety		2		1
Marital paranoia		1		1
Acute schizophrenia			1	
Personality disturbances[b]				
Immature	1	3		
Explosive		2		2
Inadequate		1		
Highly emotional			1	
Moody and tense				2
Teenage (acting out)			1	2
Extreme premenstrual tension			1	
Total	15	16	12	12
% of total (N = 66)	22.7	24.2	18.2	18.2

[a]Differences not significant.
[b]All untreated.
[c]Two autistic fathers and 3 normal mothers untreated.

major way; these mothers were able to go about their routine duties without interruption. In all cases, the autism played a primary or highly contributory role. It must be said that all autistic mothers felt saddened by their child's problems and we were not sure where to draw the line at diagnosing a mild situational depressive reaction. The raters used the presence of the following as criteria:

(1) Depression not present before situational stress.
(2) Presence of one or more symptoms of depression in addition to sadness; e.g., serious diminution of enjoyment in life, interruption of sleep, elimination problems, frequent crying spells.
(3) Routine functions not interrupted.

An additional 9% of autistic mothers had depressions that did interfere with function and in one case severe symptoms antedated the advent of the autistic child's problems. Two cases were definitely not primarily reactive to the child's problems but were affected by them. About 15% of the mothers took medication for a short while. An additional 15% were given prescriptions for medication but either did not have the prescription filled or took only a few tablets. Psychoses were not present in any of the autistic parents and in only two normal parents; these were in remission at interview time. Three autistic and three normal mothers received short-term psychotherapy. Depressions in normal mothers (9%) did not stem primarily from problems with the normal index child.

Incidence of personality disturbances, trouble with alcohol, and miscellaneous conditions did not differ significantly between the two groups. Thus it appears that psychiatric illness occurred much the same in our sample of autistic and matched normal parents except for reactive depressive symptoms of the autistic mothers.

Wanting to Escape

The severe frustration of the mothers over their inability to solve their autistic child's problems was revealed in response to a question designed to uncover depression and suicidal thoughts. We asked: "Have your problems ever seemed so great that you didn't want to go on?" Only two mothers and two fathers reported thoughts of suicide and only one mother had made a suicidal gesture. About 42% of the autistic mothers stated they sometimes had feelings that they couldn't deal with their situation any more, and that they would like to "slip away someplace." Only one normal mother reported this feeling. Most mothers denied these were suicidal feelings or that they would in actuality ever run away. Their autistic child's problems were so baffling, so serious, and so resistant to their maternal efforts that they didn't want to have to think about their situation or try to manage it any more. Indeed, most of these mothers did not try to run away from the situation either by staying long periods away from the home or by going to work. Only four mothers often managed to get away physically or psychologically. Two mothers worked regularly, one increased her alcohol intake, and the fourth one left home a great deal to visit with friends, leaving the child in the care of the father.

Most mothers stuck it out despite the feelings that they were managing poorly or that the whole situation was too frustrating to try to deal with any longer. Some mothers spoke of this as "just living one day at a time," or "muddling through from one hour to the next," but most denied any possibility of acting out their thoughts of escape. None of them "took off running." If fathers weren't willing to stay at home with the children, and a few were not, then mothers had little time away from home for themselves. If this group of mothers erred, it was on the side of not taking enough time away from home and children and in not fighting hard enough for father to take his turn babysitting. Here is one mother's account of how the frustrations and uncertainties affected her mental health. The effect of several uncertainties seemed additive.

Question: Did your problem ever seem so great you couldn't go on?
Mother: Not any more. Oh, I get the feeling at times that I'd like to go out the front door and not come back. I wouldn't do it now. There was a time that—after we got the diagnosis on Ronnie that things did seem that bad and I went to a psychologist.

Question: Did you ever seriously consider suicide?
Mother: No, I don't think so—but for awhile I wondered if I was heading for a nervous breakdown—I wasn't remembering to get the meals on the table. One day only I had a period where things seemed a little unreal—like I was observing myself—I must have been groggy from lack of sleep.

Question: What was particularly troubling you at that time?
Mother: Well, I was considerably worried about Ronnie, and it became apparent we weren't going to get treatment where we lived then, and this worried me a lot. My husband was thoroughly wrapped up in his work and was hardly home—then his company told him he was to be transferred—we were going to move—but I didn't know where. This much insecurity threw me.

Another way of estimating the degree of psychopathology in the autistic parents was through the Minnesota Multiphasic Personality Inventory (MMPI)

(McAdoo & DeMyer, 1978). If autistic parents were truly deviant in terms of psychopathology, then their MMPI profiles should resemble those of parents who were patients in an adult psychiatric clinic. Instead we found that the psychiatric patients had significantly more psychopathology than the autistic parents, whose scores were more like the normal adult standardization population.

Many authors, especially in the past, have said that parents of autistic children have extreme personality traits such as overrigid perfectionism (Kanner, 1943) or extreme rage (Bettelheim, 1967) to name exponents of two of the more widely held views (Kanner has since changed his mind). The Edwards Personality Preference Test (EPPS) was chosen to investigate those ideas. The intent of the test author was to measure the 15 human needs defined by Murray (Murray, 1938). The test materials were given to each parent singly (24 autistic parents and 30 parents of handicapped, nonpsychotic children). As with the MMPI, the answers were scored without regard for the diagnosis of the child.

Parents of autistic children were not unusual in personality preferences either when compared with the standardization population of heads of households or with the control group. If the parents had been rigid, unaffectionate perfectionistic, mechanistic people, they should have scored high on achievement, order, autonomy, endurance, and low on exhibition, affiliation, succorance, nurture, and change. To conform to Bettelheim's view, they should have scored high on aggression and low on nurture. Instead, in all the comparisons between the autistic and control parents, using mean percentile scores, there were no singificant differences. The only scale that tended to differentiate autistic from control parents was heterosexuality, which measures interest in members of the opposite sex as people and as sexual objects. The autistic fathers tended to express more interest in heterosexuality than control fathers. Otherwise, there were no differences between autistic and control groups in mean scores, number of extreme scores (> 85 or < 15), or in the profile of scores.

Still another way of estimating the personality types of the autistic parents was to compare their preferences in parenting practices and personal traits of their spouses as marital partners with those same qualities in the matched normal parents. There were no significant differences between these groups in the way they responded to the questions: "What are your best/worst points as a mother/father?" "What are your spouse's best/worst points as a mother/father?" "If something were to happen to this marriage, what qualities in your husband/wife would you like repeated/eliminated in a second spouse?"

In their own and their spouses' parenting role, the parents admired most open expressions of affection and love for the children (about 70%, both groups). Fathers also admired in their wives a character trait that facilitated smooth mother-child interaction. Mothers also admired in their husbands participation in the children's activities and character traits that allowed them to be good models, teachers, and disciplinarians.

The most frequently cited "worst" motherly trait by the mothers about themselves was too frequent displays of bad temper or impatience (autistic mothers, 66%; normal mothers, 73%). Fathers tended to see mothers as more patient. A mother could be regarded by herself as too impatient with the children, and still regarded by her husband as generally patient. Most mothers expressed chagrin or even guilt that they ever lost their tempers with their children, thus setting standards for angels and not for ordinary mortals.

Poor disciplinary procedures were reported most frequently as the "worst" fatherly trait. In several cases the mothers admired the fathers' capacity for firm discipline but also reported in one and the same father a "worst" trait as being "too stern" or "spanking the children too hard."

Disturbing character traits of various kinds with regard to the children and too little participation in their activities were frequently mentioned. The fathers in both groups who actually were devoid of interest and affection for the children and who refused to play and talk with them at all caused mothers much pain and anger. Fortunately, these fathers were a small minority in both groups.

The most admired traits in marital partners were expressions of affection, listening and talking to the spouse, and being a "good parent." Most frequently mentioned disliked traits in marital partners were personal qualities or "bad habits." These ranged from the trivial, such as "eating crackers in bed" and "not pulling down the blinds," to the important, mainly bad temper (autistic, 54%; normal, 60%). Verbal abusiveness was reported of some wives while several husbands were reported as both verbally and physically abusive. In no case was injury reported. The spouse who would not talk or listen was mentioned about the same for both groups (autistic, 39%; normal, 33%). Examples of other disliked marital traits were laziness, procrastination, pessimism, lack of humor, too many absences, sexual coldness, and religious differences.

While no formal analyses were done, it was the raters' impression that parents of both groups were better prepared and less defensive about evaluating each other as parents than as marital partners. This is an interesting phenomenon if true and is deserving of fuller study by social scientists. We noted that descriptions of "best" and "worst" parenting practices came rather easily to the parents' minds. Several parents refused to discuss the question about admired and disliked traits of their spouses as marital partners. It was clear that many did not understand with any depth the nature of their relationship with their spouses. Some parents found it threatening to examine this topic with us. Many parents had difficulty dissociating their spouses from a parenting role, which of course underscored the importance of parenting in the marital relationship itself.

In summary, despite the stress of rearing a difficult to understand, developmentally deviant child, autistic parents did not have any greater incidence of severe psychopathology than normal control parents. On objective tests of personality disturbance (MMPI) and personal preference (EPPS), autistic parents most resembled the normal standardization populations. Autistic parents had significantly less psychopathology than parents who were patients in an adult psychiatric clinic. The interviews revealed that personality traits and preferences were not expressed in extreme degree by autistic parents as a group. The autistic mothers differed most from normal matched control mothers in having a greater incidence of reactive depression, probably as a result of trying to deal with the continuous stress of rearing and finding help for an autistic child.

The Marriages

While general ratings of marital happiness and unhappiness were not significantly different between couples who had an autistic child and those who did not (see Table 46), there were obviously more strains in the autistic marriages as determined by examination of several aspects of family living. Also, there tended to be more extremely happy or happy marriages among the normal couples (autistic, 30%; normal, 42%) and more extremely unhappy marriages among couples with an autistic child (autistic, 30%; normal, 18%). An example of an extremely happy normal marriage written in thumbnail form by a rater is as follows: "The mother is outgoing, sensitive to her own and family's needs, and sensible. The father is enthusiastic about his work and admires his wife. They have many mutual interests and good sex." A happy autistic marriage of longer duration than the foregoing was described as: "Both parents happy and contented with each other. Autistic child is low

Table 46. Marital Happiness Rating Scale[a]

Scale	Autistic		Normal	
	N	%	N	%
Extremely happy or happy	12	36	14	42
Bored (happy–unhappy)	13	39	13	39
Unhappy or very unhappy	8	24	6	18

[a] Differences not significant.

point of marriage. Parents have not blamed each other but have been mutually supportive. First year they had marital problems as father felt inadequate over poor paying job. As finances improved, he felt better and the marriage improved."

Examples of unhappy or very unhappy marriages are the following:

(1) Father often angry at mother and one child in family. He feels too tied down by large family. Parents sometimes try to solve impasses by open discussion. Mother often reacts to father's temper by feeling sorry for herself and giving father silent treatment, which further angers him. Mother is often tense about the children.

(2) Marriage has always been stressful. Parents recently discussed separation and divorce. Mother reports father angry, unfeeling, and verbally abusive. Father feels mother withdrawn from him and uncaring. House untidy.

A similar proportion of autistic and normal couples had "so-so" or "bored" marriages (39%), an example of which follows: "Neither parent sees serious problems in the marriage but neither is enthusiastic about the other. Both seem bored; mother hates housework and has no other outlet. They have few interests together. Marriage is probably stable."

Table 47. General Effect of Autistic and Normal Children on Marriages

Effect	Autistic[a]		Normal	
	N	%	N	%
Restrict activities or cause worry but bond not particularly lessened	15	45	10	30
Emotional bond somewhat weakened by problems concerning rearing of index child	13	39	6	21
Emotional bond seems virtually broken (index child played major role)	3	9	0	0
Marital bond strongly strengthened by index child	1	3	1	3
Emotional bond broken—index child did not seem to play a major role	1	3	0	0
Effect generally positive and no particular worries or restrictions posed by index child	0	0	15	45

[a] $p < .01$.

General Effect of Index Children on Marriages

Normal index children were likely to have a generally positive effect on a marriage (45% of normal cases). Normal parents said such things as: "He's a delightful child"; "Very good to have around"; "We get a big kick out of her." Problems associated with rearing the index child seemed to weaken the affectional bond in about 51% of autistic marriages as compared to about 21% of normal marriages.

That problems in childrearing cause friction and tension and sometimes lessening of affection between couples whose children are normal comes as no surprise. One example is of a normal father whose ire was stimulated by a son who had a long bout of illness due to bacterial infection. The mother's feelings for her husband were eroded by his attitude. A normal mother said: Gearry is such an aggressive boy—he just grates on me. I don't get along well with him—it can't be his fault and I'm afraid my feelings aren't the best for him." While she acknowledged the "irrationality" of her feelings, the father deeply resented her attitude. These examples may represent displacements of feelings from marital partners to children but on the surface at least they appear to be a response of the normal parents to particular features of a given child.

Principal Issues in Considering Divorce

The autistic index child figured more prominently in thoughts about divorce than did the normal index child (autistic, 27%; normal, 0%). Other issues such as attention to other people, fathers who were unsupportive emotionally or had job problems, finances, and sex did not differ, at least according to parental statements. In some cases, the tensions building up about handling the autistic child seemed the most damaging to the marital bond when either mother or father was especially bitter. "Our marriage has gone downhill since our child's problems. There's just too much tension and bickering and bitterness." In other cases, the parents realized one of the main reasons they were thinking about divorce was to escape from their frustrations over the child.

Here is what one father said in response to the question, "Have you or your wife ever seriously considered divorce?"

> One night we got to talking about our marriage. She said she had been thinking about a divorce, and I said I had too. We made some plans about when we would do it and all—then we both looked at each other and said we really didn't mean it—we just wanted to get away from our problems with Clare—and of course divorce was no way to do it.

Table 48. Principal Issues in Considering Divorce

Issue	Autistic		Normal	
	N	%	N	%
Child's problems	9	27	0	0
Interest in others	5	15	6	18
Father emotionally unsupportive of mother	5	15	3	9
Finances	4	12	6	18
Miscellaneous[a]	4	12	8	24
Job problems of father	2	6	3	9
Sex between parents	1	3	3	9

[a]Includes crowded quarters, readjustment after military service, inlaws, death of another child, depression in mother, alcohol abuse.

Factors Adversely Affecting Autistic Marriages

The effects of the stress of the autistic child's symptoms seriously affected parents as individuals and spilled over into the marriage itself. The "nerve-wracking" effects of worry and some of the children's more irritating symptoms, such as screaming and hyperactivity, put the parents on edge and "made" them say "hurtful things to each other." This edginess particularly made mothers "take things the wrong way." Here is how Elmer's father replied to the question, "How much trouble is there between you and your wife because of Elmer?"

Father: Well—his actions put her nerves on edge. They do mine too—but her more than me; and things that wouldn't ordinarily bother her, bother her now. He gets out of bed—the day'll go along and the farther into the day we go, the worse it gets. I'd say nine-tenths of the disharmony would stem from him.

The sadness, depression, and worry often took the joy out of marriages. As one mother said, "I think I feel old before my time. I think we used to laugh and cut up more before all this." George's mother said she would take all of her husband's "less than perfect" characteristics in a "much worse light" when she was feeling blue and would have thoughts of divorce. When she felt a mood swing upward, she felt better about him. Several parents said they covered up their feelings in front of their mates in order to cause less worry. By so doing, they seemed to shut off valuable communication and increased their feelings of isolation from each other.

Those parents who had two children who were not developing normally were especially stressed. There were 28% of parents who had another child with a learning disability, in three cases a severe one. These parents, particularly the mothers, were so sad that at times they felt demoralized.

Question: How is your relationship with your husband?

Mother: I think a lot of our problems are the children. Both take a lot of care and patience and sometimes we don't have it. You get tired of hearing them scream all the time and it's hard to keep on working with no response back—it's heartbreaking. You don't always want to walk with a long face. There are times it makes you feel badly and you take the hurt out on each other—you can't take it out on the children. I think after each tragedy, things between us got worse even though we tried. Also we try to cover up our bad feelings so we don't always feel so low.

The autistic mothers' most frequent and fervent complaint about their husbands with respect to their own problems in mothering an autistic child was: "He doesn't give me enough support. He doesn't boost my morale." This lack was felt from the time some mothers first thought something was wrong with the child. In this regard, they were ahead of fathers who frequently doubted the accuracy of their wives' observations and criticized their efforts to get help. Freddie's mother said:

After I took him to the doctor my husband was just incredulous. The doctor said we should have an expert look at Freddie and I came home quite upset and he still refused to believe that anything real was wrong. That was rather—rather cruel. But it's the times that we become very accusing of each other about little things that puts a great strain on things.

"Moral support" from fathers was extremely important to the mothers and important to the survival of the marriage. Nearly every mother told us whether she received such support (see Table 49).

About a third of the group said they were satisfied with the way their husbands helped. "He really pitches in and helps. He's a good father. I have no complaints." Another mother: "He calls during the day to see how things are going. He's just so good." About 27% were at the other end of the spectrum. These mothers believed that the father either showed insufficient interest in the child's problems or was so insensitive to them and their efforts that they felt mostly bitterness and animosity toward their husbands. On

Table 49. Mothers' Reports of Support Received from Fathers in Care of Autistic Children

Degree of support and feelings	N	%
Father shares burdens; mother feels supported	10	33
Father shares burdens; mother reports some lack	5	15
Mother seems fairly upset, but won't openly discuss feelings	4	12
Mother generally feels lack of support, except for occasional help	5	15
Mother feels acutely the lack of support	9	27

follow-up, most of the divorces among autistic couples had occurred in this group (five of the nine members were divorced). One mother had become seriously depressed. Another 15% of autistic mothers expressed serious dissatisfaction with the way the fathers failed to appreciate or help with their efforts, but without such bitterness. Mothers cited the following as important evidence of lack of support: critical attitudes, failure to praise, not taking the family on outings, never helping with the physical care, unreasonable or too harsh discipline, not talking with their wives about problems, or belittling their efforts to obtain help. Mothers did not appear to want perfection, but they more often than not (70% of cases) wanted a little more, or a great deal more, than the father could give. Joel's mother said this while sobbing:

> My greatest beef is that he's so often not at home. He leaves nearly all the care of Joel to me—also the rest of the kids. I think of him going to all those business lunches and I am stuck in the house literally 24 hours a day. But then what would we do as a couple if he didn't work! We can't weekend because Joel is so difficult. We can't go out much—babysitters won't stay. Maybe I can't expect any more—at least *he* can get away awhile. Maybe this is the way he can stand it.

That marriage survived but Marjorie's parents divorced. The mother said: "Not only is he never home, but he spends his money other places. When he is home, he wants me to wait on him hand and foot along with all the other things. He wanted this when I had two in diapers."

One of the few mothers who was loath to tell her side of the case nevertheless was heard through her husband.

Question: Tell me your worst points as a father.

Father: I don't give my wife enough moral support. I think she has a difficult job and I criticize her too much.

Question: Now tell me about your worst points as a *father*.
Father: I think that's it. Part of being a good father is being a
              good husband and a good husband has to help his wife.
              The worst problem of my life is to have my son have
              something wrong that I can't do anything about. It's
              heartbreaking.

Fathers were made uncomfortable by the increase in emotionality,
"edginess," and involvement with the child's problems that they saw in their
wives. "I just don't like to have her cry so much." "Her mind is always on
that child." "She cries about him too much." "I'm sad too, but you have to
get away from it sometimes."

Sexual Adjustment

Normal parents tended to have a better sexual adjustment than autistic
parents (see Table 50). While groups were equal as to minor and moderate sex
difficulties, there tended to be fewer autistic parents reporting a superlative
sexual relationship and more reporting severe problems. Autistic mothers
tended to report more often than normal mothers that worries about the
index child interfered with their interest in sex (see Table 51). We failed to
ask a direct question as to whether the index child directly interfered with
sexual relations, but such was spontaneously reported more often by autistic
parents than normal parents (autistic, 45%; normal, 3%). In an additional 21%
of autistic cases, raters inferred from the discussion that problems of child
care probably interfered. An example of a direct reference is that by an
autistic mother: "Since the last baby was born and with all of Cora's
problems, I'm tired all the time. My husband seems to understand. When we

Table 50. Sexual Adjustment of Parents of Autistic and
Normal Children[a]

Severity of problem	Autistic		Normal	
	N	*%*	*N*	*%*
None	4	12	7	21
Minor	13	39	13	39
Moderate	10	30	10	30
Severe	5	15	2	6
Relations ceased	1	3	1	3

[a] Differences not significant.

Table 51. Interference in Sexual Compatibility of Parents of Autistic and Normal Children

Type of interference	Autistic	Normal
Parents worried/tired	11	4
Loss of affection, respect	7	1
Unfeeling, dislikes sex (mother)	4	10
Fear of pregnancy	4	1
Preferences/frequency different	3	6
Parent uninterested (father)	2	6
Sick/disabled	2	1

do it, it's still satisfactory." Indeed her husband did understand. In his interview he reported: "Our sex is fine—except she's tired a great deal. It's not the same as it used to be before we had this trouble with Cora. I realize the situation—she just can't turn it off and on." George's mother could only hint at the effects of the problem because she seemed embarrassed by the questions. Her husband was more open: "It's very good except since George's difficulties and his brother's illness--my wife is upset about these things and so we get along but it's not like it was."

Fathers seemed less directly affected by worry over the child. Only one reported that it had affected him. Autistic fathers as a group seemed to want intercourse at the same frequency as they did before their problems began. Autistic mothers were the ones who had their libido reduced by worries and tiredness. Normal mothers were also affected more than normal fathers by the cares of daily life. Both agreed that mothers see their husbands as innately more interested in sex. When sex was a problem in both autistic and normal marriages, and even when it was not so reported, fathers, as a whole, were described as wanting sex more often than mothers. These were marriages of the 1960s and perhaps—perhaps—these findings might not apply to young people's marriages of the 1970s. One mother spoke for about 85% of all of them: "Sex isn't just what happens in bed. It's everything that happens during the day. If the little things aren't good, then sex isn't good for me; it isn't there at all."

From a father's point of view, sex can proceed satisfactorily if not superlatively despite worries and cares and a certain loss of affection. Fathers who felt their wives were withholding sex as "punishment" or who were basically "frigid" or unwilling to "experiment with new things" were extremely unhappy. Most fathers, both normal and autistic, understood that their wives' sexual desires were diminished by the cares of life. If a mother's sexual interest dipped below a certain level, then her husband felt deprived and bitter. A father of a normal child expressed this feeling: "I know that for me all the problems of daily life can be made much less by good sex. I have tried to tell my wife this, but it is hard to say to her, and she doesn't think this way. This is a great difficulty to me."

Sexual unfaithfulness was a rare event for mothers and was reported in about 15% of both normal and autistic fathers. Unfaithfulness (like cruelty) brought about extremely painful reactions from the mothers, who were not only angry but demoralized and carried these painful feelings long after the event. The fathers, at least those who were open, expressed acute pain about mothers who were sexually cold. Herein lies one of the dilemmas of the autistic marriage, or of any marriage. Women are likely to be less interested in sex in a stress situation while men seem to need sex the same as usual or perhaps even more. Thus in the marriage under stress, a man may be likely to seek or strongly desire other sexual partners because his wife is less interested. On the other hand, a woman is likely to be demoralized by her husband's unfaithfulness or lack of interest, thus further compromising her interest in sex. There were marriages in both the normal and autistic groups that did not follow this pattern but they were the exceptions.

Factors affecting the marriages of autistic parents more than those of normal parents were housekeeping, finances, and family outings. Autistic mothers spent a greater proportion of their time cleaning up and some did not meet their own or their husbands' housekeeping standards (autistic fathers, 36%; normal fathers, 15%). Autistic fathers agreed with their wives that autistic children posed a special burden in physical care of the home, yet they wanted a reasonably neat home. On a happier note, 21% of autistic fathers praised their wives' housekeeping, sometimes in the face of serious hindrances. "I think she does a marvelous job under trying circumstances." A few mothers in both groups complained their husbands were unreasonable in their demands for a super-clean house at all times.

More autistic couples reported a money shortage (autistic, 63%; normal, 45%). At least part of the financial strain came from extra medical and educational expenses for the autistic child, but autistic parents tended to report more often than normal parents that at least one of the pair was a good money manager (autistic, 67%; normal, 54%). The groups did not differ with respect to quarrels about money.

The relative infrequency of family outings was a particular complaint of mothers. Behavior of the child on community excursions was sometimes embarrassing and often difficult because of hyperactivity, wandering away from the family, unusual body movements and use of toys, and sometimes unusual approaches to strangers. Mothers felt the isolation more than fathers. "My husband won't take us out much. I really miss not going any place with the family together. I think it would be good for all of us—but if we do go somewhere and she makes the littlest noise, he comes right home."

What Parents of Autistic Children Want from Each Other

When all the verbiage was cleared away, mothers seemed to be asking of fathers:

> Please support me in trying to do the best I can with this different and trying child. Tell me I'm doing a good job. Let me cry on your shoulder, listen to my observations about our child, go with me to see the doctors, don't retreat from us. Take us out for some fun even though you are embarrassed by our child in public. Don't criticize me, but help me.

In turn, fathers seemed to be asking of mothers:

> I'm trying to do the best I can to earn a living and to understand what's going on, but I understand our autistic child less than you do and I'm uncomfortable because of all your painful emotions. Society has taught me it's not brave to cry and you do a lot of it. One of the reasons I married you was because you were laughing and joking and affectionate. You're not that way any more and you are immersed in the problems of one child. Let me have some fun alone even if you yourself can't get away from home or your thoughts enough to have your own fun.

Major Effects on Siblings

The increased parental tension and worry inevitably affected the siblings and many parents described such tension in terms of the whole family as well as of themselves as individuals: "I think the whole problem has been a terrible strain to all of us—to our other children. We can't sleep right or enjoy our meals or go out much. I feel sorry for us all." In addition to increased general tension in some of the siblings, more specific effects were described for many siblings. The most common mentioned effect (54%) was that the special problems brought out the helpful side of one or more of them. They did such things as amusing and diverting the autistic child, participating in physical care, and "understanding" when the autistic child received preferential or special treatment from the parents. Jana's mother said: "My oldest daughter is my strong right arm. She can do everything I can do." Some siblings tried to teach the child speech or persistently offered affection until it was accepted. Most of the truly helpful siblings were at least of school age or older but occasionally very young ones seemed to grasp that their autistic brother or sister was different, and didn't resent the extra attention they received. Some high school and college age children chose careers in medicine, teaching or psychology, in part spurred by the desire to help.

On the other hand, the most prominent negative effect (in 30% of families) was that one or more children in the family felt neglected, or the parents reported relative neglect, because so much attention was paid to the autistic child and so much time was spent in finding help. "There's just so much time in the day and sometimes I know I give too much of it to Jaimie. My daughter is at a stage where she needs more of me and no matter how hard I try, she doesn't get enough of my time." Another mother told how their 5-year-old daughter had changed from loving and accepting the autistic child into resentment because "he has gotten too much attention—I don't blame her for resenting it, but we literally have no choice right now."

About 18% of the parents reported that at least one sibling seemed worried and upset about the autistic child's condition. "One of my children continually asks me why she won't talk and why she doesn't like him." About 15% reported regression in habit training (toileting and eating) that seemed related to their autistic child's effect on the sibling. Other effects reported in one or two families each were inordinate teasing by school friends, nearly complete ignoring of the autistic child, and an unusually high level of jealousy. Two siblings ran away from home saying that their responsibilities to the autistic child provoked it. One sibling refused to go to school. Whether the autistic child actually stimulated these reactions is a moot point since most of these events occurred also in normal homes, but in these cases the normal index child was not blamed. Nevertheless, being a sibling of an autistic child undoubtedly is a deeply affecting experience. In families with 2 children of which the older is autistic, the younger child will be at greater risk than older siblings in families with several children of which one younger is autistic.

From parents' descriptions of the behavior of each sibling, a psychiatrist made a judgment of whether emotional disturbance was probably present in each one (see Table 52). There were no significant group differences in probable emotional disturbance of siblings (autistic, 15%; normal, 13%).

Examples of behavior of siblings indicating probable emotional disturbance are as follows:

Table 52. Incidence of Emotional Disturbance in Siblings of Autistic and Normal Children

N and %	Autistic[a]	Normal
Total N of siblings	59	67
N of emotionally disturbed	9	9
% of emotionally disturbed	15	13

[a] Differences not significant.

(1) Female, 7 years of age: fearful, insecure, teased by peers. At 2 years of age did not talk and had some unusual repetitive behavior; however has always been friendly to adults and plays with other children.

(2) Male, 5 years of age: neighborhood discipline problem; fussy, demanding, beats his head on the floor.

(3) Male, 9 years of age: wets his bed regularly, fearful of dark, no sense of responsibility at school or home.

While stress on parents, and probably on siblings, is great during the preschool years of the autistic child's life, the probability of emotional disturbance in siblings of autistic children does not appear greater than in those of the matched normal index children. A study of sibling groups using face-to-face interviews and reports of their school teachers would give a more accurate estimate of such incidence. At this time a major study of siblings is in progress (Campbell, Cleary, Geller, Hardesty, & Cohen, 1979) and will be published in book form.

Concluding Note

While the stress of rearing an autistic child is considerable, there are only a few detectable differences in stress effects between families with an autistic child and families without such a child. One hesitates whether to conclude that autistic parents are exceptionally resilient or that raising a normal family is almost as stressful as raising one containing an autistic child. The incidence of serious psychiatric disorder in the two groups is about the same, and autistic parents do not, as a group, show the pathological personality characteristics suggested by some psychodynamically oriented clinicians. Not surprisingly, the incidence of reactive depression among mothers of autistic children is about twice as great, but most mothers were not incapacitated. The resulting stress of living with an autistic child seems to have weakened some marriages. It should be noted, however, that it also has strengthened many a marriage. As to the siblings of autistic children, the forthcoming study by Campbell and her associates (1979) promises to enhance our knowledge regarding incidence and severity of emotional disturbances among them.

REFERENCES

Bettelheim, B. *The empty fortress: Infantile autism and the birth of the self.* New York: Free Press, 1967.

Campbell, M., Cleary, P., Geller, B., Hardesty, A. S., & Cohen, I. L. *Autistic children and their siblings.* Washington, D.C.: V. H. Winston & Sons, 1979, in preparation.

Kanner, L. Autistic disturbances of affective contact. *Nervous Child*, 1943, 2, 217.

McAdoo, W. G., & DeMyer, M. K. Personality characteristics of parents. In M. Rutter & E. Schopler (Eds.), *Autism: A reappraisal of concepts and treatment.* New York: Plenum Press, 1978.

Murray, H. A. *Explorations in personality.* New York: Oxford University Press, 1938.

Chapter 11

PROBLEMS IN FINDING AND USING PROFESSIONAL SERVICES

Introductory Comment

Over the years, as I have tried to help parents find services for an autistic person, I have come to recognize that certain problems arise in nearly every case and that there are certain phases in parents' adjustments. Also, I have come to recognize common assets and liabilities among parents as seekers of help and among professionals as givers of help. We shall look at some of these issues in three phases of the help-seeking process. The early period comes during the autistic child's preschool years when the parents are recognizing that the child has a severe problem and searching for a source of initial therapy. They seek advice from family and friends, then from the family physician and pediatrician, who refer them to professionals whom the parents expect to be "experts." The middle period (Chapter 12) encompasses roughly kindergarten and grade school age when the child receives some treatment and special education, and the late period (Chapters 13 and 14) involves the adolescent and adult years when the autistic individual's final level of education and work becomes apparent to the parents. During all of these periods, the parents have enormous adjustments to make as they learn about autism in general and their own child in particular. If they are to find the best

Table 53. Role of Grandparents of Autistic Children in Help-Seeking[a]

Grandparents' reports	N	%
Supportive of plans to get help	15	45
Thinking autistic child will get better without help or doubting that child had problem	11	33
Critical of parents' child care methods	8	24
Not close enough to have an opinion	5	15
First to urge parents to get help— parents resented or dragged feet	3	9
Too "pessimistic"	1	3

[a]Total N of grandparents = 33; reports by one or more.

in education and terhapy that their community has to offer, they must generally become diplomatic evaluators of educators, physicians, psychologists, and social workers. There are some real hazards to the parents who may become so overinvolved in their autistic child that they lose sight of their personal growth, their marriage, and perhaps of their other children as well.

About 70% of parents reported some strain over the part played by at least one grandparent. The most frequent problem from grandparents (about 33% of families) was unwillingness to admit the autistic child had a problem severe enough to warrant professional help or even that the child had a problem at all. In some cases, this was a mild irritant; e.g., "Oh, I think they try to look at it through rose-colored glasses. It's pride but eventually they will accept it." In other instances, it created major breaches among family members; e.g., "She (grandmother) actually got belligerent when she found out about the psychiatric treatment. It caused a revolt in the family because we were going to do what we felt best." For most parents this grandparental attitude was not regarded as crucial, but it was one more burden to bear as the parents came to a painful and lonely decision to get help. As one father said, "Either my wife's mother won't believe something is wrong or she won't accept the fact. I know my wife would like her to understand. She is not too dependent on her mother, but she would like this."

In about 24% of cases, a grandparent or other family member was critical of some phase of childrearing that particularly hurt the mothers in their overly sensitive, anxious state. As Maryanne's father said, "My mother-in-law at times will say things that are OK. Then she can get critical. The whole thing has affected my wife. Her mother will call and say that Maryanne may feel rejected or unloved. This is very hard for my wife to take." Another father spoke of his own father's "unreasonable" suggestions. "I think my wife has done a fine job. Advice is fine, maybe, but it should be given carefully." Another father "stayed out" of such discussions and his wife felt the lack of his support.

In about 15% of cases grandparents were seen as too old or too removed from the scene to have an opinion. In most cases the parents were not resentful, but one mother said, "My mother and father aren't at all interested. I wish they were but why should I expect it, because they were never very interested in me." Some grandparents were the first to urge treatment and persisted in making the suggestion. Parents ultimately acceded with varying amounts of resentment. Here is one parent's account:

> My mother gave me the dickens for not seeing to it that Eliza was attended to much earlier. As long as 2 years ago they recognized it. When we did start, it seemed to take so long—one referral was lost at the first hospital we were sent to. It took 3 months to get that straightened out. Oh, I was glad she was so interested.

In one case, the parents were still not sure that "anything was wrong" but were reluctantly seeking consultation at the grandmother's urging.

After the parents, generally the mother, realized that something was amiss in the autistic child, the family physician or the pediatrician was usually the first professional consulted. In about 73% of cases, after a variable period of time, these physicians recommended further diagnostic study, often in a pediatric medical hospital (about 48% of all cases). In about 27% of cases, nothing further was done for about a year because parents were told "there was no serious problem." No great bitterness accrued unless the message was

Table 54. Actions by First Professional Consulted on Child's Disorder

Action	N	%
Referred to pediatric hospital for further diagnostic study	16	48
Nothing done for several months	9	27
Parents told "don't worry"	5	15
Parents offended by doctor's approach	4	12
Referred to psychiatrist, psychologist or child guidance clinic	6	18
Referred to speech and hearing clinic	2	6

given in an unkind or perfunctory manner, but parents generally wished for the earliest possible help and regretted the wait (see Table 54). In some cases, fortunately only 12%, the parents were so offended by the physician's manner or words that they changed physicians. "He (the physician) was very impatient with out child, and he had no time for us. I instinctively didn't like the way he treated Maria, and we just left and went to someone else."

Brenda's mother said of a physician who said to give her child "time to grow":

> He wasn't any help at all. He wouldn't even sign the papers for Brenda to go to the speech and hearing clinic. He got after me for not bringing her back for more nerve medicine—but it hadn't helped. Finally I took my sister and mother-in-law with me to get the papers signed for her to go to the speech and hearing clinic.
> Question: Did you feel you needed protection?
> Mother: Yes, I did. It turned out I didn't need it. The doctor signed the papers without knowing they were in the waiting room, but after that we went to another doctor.

One of the strengths demonstrated by parents in this early phase was their persistance in seeking diagnosis and treatment of their child's condition despite criticism and discouragement from many grandparents and some family physicians. When at least one grandparent supported the plans to get help (45% of cases), the parents felt grateful. "We are so thankful about our parents' attitude. They have been like the Rock of Gibraltar. I don't know what we would have done without them."

Parents also had some good things to say about their family physicians and pediatricians. As Ronnie's father said, "Our doctor expressed his deep concern even though he said Ron's problem was beyond his reach." Another mother said, "We couldn't have felt better about our doctor, who knows how we feel and talks to us." The good listener was greatly appreciated, as a father described: "We are fortunate in having a doctor who makes you feel better just by saying 'hello'. She really listened to us, unlike some others who wanted us out of the office as soon as possible."

It was apparent that parents had fewer complaints about family physicians and pediatricians than about the "experts" to whom they were later referred. By and large, parents did not expect the family physicians to be experts in their child's problem. They expected an early referral to a "specialist," which many general physicians tried to provide. Parents then looked forward with high hopes to getting a clear and definite answer about the nature of their child's problem and also referral to an easily available and affordable treatment program that would effect a cure. They also expected, admittedly with some trepidation, that the "experts" would be able to spot their own

Table 55. Parents' Evaluation of Professional Helpfulness

Evaluation	N	%
Definitely helpful	5	15
Somewhat helpful	9	27
Not helpful	14	42
Evaded answer	5	15

deficiencies in parenting and would given them practical advice about changing. In a word, they expected "the specialist to run some good tests and then do something helpful." We asked the following: "Some parents feel helped by their visits to professional people and some don't feel helped. What have been your experiences in this regard?" (See Table 55.) Unfortunately, in about 57% of cases parents found nothing positive to say about their experiences with "the experts" and 28% had a mixture of good and bad things to say, leaving only 15% with strongly positive feelings.

Examples of "dissatistifed" answers were: "No, we weren't helped. We don't know any more than we knew when we first started out." One mother said, "The doctors just gave us their opinions—just looked at her—really didn't do anything—both said it might be brain damage or an emotional problem." Question: "Did you feel helped?" Mother: "No, just bewildered."

An example of a positive answer was: "Yes. The man at the Child Guidance Clinic has given us very simple and forthright explanations. You ask him a question and he takes time to explain things. It makes me feel more relaxed."

Two examples of mixed feelings about the helpfulness of professionals were:

(1) "The people—the doctors—at the Rehabilitation Center have bent over backwards to help. We would have given up without them. Some of the doctors at home have been no help. One doctor wouldn't discuss anything and scoffed at everything we tried."

(2) "Well, after beating at so many doors with no response, you begin to get weary. We appreciate the small gains but we feel we have wasted a year and a half of our child's life." Question: "What could they have done to be more helpful?" Father: "Nothing. They did all they could do. They were very nice to us. It was their idea that their treatment was too slow."

Unfortunately, parents named three times as many complaints about professionals as admired qualities (60 vs. 20). The most frequent complaint

Table 56. Complaints about Professionals

Type	N	%
Defective communication with parents	16	48
Questionable accuracy of diagnosis or adequacy of diagnostic process	9	27
No direct help for child	9	27
Child needs more treatment time than is receiving	5	15
Unfair in assessment of parent	3	9
Failed to take observations of parents seriously	3	9
Doubted competency	2	6
Waited too long for appointments	2	6
Actively avoided seeing parents	1	3

(48%) was that the professionals failed to communicate adequately with them (see Table 56). Parents wanted more information about the exact nature of the child's problem; e.g., "They kept him in the hospital a week but after all that I don't know what they thought was wrong with him. All they said was it was an emotional problem." A common plea of parents was: "I wish the doctors would tell us more." Parents wanted more definite recommendations for improving their methods of child care. Here is one mother's account of her encounter with a professional in trying to get some specific advice:

> He told us Barry had infantile autism and we asked if we had caused it. He gave us an indirect answer that wasn't very clear. At that point, we were having a terrible problem with things being torn up and we didn't know how to handle it and asked him for advice. He told us we ourselves would need several months of work before we could tamper with Barry's destructive behavior or we might do something bad that would make it hard to treat him in the future.
>
> Well, I was doing something that I wasn't sure was right. When my husband isn't around to help with Barry, I often can't get meals ready without a terrible hassle that gets me and the other kids' nerves on edge. I finally came to putting Barry alone in his room. I get us fed and then turn all of my attention to Barry. Well, he told me that was just like saying to Barry that I wanted him out of the way and I should do something different. I didn't know what else to do and he wouldn't discuss it with me. It was terribly frustrating.

Professionals were seen as being too taciturn; i.e., "I got the idea he didn't want to talk at all—he wanted us to do all the talking"; "One thing I've noticed about doctors is they don't talk to you—they'll hardly tell you anything at all."

Professionals were seen as using big words without explaining them. Jerrold's mother said, "I have been confused quite often. I think I have everything straight then I find out later I don't." Her husband added: "Yes. I think they use terms a little above our heads—maybe quite a bit above our heads."

Not listening, not believing what the parent said, or belittling what the parent said caused much anger and even bitterness; e.g., "I get mad when I've told her (the doctor) something, especially if it's important, and she either doesn't hear it or forgets it." One mother, with great feeling, told of recounting her son's speech problems and worries about future development to a clinician whose main response was a sharply spoken, "What do you want of your child? Not every child is the same!" Her inner response was to "feel about an inch high." The father added, "We didn't get any help at all—we were just put off and told to wait."

Some parents (27%) complained that they doubted the diagnosis. "The first place we went they told us he was mentally retarded. We weren't satisfied with that diagnosis." Parents were especially upset if a diagnosis was made on the basis of a short interview without any special tests. As Joel's mother said, "All they did was to look at him for 20 minutes; then they told us it could be retardation or an emotional problem. I don't see what they could have told from that—they didn't do anything." If the child was hospitalized for diagnostic procedures, as were 48% of the children, there was not apt to be a complaint about too cursory an evaluation. The parents assumed that if a child was in the hospital for several days that a thorough diagnostic workup had been completed. However, complaints were frequent that parents learned little or nothing of "what the doctors found after all those days in the hospital."

Parents who had been to several agencies or physicians were apt to become frustrated if no direct help was offered. They reported: "We were just being shuffled around—no one did anything but look at him and ask us the same questions over and over again." Two sets of parents made direct statements that they doubted the competency of at least one professional they consulted. One mother who had received professional counselling for several months said this: "Well, I don't think the person I was supposed to talk to every week knew any more than I did about it. He didn't know the difference between autism and schizophrenia and always had to run to somebody else whenever I asked a question."

A few parents thought they were assessed unfairly. One mother asked the family physician to explain the results of a diagnostic study of her son hospitalized over a week in a distant city because she had been told "so little." The physician gave her the hospital report to read. The mother's reaction to the report was this:

The word *autism* was in it, but I didn't know what that was. Later I found it was the same thing as schizophrenia. They could have been more fair. Part of the report was true and part wasn't.

Question: "What part was untrue?"

Mother: Naturally I see myself different. They said I stayed there and refused to leave. It wasn't that way. In fact, I was at the hotel and the nurses called me and asked me to come over—they couldn't get him to stop crying. I got my clothes on and went back. I'd rock him—he was awfully tense, but he'd doze off and I'd lay him gently down. As soon as he'd hit the bed, he'd scream—all night it went that way. Pretty soon dawn cracked and they said "the mother just stayed all night, so he didn't sleep."

Parents mentioned five principal types of admired qualities, the most frequent of which (24%) was good communication, including the ability to listen well. Parents liked open expression of concern, interest, and warmth which, of course, involved an attitude as well as communication. They admired a knowledgeable, clear, and open discussion of diagnosis, prognosis, and of their questions. "I can really talk to my doctor. I ask him about things I don't understand and he gives me a few pointers." "He explained things to us as he saw them." Some parents, but not all, who took their child for treatment felt that their questions were given enough consideration.

An active effort to be of help to the child after the diagnostic process was over was named by 15% of the parents, most of whom were enrolled in a child guidance treatment program. The remaining admired traits included a friendly approach (9%) ("He put us at ease."), special understanding of handicapped children, thorough diagnosis, and a hopeful attitude.

Table 57. Admired Professional Traits

Trait	N	%
Good communication of concern[a]	8	24
Active efforts to help	5	15
Friendly; nice; aware of limitations	3	9
Specific, understanding, hopeful	1	3
Thoroughness of diagnosis	1	3

[a]Also of interest, warmth, diagnosis, prognosis, as well as good listener and thorough in discussing questions.

Is the parents' assessment of the professionals a fair one? Are we as unclear, taciturn, and unhelpful as the parents see us? I think the answer is a mixture of yes and no. Part of the problem lies in the condition itself and in the level of knowledge of child mental health practitioners about autism.

The expectations of parents that they will receive definite answers from child mental health professionals about diagnosis, prognosis, and treatment are unrealistic. Autism is a relatively rare condition. Most professionals have relatively little experience with it and must depend on their book knowledge. While nearly all recent research has demonstrated that autism is a neurobiological disorder and that parents are not the cause, many practitioners still adhere to earlier notions. It takes time for new research to become part of regular psychiatric practice. Those who believe in parental causation will handle parents in various ways, but commonly they are evasive or extra silent. A mother has written in a telling way the effect of such silence on the parents (Park, 1973). This book should be required reading for all mental health professionals, and some will profit from other accounts of contacts with professionals in a recent collection (Turnbull & Turnbull, 1978), especially Mary Akerley's contribution. It is my impression that professionals who believe in the theory of parental causation tend to be more evasive than those who see the cause as biological. Early in my experience, when I was taught such a theory, I tended to be so. Rather than say something that the parents could not use or understand, I said as little as possible. Naturally enough, I found no way to tell them early in our relationship that they had caused the autism without increasing their anxiety to unmanageable proportions.

A dilemma for both the doctor and the parent, however, is that there is one part of the parent (especially mothers) that wants to believe the autism is the parents' fault, reasoning that the parents can change themselves and their approach to the child and thereby cure the autism. Yet there is another large part of the parent that wants to deny parental causation. Most parents reported horrified shock and anger when a doctor suggested that they had caused such a serious disorder. These two opposing desires cause them to be apprehensive about every causal theory they hear except perhaps that it is a metabolic disorder which can be cured by diet or a derangement in the timing of nervous system development which may be treated by retraining.

The other factor causing all doctors to choose their words with care in diagnostic interviews is that we know from experience that parents can digest only a few new facts at any one session. To inundate parents with too many facts or too detailed explanations in a short space of time (even an hour's interview) creates confusion rather than enlightenment. When the parents hear the diagnostic words "autism" or "mental retardation" or "childhood schizophrenia," we have learned that they "are shocked" and in such a state they comprehend little of what the doctor says. Here is what one mother reported happened to her:

> When we were told Albie had autism, I was stunned. I didn't know what it meant but I knew it was serious. I don't know—it was just—I was in shock. She explained it again—but I didn't quite get it—I was still stunned. I should have had her write down what was wrong. I remember asking a couple more questions, but she was indefinite about the cause or whether anything could be done. I have come later to realize there are many mental disorders that doctors don't know all about and can't cure, but then I couldn't get anything—I was too shocked.

Despite this shock, most parents said they wanted and expected practical advice about managing some of their child's most troublesome behavior problems, at least in the final phase of the diagnostic process. This issue is often evaded by counsellors in the diagnostic phase because professional people have found they do not know the parents well enough to give them advice they can use. Most counsellors follow the principle that parents can best change their own behavior toward a child if they have participated in deciding about the exact process of change. As an example, Mary's mother wanted to know how to keep her child in bed at night. Ideally, the counsellor and the mother together should work out the exact method of accomplishing this goal, and in subsequent appointments determine how the chosen method was working and what forces in the mother aided or hindered reaching the goal.

Until the recent research concerning the neurobiological nature of autism becomes part of the teaching of every student and the updating of every professional in medicine, psychology, social work, and nursing, parents will meet diversified opinions about the cause of autism among the various professionals they meet. Until professionals themselves agree upon exact criteria to use for the diagnosis of autism and the relationship of the disorder to allied conditions such as childhood schizophrenia and mental retardation, then parents are going to continue to get differing answers about these questions. The parent who has heard these diagnoses is going to feel shocked, stunned, frightened, and angry for a while, no matter who has pronounced the diagnosis. Parents must be mindful not to project their angers and fears on the person who gave them the diagnosis but give themselves time to digest the information and then decide, in a clearer frame of mind, what their next action for their autistic child should be. To make these decisions wisely, they generally need the help of a trusted professional counsellor who has a good picture of them and their child.

Parental Acceptance of Diagnosis

After the parents have heard a diagnosis from the mental health professionals, they are generally given a suggested course of action. There are many possibilities of response, but only the common ones will be discussed in these next three chapters. The first is to doubt or even discount altogether the diagnosis and therefore the recommendation. Among factors that lead parents to doubt the correctness of the diagnosis are:

(1) A cursory workup, or the parents' belief that the workup was so. Hospitalization of the child generally prevents this problem and will give the doctor a better picture of the child's range of behaviors.

(2) Failure of the clinician to give the parents time to tell the history in detail.

(3) An attitude of hurry, disbelief, or lack of interest on the part of the clinician.

(4) Failure of the clinician to explain the evidence used to reach the diagnostic conclusions and recommendations.

(5) A diagnosis of mental retardation.

Elements of an Adequate Work-up

The first requisite is for the clinician to understand some of the medical and psychological practices that elicit parents' perceptions of an inadequate or unfair workup. Since nearly every treatment measure must have the understanding and backing of the parent, it is essential that good management practices begin with the first consultation interview.

Some of the problems many clinicians bring to the diagnostic evaluation are:

(1) They try to handle the problem too quickly. Parents perceive 50 minutes with them and a half hour with the child as too short a time to make far-ranging judgments about themselves and their child.

(2) They let the old myths about autism color their judgments about what the personalities of the parents and the basic intelligence of the child might be.

(3) They doubt and underplay the significance of parents' observations about the child.

(4) They tend to misread the appropriate anxiety of parents about their child as a cause rather than as an effect.

(5) They fail to understand the devastating effect on parents of a diagnosis of autism, child schizophrenia, or mental retardation.

(6) They fail to explain clearly the evidence used to support their diagnosis and recommendations.

(7) They hide their own diagnostic confusion and uncertainty behind a screen of evasive talk and big words.

A proper diagnostic workup should consist of (a) a careful history, (b) appropriate laboratory testing, (c) thorough developmental assessment, (d) pediatric and neurological examination, and (e) summation interview as detailed and candid as the parental situation allows, with follow-up interviews. The evaluation can most effectively be carried out in a pediatric or child psychiatric hospital with 2 to 4 days as a minimum hospital stay.

Mandatory is a careful history taken by a sympathetic, unhurried clinician who brings an attitude of belief while listening to the parents' account. I know of no more certain way to antagonize parents than for the clinician to say, in word or attitude, "I don't believe you." Such an attitude of belief does not mean that the clinician is being naive or duped or conned or that he should not explore discrepancies in the history. In my experience, most parents are sincerely trying to give a clear picture of their child's and their own behavior. For the doctor to summarily doubt them is an insult and a sign of poor judgment that they do not forget or forgive easily.

This is not to say that parents tell the full story of their personal lives or that they don't shape their stories so as to appear in a better light to the doctor, for this tendency is part of the human condition. However, paradoxically, parents will reveal things of which they are ashamed more readily to a clinician who sympathizes and trusts than to one who downgrades and doubts. Youthful, inexperienced clinicians have special trouble with this point. Like everyone else, autistic parents tend to lie or distort problems in certain aspects of living, notably drinking and their sex life, and like other people they need time and trust to reveal behavior of which they are ashamed.

The history should describe the current behavior of the child and how parents attempt to cope with the problems, how the problems developed, motor and perceptual-motor development, and comparison with the siblings. Family interactions and parent attitudes are especially important. Marital interaction is also extremely important, although I find some parents need an open discussion of the necessity for the diagnostician's interest in this aspect of family life before they can believe it has any relevance to the questions in hand. The mother's obstetric-gynecological history should be taken and particular attention paid to the gestation, birth, and health history of the child. Family history of mental illness, neurological conditions, and learning problems, both general and specific, should be part of every history.

The physical evaluation ideally should not only include a pediatric examination but also a neurological examination by a physician skilled in examining children. A simple measurement often overlooked in the neurological exam is the measurement of the occipital-frontal circumference (OFC) using a steel measuring tape marked in centimeters for the diagnosis of micro- or macroephaly.

The minimum laboratory workup should consist of:

(1) Electroencephalogram while the child is awake, in a light sleep, and in transition between wakefulness and sleep. The record should be interpreted by an individual thoroughly familiar with children's records.

(2) Urinary genetic screen for inborn errors of metabolism.

(3) Skull radiographs.

(4) Any other pertinent tests called for by findings in the physical examinations.

The developmental assessment should consist of:

(1) Verbal tests, both expressive and receptive. These must be administered even though the child does not speak or uses only a few words.

(2) Perceptual-motor tests.

(3) Tests of gross motor competence.

These three types of tests allow the clinician to estimate the verbal, perceptual-motor, and gross motor developmental quotients and thus provide the best prognostic tool yet developed for estimating the outcome of autism. A good estimate of the mental age also gives information important for educational placement. If the general developmental quotient (DQ or IQ) is below 40, the outlook is poor for independent living. If the general DQ (IQ) is 60 or above, it is better. A list of developmental tests for preschoolers for appropriate assessment is given below:

> Alpern-Boll Developmental Skill Age Inventory
> Bayley Scales of Infant Development
> Beery Test of Visual Motor Integration
> Cattell Infant Intelligence Scale
> Denver Developmental Screening Test
> Yale Child Center Developmental Schedules (Gesell)
> Peabody Picture Vocabulary Test
> Stanford-Binet Test
> Weschler Preschool & Primary Scale of Intelligence

No autistic child is untestable. No diagnostic workup is satisfactory without developmental testing.[1] If the diagnostician is inexperienced with infantile autism, a consultation with a highly competent and knowledgeable professional should be sought.

Mental Illness in the Parents

During the course of the interviews, the diagnostician should also be assessing the mental health of the parents. Unfortunately, the myth of parental causation of autism leads many diagnosticians to overdiagnose parental mental illness or to magnify parents' personality traits or manifestations of anxiety. A diagnosis of parental illness should be made only on the basis of the usual criteria for any other adult. Recommendations for appropriate treatment should be made for reasons of personal growth of the afflicted parent and the good of the entire family. No special onus should be placed on the mentally ill parent as the cause of the autism, and no guarantees, implied or overt, should be given that the cure of the parent will also cure the autistic child.

Presenting Diagnostic Findings to Parents

We have seen how the parents may perceive faulty communication of the diagnosis as a problem. Part of this problem lies in the names—or diagnostic terms—that we professionals use. We asked 28 sets of parents what names had been given to them as possible diagnoses. About 39% had been given two or more diagnostic terms, and most parents found this circumstance confusing. In some cases, parents did not clearly realize that the diagnosing clinician was probably saying that two or more diagnoses were under consideration and it was not clear which one might be correct. In other cases, it was apparent that the parents had seen several diagnosticians who in actuality had opposing views. One mother whose child had been evaluated by an unusually large number of diagnosticians said, "I don't know of any two doctors who fully agree on what his problem is."

In Table 58 are listed the different names of diagnostic terms given to parents. "Autism" headed the list (46%). Most parents felt they had only a vague idea of what this term and also "childhood schizophrenia" meant.

Table 58. Diagnoses Formulated for Child's Disorder

Diagnoses	N	%
Autism	13	46
Emotional or nervous problem	7	25
Mental retardation	5	18
Childhood schizophrenia	4	14
Brain damage	2	6
Hearing problem	1	3

Table 59. Different Diagnoses for Same Child Formulated by Various Professionals

N of diagnoses	N	%
One diagnostic term	12	43
Two diagnostic terms	7	25
Three or more	4	14
No diagnosis	5	18

Despite a lack of understanding, they knew both the terms had serious connotations. Following are a series of quotes indicating parental gut reactions to hearing these terms: "It was a kick in the stomach"; "It was tragic"; "It tore me up"; "I was worried and heartbroken"; "A complete shock"; "It made us more concerned—I knew it was serious."

The terms "emotional" or "nervous" problem were of unspecific meaning for most parents but connoted that "something in the environment" was at fault and therefore meant that the conditions were treatable.

The most feared diagnoses were "mental retardation" and "brain damage." Parents thought that such diagnoses meant that irreparable damage to the brain had occurred and treatment could not be curative; for example, "I would like to know if it's brain injury or emotional. We've been worried more about brain injury because if it's emotional, then maybe treatment would help." Even though the terms autism and childhood schizophrenia struck fear into the hearts of parents, they would rather hear those diagnoses than mental retardation or brain injury. As one mother said, "Autism is a frightening word, but it's better than the other choice of mental retardation."

If the diagnostic terms autism or childhood schizophrenia are so demoralizing to parents, then a legitimate question can be asked whether to use them at all. I have no good answer because most parents want a diagnosis and will seek out people who will given them one. It is vitally important for the clinician to appreciate the depth of shock and fear that overcomes parents when they hear these terms, for they may hear little else in the interview after they are spoken. The words mental retardation and brain damage give the same shocking effect. Thus, before a diagnosis is mentioned, the results of the interviews with the child, the physical and laboratory findings, and developmental levels should be discussed in everyday language that the parents can understand. I always graph the developmental levels of the child with chronological age lines so that the parents can see exactly where their child stands with respect to the average child of the same age with respect to verbal, perceptual-motor, and motor development (see Figure 2). This practice

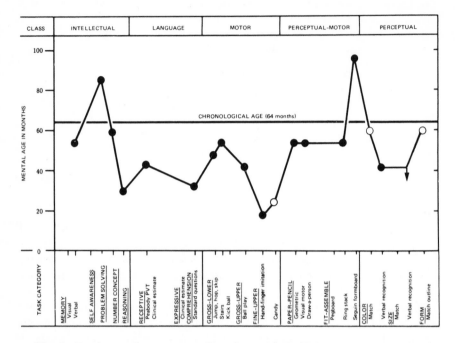

Fig. 2. Testing performance profile of an autistic boy.

Note: Developmental mental ages, represented by black circles, are compared with chronological age (horizontal line cutting across graph), 64 months, or 5 years 4 months, for an autistic boy. Note that expressive language (6th circle from left) and reasoning (4th circle from left) are among his lowest mental age scores, while problem-solving with objects (second circle from left) and perceptual-motor scores are among his best. He used a form board exceptionally well. This autistic boy could repeat words and digits (first circle on left) and do arithmetical computations (3rd circle from left) about like the average child his age, which made his parents think he was bright, but he couldn't talk to or converse with others or understand verbal concepts the parents explained to him. This simple graph of a developmental test could be used with good effect to teach the parents and examiner that expressive language disability and reasoning disability are at the heart of the boy's problem and that part of the hope for the boy's future depends on whether he can make accelerated progress in these skills. Note the lowest skill is that of hand-finger imitation (developmental age 18 months, 10th circle from left). This disability is an extremely common finding in autistic children, but its significance is not understood. Note also the comparatively high scores in gross-motor skills.

runs counter to the conventional idea that it is wrong for parents to have this information. In 10 years of giving parents such information, it is difficult to find a case where it was harmful, and in most cases it was useful. It was the first step in educating the parents about the exact liabilities and strengths that had been puzzling them in their autistic child. Most autistic parents report their child "seems so smart about some things and can't catch on to others." Developmental testing points out these ups and downs which psychologists call "scatter." The motor abilities of autistic children are generally their best and their language abilities their worst points. Perceptual-motor abilities vary, but generally autistics do relatively well in fitting and assembly tasks, such as fitting forms into formboards, and they generally do poorly in graphic activities, such as geometric figures and draw-a-person tests. Using a simple graph, I can point out that the language disability is one of the core problems and that we will want to check progress yearly at least, while the child is receiving special schooling and possibly other treatment.

After presentation of the evaluation findings, I ask for parents' questions and then if they have been given a diagnosis by other clinicians. Their answer gives me a lead as how to present my diagnosis and discuss in broad outline the controversies among professionals in the field. In most cases, another appointment is made in a week or two to let the parents have time to mull over the findings, to ask more questions, and to complete recommendations for education and treatment. The clinician who is available for follow-up conferences is at an advantage in managing the diagnostic summation interview. For about 95% of the parents, autism will be a lifelong responsibility: The beginning steps in search of a school and treatment are taken in fear and lack of knowledge. The clinician can be of great service to parents just by letting them know he will talk with them when problems arise. Short phone conversations can be very helpful and are less time consuming than formal interviews. Some clinicians I have talked to say this practice fosters too much dependency. I have not found this to be the case. When parents get over their initial shock, if given sensible advice and support from a professional person, they soon resume their natural independent spirit.

Somewhere during the interviews questions arise, implicitly or explicitly, about parental role in causation and outlook for the future. After our research findings had linked autism so strongly to neurobiological disability, it was the practice of the staff of the Clinical Research Center to tell the parents directly that they were not responsible. Also, we told them that undoubtedly there were ways they could deal better with their child, and that these ways would be explored subsequently during the education-treatment program. Many diagnosticians will not have responsibility for treating the child. If the parents have specific questions about a specific problem during the diagnostic process, they should be faced squarely after the diagnostic summation interviews and various ways for the parents to handle their problems should be explored. Follow-up appointments are mandatory in order to discuss how the child and parents have fared in using any new techniques.

Discussion about prognosis during the preschool years should emphasize a wait-and-see attitude. If the child is capable of accelerated progress, it usually begins between the ages of 4 and 6 years, and occurs in those preschool autistic children whose general developmental quotients are 60 or above. However, to complicate the picture, not all of this latter group will accelerate. Those children whose general DQs are below 40 have a dim outlook for anything but retarded development; however, even they can make some accelerated progress and a wait-and-see attitude is appropriate for this group also.

While many aspects of autistic development are difficult to predict at an early age, one factor is almost certain: By the age of 6 to 7 years of age, if the autistic child is not speaking for communication, he will develop no useful speech. This fact, reported first by Eisenberg (1956), has been confirmed by Rutter and Lockyer (1967) and by DeMyer, Barton, DeMyer, Norton, Allen and Steele (1973), although exceptions have occasionally been reported. Nearly all of these nonspeaking individuals also have great and continuing problems with abstract thinking and do poorly in all endeavors at study and work. There are occasional exceptions; for example, I know of one nonspeaking autistic adult who partially supports himself tuning pianos and another who can do skilled factory work with supervision. The prognosis in preschool children thus cannot be made with exactness. Parents should be told this fact, advised to have developmental progress checked yearly, and told that by the age of 6 to 8 years a more exact prognosis can be given.

Such a pronouncement is difficult because the parents have to live with uncertainty. One father said, "We hate the uncertainty of not knowing how he is going to turn out." After the initial shock and uncertainty, parents begin to live on hope, and we come next to parents' experiences with early treatment.

Note

[1] Parents and professionals alike can avail themselves of my developmental testing procedures which I shall be pleased to forward on request.

REFERENCES

DeMyer, M. K., Barton, S., DeMyer, W. E., Norton, J. A., Allen, J., & Steele, R. Prognosis in autism: A follow-up study. *Journal of Autism and Childhood Schizophrenia*, 1973, 3(3), 199–246.

Eisenberg, L. The autistic child in adolescence. *American Journal of Psychiatry*, 1956, 112, 607–613.

Park, C. C. *The siege.* Boston: Atlantic-Little, Brown & Co., 1973.

Rutter, M., & Lockyer, L. A five to fifteen year follow-up study of infantile psychosis: II. Social and behavioral outcome. *British Journal of Psychiatry*, 1967, **113**, 1183–1199.

Turnbull, A. P., & Turnbull, H. R. *Parents speak out.* Columbus, Ohio: Charles E. Merrill, 1978.

Chapter 12

TREATMENT AND SPECIAL EDUCATION PRIOR TO ADOLESCENCE

The diagnosing professional makes recommendations for therapy and education under several constraints. Mentally he may design a program that would be ideal for a particular autistic child and his parents but rarely can the ideal be realized. The community may lack special education facilities suited to the child in question. The educational facility may be too far from home, too costly, or the parents may reject a good program for reasons that seem important to them but unimportant to the professional. I have found that parents are apt to reject a recommendation of counselling for themselves. In every case, the diagnostician needs to be aware of facilities in the community suitable for autistic children and aware of what program any particular set of parents can support both psychologically and financially. The best diagnostic evaluation in the world is of little use unless it is followed by a program of education and treatment that the family can feel confident about and can afford.

If the diagnostic evaluation takes place in a city other than the home community, then the ability of the diagnostician to help find a suitable program is severely curtailed. Any person working in the field must keep his knowledge of available facilities current each year because they may change rapidly in quality and in the types of individuals they serve. Out-of-towners do not have this intimate knowledge. Reports can be sent and phone calls made to facilities, but the ultimate burden rests on the parents for the necessary follow-through and this can be · a bewildering process for the neophyte. In our own city, a group of parents have started a clearing house for information concerning professionals and schools serving the handicapped and learning-disabled child to reduce wasted time and uncertainty for the searching parent. There should be universal statewide networks of treatment, education, and information services, such as Eric Schopler and his group (Reichler & Schopler, 1976) have established in North Carolina. Every professional advising families of autistic children should have available the latest edition of the NIMH directory *U.S. Facilities and Programs for Children with Severe Mental Illnesses.*

In the past decades the cornerstone of therapy was individual psychiatric treatment for the child coupled with individual counselling for the parents, heavily concentrated on the mother. Of the children in our study, 25% were previously enrolled in a treatment program, most of them in the traditional child guidance setting. Those parents whose children had been in such a program for a year or more were likely to complain that the program was inadequate because not enough time was devoted to the child. A typical statement was: "One hour a week isn't enough. He needs more treatment than that." One father said, "The doctor is a very nice man, but he didn't move our child along fast enough. Still, what could he do in one hour a week?" Those parents whose child had been in a treatment program only a few weeks were not complaining and were full of hope.

This attitude that the autistic child needed more treatment time than the average child guidance patient was held by professionals as well as parents and led to the establishment of residential care or the so-called 24-hour treatment program. People held the belief, or hope, that individual psychiatric treatment, as it was practiced in the '60s and earlier, was the treatment of choice except that in the case of autistic children it needed to be applied nearly continuously. Many professionals also believed in complete separation of the child from his parents.

Experience has shown that residential care probably does not give any better "cure" rate than any other approach, but nevertheless it has an extremely valuable effect on the family and child if the parents maintain close and continuing contact with the child and treatment personnel. At our Center, we found that complete and prolonged separation of the child from his family was almost a sure way to seal over the place he had left in the family. On the other hand, if the child went home on weekends, the parents' positive contact with the child was maintained while family members were allowed relief from the consuming problems of sleepless nights, screaming spells, and worry that other symptoms brought.

As a practical measure, residential treatment facilities for autistic children should be no more than 60 or 70 miles from the child's home, but most states do not provide such nearby facilities for all residents. Because good residential treatment is very expensive, state and private facilities are small in number and thus available to only a limited number of children. Preschool residential facilities are extremely scarce, and ours at the Clinical Research Center was one of a handful in the country.

When should the diagnostician strongly recommend residential care for the autistic child? There is no hard and fast answer to this question, but the general rule is that when no adequate outpatient and educational facilities exist, and the problems associated with symptom management in the home are so grave as to compromise the mental and physical health of parents or siblings, then residential treatment should be sought. The current idea of not considering family needs when recommending hospitalization for an afflicted person is absolutely wrong. Good emotional health of parents is necessary to maintain an autistic child in the home. The practice of withholding third party insurance payments if the decision to hospitalize is made on the basis of family health as well as patient need is malpractice. The medical profession and those in government and insurance policy-making should fight against this policy, which is not only nontherapeutic but is more costly to society in the long run. Fortunately, autism now has a long and intelligent definition in the latest *Diagnostic and Statistical Manual*, DSM-III, and so expenses of treatment will become reimbursable under health insurance plans.

As more day schools establish special classes for children with learning disorders and counselling is made available to parents, the need for long-term residential care during early and middle childhood years becomes less pressing. The most urgent need for all intellectually disabled children, including the autistic, is to upgrade the quality of private and public school classes and to extend them universally to preschool children, adolescents, and adults who need them. Those who counsel parents and do individual therapy with the child need to become well grounded in the nature of the intellectual disability of the autistic child as well as in psychological principles so that their counselling is based on reality.

"Ideal" Therapy/Education Settings for Preschool Children

Having been associated with both inpatient and outpatient services for preschool autistic children, I have seen the positives and negatives of both settings.

The positives of 5-day a week outpatient treatment are:

(1) The child and his parents are allowed to maintain day-to-day contact and the parents maintain emotional closeness while developing further their

special knowledge of the child through daily contact with the education/ treatment staff.

(2) The mother is given sufficient freedom from time constraints and worry to further her personal growth, attend to the needs of her other children, and nourish her marital relationship, all of which are generally neglected if a preschool autistic child must be cared for by the mother all day, every day.

(3) The child's growth is fostered by a teacher-therapist who gives him educational material pitched to his developmental level, each day of the week. He learns to master some of his anxiety about adapting to "new" places and faces.

The negatives are:

(1) Some parents and children need longer separation periods to gain perspective on their problems.

(2) Some children's symptoms, especially those of the self-destructive variety, need concerted and highly controlled behavior modification techniques which demand good control of staff reactions. Such tight environmental control rarely can be attained in outpatient settings or the home.

(3) Some symptoms, and again these are often the severe self-destructive or destructive variety, can demoralize all family members until inpatient treatment becomes mandatory.

Whatever the treatment setting, I have come to realize that appropriate education for the child is a cornerstone of good case management and this process must begin during the preschool years. We have seen in Chapter 9 that autistic children learn best in familiar surroundings where they can become psychologically comfortable and where daily repetition of the material is possible. In my experience, this situation occurs when school is held both morning and afternoon, 5 days a week. For many children, a summer program also is advisable to maintain gains made during the fall and spring terms. Classes should be small, from five to seven pupils, with two teachers for each class. Each child should be assessed for developmental levels at the beginning of each school year and the teachers should be thoroughly familiar with each different level in each child so that the level of teaching can be matched to him. Wing and Wing (1966) emphasized the need for teachers to know the various abilities of the autistic child and to teach them as they would intellectually disabled or learning disabled children. These investigators also rightfully stress that the school environment should be highly structured, should not be permissive, and that emphasis should be placed on effective training because the pupil-teacher relationship will naturally follow from the education process.

Mental health professionals should have an important role in school programs to help the teacher understand her feelings for the child and the child's psychological reaction to the program. Psychologists often help design specific techniques for teaching children and modifying problem emotional reactions. Mental health professionals also play a crucial role in helping parents make the best use of the program. Once parents enroll their autistic child in any school, they begin with the strong hope that the program will advance him toward normal. They have some initial fears, but they want to put their trust in the program and do so, in large measure, during the first few months.

As is sadly too often the case, many autistic children do not progress as far or as fast as the parents wish and so they begin to wonder if their child might do better with another program. Yet the autistic child in an adequate education program does learn something and often becomes easier to live with at home. The parents see a skilled professional teacher deal with temper tantrums and negativism and they begin to incorporate the teacher's methods into their own. They learn how often their own methods serve to reinforce the very behaviors they are trying to deal with, and they learn the reinforcement strategies that accomplish what they want. They watch how teachers take a class of autistic children on excursions into the community, and they begin to take their child out more often. The very fact that parents have someone to help them understand their puzzling and difficult child binds the parents tightly to the staff of a school or treatment center. On occasion a mother may be jealous of a teacher or therapist who succeeds relatively well where she perceived herself as failing. She likes the teacher's success, but she hates her own feeling of failure. Some parents may project feelings of hostility onto teachers and magnify small lapses in management or communication.

In short, parents develop strong positive and strong negative feelings, side by side, about most education/treatment programs. In the top-notch program, the teaching staff understands these powerful and opposing feelings and does not react so as to create unnecessary conflict. The top-notch teacher will listen carefully to parents' complaints and sort out which are justified and which reflect underlying anxiety over lack of progress in the child or other negative feelings. Mental health professionals who have as strong a concern for parents' problems as for the child's can be of great value in promoting good working relations between the teaching staff and the parents by helping them understand each other. Educators, in my experience, tend to become anxious themselves in the face of parental hostility and criticism, while mental health professionals are, or should be, trained early to expect and deal with such feelings.

The pitfall for parents, teachers, and therapists to avoid is that of an adversary relationship. All three groups are vitally interested in the child's welfare, and all should understand the fears that develop in parents as they begin to ask themselves questions: "Is this the best program available for my child?" "Does my child love the teacher or therapist more than me?" "Am I a bad mother because the teacher or therapist controls him better than I do?"

If the parents are strongly dissatisfied or anxious, they may look elsewhere, only to find there are no other programs and they must make peace with the old program or again face their problems alone. Most parents have eventually seen more good than bad in the preschool programs with which I have been acquainted. Eventually the positive feelings have won over.

When the child arrives at school age, 6 or 7 years in most preschool programs, there comes another stressful time for both child and parents. The child must leave the old, familiar scene for a new one. The stress is not too severe if the new school program is perceived by the parents to be as good as or better than the old one. After a year or two of seeing their child in special education program, they become better educated about the facilities in the community, about their rights as citizens to get high quality education for their child, and about the kind of program to which their own child will adjust best. At this point, autistic parents feel stronger within themselves and have formed alliances with other parents which give them additional assurance.

If the new program offered to the child is deemed of inferior quality, then the parents will fight to get it upgraded or they will defy the board of education's right to specify the school the child may attend. Public school educators believe they need time to develop new programs and generally resist bending their policies for individual children, especially if it costs additional money. Their point of view is to provide the best possible education for the most children with the money they have to spend. Currently, if it is financially feasible, parents will fight these decisions in court. Extreme cases are rare, but feelings of strong resentment are common toward educators perceived as providing less than optimum education. How to avoid costly showdowns is an important problem for educators and parents to solve together with good will on both sides. The recent enactment of Education of the Handicapped Act, Public Law 94-142, makes it a federal offense not to provide an appropriate, individually designed educational program for every handicapped child, and parents and their advisors should all be familiar with the terms of this legislation and the proper steps to be taken when school authorities are felt to be violating the law.

One cannot fault the parents for the drive to get the best for their child, but there are certain pitfalls that can trap the parent who fails to achieve some balance in his search for help. Some parents who fall into these traps don't extricate themselves, and they and their children are the ultimate losers for they lose sight of other important aspects of their lives. These pitfalls are:

(1) Failure to appraise realistically the basic biological mental retardation of the autistic child as the years progress.

(2) Developing driving anxiety in the search for new "treatment" ideas.

(3) Alienation of professionals truly interested in their problems by being overcritical.

(4) Keeping the autistic child in the home despite evidence that both he and other family members are paying too heavy a price.

(5) Allowing overinvolvement with the autistic child and his problems to block solution of marital problems.

(6) Developing a feeling of "elitism" sbout autism.

(7) Adhering too slavishly to current ideas of parents' groups without critical examination of those ideas.

Failure to Appraise Realistically the Child's Basic Retardation

In the preschool years, we have seen how it is realistic to hope that the autistic child, especially one with a general development quotient of 60 or above, may make accelerated progress and become capable of doing average or above-average work in a normal classroom. Although such an outcome is rare, it does occur. The routine practice of periodic developmental testing begun in preschool years plus teachers' observations allow parents to become better judges of the basic developmental levels of their child. For the very few parents whose children spurt ahead until their performances catch up with their chronological ages, there is great rejoicing. For those parents whose children remain retarded in general intelligence, there are two courses of action: They can realistically accept the limitations of their children while still appropriately finding the best programs available, or they can disbelieve the tests and their senses and become hypercritical and bitter and begin an expensive and generally futile search for "the key," the magic treatment that will unlock the "shell" within which the child supposedly has retreated. These parents will look upon each small gain the child has made as a sign of superior ability rather than as an expected gain based primarily on the anatomical maturing of the nervous system. As we learned in the chapter on intelligence, for an increase in mental age to be indicative of accelerated progress, the child must progress in mental age faster than his chronological age.

Society, as well as overweening parental hope, prods parents to search. Television and newspapers contain programs and articles describing new treatments that promise cures or treatments that are "better" than all others. These sources often allude to gross environmental irregularities which have made the child "retreat into a shell." Such practices reinforce the parents' natural desires for a miracle cure, whether it be from some about-face in their parenting practices, such as giving "unlimited- love," or from a new diet of megavitamins or a behavior-modification program or repatterning of muscular control. It reinforces the parents' overwhelming desire to see their autistic child as basically normal neurologically, since they reason that a normal nervous system augurs a better outcome. The reasoning is correct but based on a false premise. Misplaced hope often causes parents to contradict their own observations of retarded abilities that have consistently resisted all their efforts and those of others.

There is nothing wrong with some of this searching. Someone may find a good treatment that seems medically implausible. We physicians have been known in the past to reject marvelous ideas that flew in the teeth of accepted medical practice. Rejections by physicians of Semmelweiss' theory that childbed fever was carried on the hands of attending physicians is one good example. Also, some treatments may help the rare autistic individual as apparently is the case with megavitamin therapy (Rimland, Callaway, & Dreyfus, 1978). Many parents have to learn through their own experience that "one more try" is not going to prove curative. The trap exists when parents seek too many "fad" treatments and when the search becomes too emotionally and financially expensive. Some parents have difficulty in seeing when this line is crossed.

What response should the mental health professional give when told by parents that they are going to try a "fad" treatment whose worth is far from proven? Some professionals vehemently condemn the practice and some go so far to say, "If you put your child in that program, don't come back to me." Most parents report a feeling of loss. If torn between pleasing "the doctor" and trying a course of action that may prove beneficial, generally they opt for the fad treatment. Other professionals try to dissuade the parents in a noncondemning way. My practice is to give my honest opinion, then discuss how set the parents are in theirs. If they are going to pursue the "fad" treatment, I ask to be a part of the evaluation process, testing and interviewing the child before the new program starts and after it is well under way. In this way, both the parents and I can become educated together about the value of that particular treatment program for their child and preserve our working relationship.

Patterns of Improvement

The grade school period of an autistic child can be among the most rewarding years of his life. Many children have improved over preschool years in sociability, emotional control, and attention span, and most are toilet trained. They seem to get more joy out of life. If they are enrolled in a school program that meets their needs, then parents can begin to widen their own horizons and feel less anxiety about the future. Parents still have great hopes or they can postpone thinking about the future, at least for a few years.

Sadly, not all autistic children reach this improved state and a few lose ground. About 74% of children in our study, even though many had improved somewhat in social relationships or acquired some speech, were regarded by parents and teachers alike as seriously isolated socially and unable to do school work except at retarded levels. Sadly, at puberty, many autistic children begin to masturbate frequently and show no restraint no matter what the situation. Some parents seem to achieve a "numbness" and deny all feeling about this compulsive masturbation. For others, it is just one more problem that leads them to seek residential care. If the child still tends to run away or attack others, then these problems can be well-nigh insurmountable. As a child grows stronger, he is harder to constrain physically. Mothers and women teachers have particular problems with the runaway, aggressive boy in these years.

As Rimland pointed out (1964), after the preschool period, autistic children diverge in their emotional and intellectual states. We found in our follow-up study (DeMyer, Barton, DeMyer, Norton, Allen, & Steele, 1973) that about 1 to 2% are so normal in emotions and intellect, they fit in like an average child with other children. They posed no different problems to parents and teachers than the average child. Parents of these children wanted to forget the preschool period and either refused to let us reexamine the child for follow-up study or did so with reluctance. I felt sympathetic with this reluctance because the parents rightfully wanted to avoid any possible repercussions in the way the child viewed himself or others important in his life saw him.

Table 60. Overall Educational and Social Outcome for Autistic Children[a]

Outcome[b]	%
Recovery to normal	1
Good	9
Fair	16
Poor	24
Very poor	40

[a] Mean age = 12 years.

[b] Residence (mean age 15 years): parental home—42%; institution—58%.

About 9% had made great improvement in that they were viewed at follow-up time, mean age 12 years, as normal or nearly so in a major feature of living, though they still had problems in other important aspects of life. Parents of these children generally were still hopeful that the child might achieve independent living. If we look at the three cardinal symptoms of autism, i.e., severe social withdrawal, noncommunicative speech, and nonfunctional object use, we find that these children no longer fit into the criteria. Nevertheless, their improvement in social interaction seems to have stopped short of normality. They failed to understand the subtleties of social interaction of their peers and made tactless remarks or were inappropriately friendly. About 35% were regarded as normally affectionate within the family circle but as having difficulties with other children their age. They were outsiders and formed no close friendships, often not because they didn't want friends but because they did not understand how to do so. They continued to have trouble in playing games and participating in jokes. Emotional control remained a problem. Most did not scream anymore, but they lost their tempers easily or were plunged into despair over the most trivial things. They failed to appreciate the feelings or points of view of other people. Only four of the most improved autistic children of school age were regarded as being about "average" in peer relationships.

So too improvement in intellectual skills in all but a few cases stopped short of normality. While there were some startling exceptions, the lags continued to be in those aspects of intelligence that were severely depressed during preschool years, namely expressive speech and understanding of abstract verbal concepts. Those who understood nonverbal abstractions in manipulation of objects continued to do so.

Some illustrations of these continuing difficulties are:

> Aaron, at age 10, was somewhat above average in all language subjects including thinking with language. He was a top scholar in arithmetic and, unlike all the other follow-up cases, could deal in a superior way with mathematical principles underlying arithmetic operations. His parents had this to say about his emotional control and social understanding:

> He gets on the school bus and immediately the kids start to tease him. We may have just reminded him to hold his temper and the kids will stop, but he just can't hold it back. He came home the other night and said he was going to hang a sign around his neck that said "DON'T TEASE ME." He really meant it and couldn't see our point that the sign would make the kids tease him more. He has no social savvy, and we are at our wits' end about how to help him learn some!

> Maryanne, at first evaluation at age 3½ years, appeared typically autistic in social isolation, continuous rocking, and echolalic,

noncommunicative speech. At age 5, on first follow-up, she still appeared autistic but was occasionally socially responsive. She had made about one year's progress in all developmental directions. During the following two years she made accelerated progress in nearly every aspect of social, verbal, and intellectual development, but the progress was uneven. At age 8 years, on second follow-up, she was finishing second grade in a normal classroom where she was receiving extra help with language. There was controversy among her teachers about how bright she was. Detailed language testing revealed why. She could repeat digits and sentences with the skill of an 11-year-old and yet her ability to think with language was like that of a 5½ year old. She had learned multiplication tables with great ease, but mathematical reasoning was less advanced. In short, her rote memory skills were "superior," but her thinking skills were "borderline retarded." Her superior rote memory skills allowed her to complete age level work in the second grade, but her concreteness and inability to understand general ideas worried her mother and some of her teachers.

She no longer appeared autistic in the psychiatric interview but related like a child younger than 8 years. She preferred to play with 5-year-old children. Her mother said, "The girls in her class—the other 8-year-olds—she doesn't understand them. If they tell her something about what they're interested in, she just doesn't get it. I don't know if they have been unkind to her, but they don't include her."

A fairly common direction of improvement (about 26%) was in emotional control and social interaction, while general intellectual ability remained in the retarded range. Rosalie's mother describes this change in her:

> Do you remember how crabby and flighty she used to be? Well, mostly she is friendly now and settled down. She trails after me at home and does some things like help me make the beds. She talks to us some, at least, and asks for things she wants. She doesn't learn much at school and her teachers feel she is doing as well as she can.

In Aaron and Maryanne's cases, the parents were still hoping for improvement, seeking therapy and special help in education in addition to placement in a normal class. In Rosalie's case, her parents felt they had done everything possible and were content to have her live at home with them as long as they could care for her. They had a social life of their own and felt in no sense they were not adequately meeting the needs of their other children. Both of these attitudes seem appropriate to the children involved.

Problems arose in households where the child's continuing symptoms were of such a nature that they could be managed only at great emotional and physical cost to the mother. In these cases, it is nearly mandatory that residential placement be sought. By the age of 15 years, 58% of the follow-up children were in residential placement. In practice, for all but the wealthy this means a state hospital. If parents perceive the state hospital to be less than optimum for their child, then they are likely to keep the child in the home far beyond the family's tolerance point. I have seen cases of physical and emotional breakdown in the parents, runaway siblings, and severe marital discord because parents would make no compromise with their concept of the residential placement that they wanted for their child.

As the autistic child of school age gets closer to adolescence, the ultimate outcome of his development becomes clearer to all who care for him. Those children who still learn at retarded rates and maintain obvious social distance settle into a period of little or no improvement. On follow-up of 107 autistic children (see Table 61), of average age 12 years, 58% were still without any useful speech, and an additional 16% communicated only their immediate needs.

Most parents who see this picture begin to lose hope. Many mothers at this period decide they want to spend more time in personal growth or take a job, and they want to place the child under residential care. The day in, day out strain of caring for their child causes physical and emotional exhaustion that contributes to their decision. Such a decision is extremely difficult to make because of the guilt and sadness over giving up their child forever to what they consider the shadowy world of residential care. A turnabout in attitudes of mother and father contributes to the strain in many households. In preschool years, it was often father who pressed most heavily for residential care. In grade school years, fathers may oppose such a move, creating severe marital strain and increased guilt and anxiety in their wives.

Table 61. Level of Conversational Speech of Autistic Children on Follow-up[a]

Level	N	%
Normal, nearly normal	4	4
Immature, unusual	28	26
Satisfy immediate needs, with or without echolalia	17	16
Minimal or no communication[b]	58	54
Total	107	100

[a]Mean age = 12 years.
[b]Mute, echolalia only.

Some parents have used their concentration on the autistic child to avoid facing problems within the marital relationship itself. As the end of the child's school age approaches, parents may find themselves with little closeness left and perhaps at serious odds over their child. This situation needs to be avoided if at all possible. Parents must start consciously working on their own communication and their own relationship as soon as they can after the diagnosis of autism. Most importantly, they must start having some fun together. Few relationships can survive unless the couple can have some pleasing, relaxing times. In the child's preschool years, autistic parents are obviously and almost unavoidably immersed in the anxieties their autistic child produces. Mothers, particularly, sadly say, "We don't go out together, and it's hard for us to take the whole family. We can't get babysitters."

During the years of school age, parents must work on communication and the fun factor for themselves. Fathers must encourage mothers to find hobbies or work that takes them from the household regularly each week. They must take time together to talk about themselves and each other and mutual interests. On the other hand, many parents report to me that the problems and mutual decisions they have had to face together about their autistic child have strengthened their relationship. Nevertheless, studies by others (Gath, 1977; Tew, Laurence, Payne, & Rawnsley, 1977) have shown that the handicapped child poses a special threat to the marital bond, especially if parents have not cemented their affectionate ties or have failed to learn to solve problems together.

If there is a divorce, autistic parents' lives can become extremely complicated. Divorced mothers who must go to work may have to seek residential placement much earlier than otherwise because of problems of child care and money. Step-parents may resent or have difficulty understanding the special feelings that biological parents have for an autistic child and they may have little tolerance for "difficult" behavior. In my experience, second marriages are even more vulnerable to the stress of the autistic child than original ones.

Role of Other Therapeutic Practices

We have seen how, in the decades of the '50s and early '60s, individual therapy of mother and child was the treatment of choice. In the late '60s, and '70s, special education for the child and supportive counselling for the parents has become standard. Rarely do I hear now that individual therapy is prescribed as the principal treatment, but nevertheless, at certain points in the child's life it can be of great use.

Pete, at 8 years of age, was living in his parents' home and was enrolled in special education classes at public school after 4 years of residential or hospital day care. His progress was gratifying to his parents. He had replaced a monumental indifference to them and others with muted but affectionate interest. At age 5 he had begun to speak and at 8 was able to communicate his immediate needs. He had stopped being destructive in his home. Several months after a sibling's birth, he began to cry and retreat to his room and destroy things. A few sessions of individual therapy centered on his feelings toward his new brother cut short his symptoms and enabled him to achieve a new sense of importance. He could respond to his mother when she gave him small responsibilities for his new brother's care.

The point to be remembered in therapy of an autistic child is that the interpretation must be pitched to the child's verbal mental age. The days are past when we expected an autistic child, say at age 5, with a verbal mental age of about 2, to understand abstruse formulations that many adults have difficulty understanding.

Group therapy can be used to help the autistic child understand his peers and react in more appropriate ways to them. George, aged 11 years and in special classes where he worked at age level, often spoke in a loud voice in class and had little understanding of how his interruptions alienated other children. His speech was pedantic and of unusual intonation and rhythm. He had crying spells at home. In an interview, he confided that "more than anything in the world" he wanted "some good friends" and for the "kids not to make fun of me." Group therapy brought him closer to his heart's desire.

I am often asked about the usefulness of operant conditioning or behavior modification therapy. These terms refer to a technique of reinforcing (rewarding) certain acts to make it more likely that those acts will occur again. For example, Maria screams more than anyone in her life finds comfortable. We can use the technique of operant conditioning to develop in Maria other responses to her environment, and we can do it in individual therapy, in group therapy, at school, in residential therapy, or even in the backyard of her home. If she screams to be swung in a swing, she will be swung only when she is not screaming. If we wish to teach her to raise her hand as a signal that she would like to swing, then we will raise her hand for her (when she is not screaming) and will then immediately reinforce her (swing her). Eventually we will swing her only when she voluntarily raises her hand—and wonder of all wonders—Maria will communicate the message "I want to swing" without screaming. If Maria has a sufficiently intact speech and language mechanism, we can teach her to signal verbally this same desire.

The power of operant conditioning or behavior modification is that it forces the therapist/teacher to think in terms of specific goals for the specific individual. It makes the therapist observe the precise, current behavior of the child and to conceptualize exactly the new behavior that the child should learn in order to advance socially or intellectually. The fuzzy or impossible goal is not tolerated by an able practitioner of the operant conditioning method. Never would the able practitioner say, "I will strengthen the ego of Maria" but always would specify precisely which part of Maria's ego could be strengthened, in what manner, and how this strengthening would be manifested in Maria's behavior.

Like all other techniques of therapy, behavior modification can be conducted poorly. I have known practitioners who seriously misjudge the current levels of a child's intelligence or verbal capacity. If levels are overestimated and the therapist expects an impossible performance and the reinforcer (reward) is food, then the child can become malnourished. Some programs are boring to the child because they are unimaginative or applied without enthusiasm. One operant technique, the use of aversive or painful stimuli, which received widespread favorable publicity several years ago, is seldom used now because its beneficial effects are generally short-lived.[1] The most usual application was painful but undangerous electric shock for self-abusive behavior. While initial response was dramatic improvement, symptoms often returned within weeks following the treatment. Positive reinforcement procedures seem to give better long-term results, especially if it is found that the best time to restrain the child is when his behavior is not self-abusive.

Role of Drug Treatment

In her review of the response of psychotic children to pharmacotherapy (drug treatment), Campbell (1975) wrote: "Experience has shown that a therapeutically effective, potent drug can make the autistic child more amenable to other therapies . . . or maintain such a child in the community." In practice, I have found wide variation in autistic children's responses. In some cases of hyperirritability, hyperactivity, and self-abuse, where a good response is most needed, a child may remain unresponsive to any one medication or even to combinations. Some children will show a large number of undesirable side effects and no therapeutic effects, and sometimes desirable effects will wear off after a few weeks or months. Some children can tolerate only small doses or may need large ones. Any physician using potent medications should read Campbell's review and other publications listed in her extensive review, as well as be prepared to devote much time to assessment of the child's progress with the aid of the parents. Even so, the placebo (sugar pill) effect and natural fluctuations in the autistic child's behavior often make it difficult to evaluate the therapeutic effects of medication. Many types of drugs have been insufficiently studied in children, which further adds to the physician's difficulties.

In my experience, most autistic parents would rather not use medication unless all other measures fail. They fear that further harm will come to the child or that the child will become "hooked" or "too dopey." Seldom do children become overdependent on drugs. If dosage is correct, short-term administration seldom hurts. There is evidence, however, that many tranquilizers can become harmful after months to years of administration. Parents need to know that a competent physician is available for all questions and worries while the child is on medication.

Parental Group Influences

Formally organized parent groups, such as the National Society for Autistic Children (NSAC) and its local chapters, have many beneficial effects, e.g., the dissemination of worthwhile knowledge about the condition, stimulation of research, and influence on national policy in the area of developmental disability (see Chapter 15). At a local level, groups can extend a helping hand to parents who have just been given the frightening diagnosis and provide information about schools and professionals in the area that are interested in working with the autistic child and his parents.

There are some problems associated with being too closely and uncritically tied to parent groups if they tend to give certain practices a "group OK" and give a "not OK" label to others. For example, one current "OK" idea is that the child must be kept in the parental home at all costs. One mother reported she was "treated like a leper" when she decided to institutionalize her difficult-to-care-for son. Some parents, after much reading, decide they can evaluate other children's dosages of medication, kinds and "OK" types of child care, and give dogmatic advice to other parents. Charlene's mother said, "I went to this meeting and told them about all of my troubles with her hitting herself. This other mother told me I should hit her every time she hit herself. She even came to our house to tell me again." The message some parents have given to me about groups is this: "Go to their meetings, help others when you can, but decide for yourself what to do about your own child."

Some groups foster the idea that autism is an "elite" condition, that it is somehow desirable that autistic children get first preference over other handicapped groups in matters of therapy and education.[2] Such an idea, parents tell me, is not unique to autism, that it is found in other parent groups such as those devoted to cerebral palsy and cystic fibrosis. Elitism in its extreme form fosters the idea that autistic children should not share education or treatment facilities or money with other handicapped groups, and that different parent groups should not band together to seek mutual funds for research. As one father said, "All of us should get together. Think what political power we could get just through sheer numbers. We could really do something for all children." The Developmental Disabilities Consortium of the United Cerebral Palsy Association, the Epilepsy Foundation of America, and the National Society for Autistic Children is beginning, on the national level, to do just that. But efforts on the local level tend to remain fragmented.

Notes

[1] In an unpublished account of a series of experiments to study and control severe self-mutilative behavior in a 6-year-old autistic boy, Churchill and Bryson (1968) concluded that the behavior was largely reflexive in nature. By this they meant that some neurobiological irregularity upset the balance of the inhibitory-excitatory systems of the central nervous system. Despite this biological irregularity, the boy also used the behavior at times to control his environment, illustrating the complex nature of such symptoms.

[2] This idea is contrary to NSAC's generally enlightened policies.

REFERENCES

Campbell, M., Pharmacotherapy in early infantile autism. *Biological Psychiatry*, 1975, **10**(4), 399–423.

Churchill, D., & Bryson, C. *Analysis of self-hitting behavior in a 6 year old boy*. Unpublished manuscript of the Clinical Research Center for Early Childhood Schizophrenia.

DeMyer, M. K., Barton, S., DeMyer, W. E., Norton, J. A., Allen, J., & Steele, R. Prognosis in autism. A follow-up study. *Journal of Autism and Childhood Schizophrenia*, 1973, **3**(3), 199–246.

Gath, A. The impact of an abnormal child upon the parents. *British Journal of Psychiatry*, 1977, **130**, 405–410.

Reichler, R. J., & Schopler, E. Developmental therapy: A program model for providing individual services in the community. In E. Schopler & R. J. Reichler (Eds.), *Psychopathology and child development*. New York: Plenum Press, 1976.

Rimland, B. Infantile autism. *The syndrome and its implications for a neural theory of behavior*. New York: Appleton-Century-Crofts, 1964.

Rimland, B., Callaway, E., & Dreyfus, P. The effect of high doses of vitamin B_6 on autistic children: A double-blind crossover study. *American Journal of Psychiatry*, 1978, **135**(4), 472–475.

Tew, B. J., Laurence, K. M., Payne, H., & Rawnsley, K. Marital stability following the birth of a child with spina bifida. *British Journal of Psychiatry*, 1977, **131**, 79–82.

Wing, J. K., & Wing, L. A clinical interpretation of remedial teaching. In J. K. Wing (Ed.), *Early childhood autism: Clinical, educational, and social aspects*. London: Pergamon Press, 1966.

Chapter 13 *

PROBLEMS AND STRESSES IN ADOLESCENCE

As the autistic person reaches sexual and physical maturity, new stresses arise from without and within imposing ensuing new stresses on parents and family. Many families have had a period of relative stability and calm during the middle and late childhood years. Some parents remark that the autistic child during such years enriches family life and provides enjoyment to all. As Chuck's mother said, "We have had such a wonderful time with him these past few years. He goes to school and enjoys the family. My husband and I are so grateful for this good time. When he was a little fellow, and he about tore the house down over our ears and was so withdrawn, we wondered if he would ever come out of it."

Over the space of the next 3 years, the picture changed as Chuck reached sexual maturity and became taller and stronger. His parents told how life was different for Chuck at age 14 and for his family. As they related their story, Chuck's father looked tense and worried and his mother was tearful, emotional states neither had experienced more than briefly about him since his preschool years.

The problem now is this: There is no school program that he likes and fits into. He is tense and unhappy a lot of the time. He just

*With contributions by Dr. David Park.

211

doesn't have enough to do. There is another problem—it is difficult to talk about it. He must be having wet dreams, and we see him rubbing himself a lot. That brings me to another problem that just breaks our hearts. He used to be the pet of the neighborhood. Now people ask him to leave their yards or tell their children to come in the house. I think they're afraid of him now.

Interviewer: How have you tried to handle these problems?

Mother: Well, the school problem is at the point where they tell us they do not have anything for him. He just doesn't seem to fit in. He can copy any assignment they give him, but he just can't go into any academic program—he doesn't speak or read well enough. He really has little interest in doing much that they offer—he couldn't handle a shop class.

Father: I have tried to talk to him about growing up, but it's difficult and hard to know how much he understands. We feel we have reached another impasse and I think we feel tired all the time.

In the ensuing year, the parents found residential treatment where he adjusted without major difficulties. On weekends, the family visited or took him home. Major reasons why Chuck's parents and many others decide on residential treatment in teen years are not only that they are tired and inclined to give up, but also that they see the time looming ahead when they will be old and unable to care for their child.

There are several problems every autistic parent must face in adolescence and adult years: physical sexual maturity coupled with continuing social immaturity, insufficient community and residential programs, and their own sense of tiredness, both psychological and physical. The autistic is a unique individual, as is each family. This chapter and the next will present and illustrate the variety of adolescent and adult autistics as well as parental efforts to cope with the continuing problems.

Psychosexual Development in Early Life

Before describing sexual development of the autistic adolescent and the problems it can bring, I will go back in time to the earliest days of life in the womb to sketch briefly how biological and environmental factors combine to shape the different destinies of a man and a woman. In prenatal development, male hormones make a male brain different (not better, just different) than a female brain. These actual anatomical differences influence behavior after birth. Money and Ehrhardt (1972) give evidence that vigorous outdoor athletic activity and self-assertiveness in competition, for example, typically found in males, are at least partially dependent on these prenatal masculine hormone influences.

During prenatal days, the parents are deciding if they want a boy or a girl or do not care which. These wishes affect in various ways how the parents will treat the infant. Immediately after birth, on first sight of the baby, people exclaim, "It's a girl!" or "It's a boy!" (Money & Ehrhardt, 1972). Thereafter, the baby is treated differently on the basis of its sex. There are many theories on what causes a child to learn the behavior regarded by his culture as typically masculine or feminine (Mischel, 1970). The parents at first are the most important environmental influences. Later, at school age and during adolescence, the child's companions may be most important. One theory that deserves special mention is the psychoanalytic one of Sigmund Freud (Brenner, 1974) which advocates the following stages of child sexuality: oral, from birth to about 1½ years when the mouth is the center of the infant's desires and gratification; anal, from 1½ years to 3 years which is the toilet training period; phallic, beginning at about age 3 and merging into the adult genital phase at puberty.

The Freudian theory is of historical significance concerning both the ideas of causation and treatment of infantile autism. Freud saw the infant's attachment and dependency on the mother as "pertaining primarily to the sexual . . . instincts" during the oral phase of development when the mother is considered the chief sexual object of the infant (Maccoby & Masters, 1970). Adherents of the Freudian theory saw the mother of the autistic infant as failing to gratify him sufficiently in the oral period and thereby unable to form attachments and to graduate into later developmental stages. Efforts at treatment of autism during the 1940s through the mid-1960s were based largely on Freudian theory or one of its offshoots, and it was thus that parental treatment and individual child psychotherapy were held to be important keys to improvement in the autistic child.[1] Time and research have proved these ideas and practices to be wrong, at least with regard to autism. Many efforts have been made to prove or disprove Freudian theory with regard to other types of children. Like all other child development theories, some aspects seem true while others do not. A useful discussion of the various theories of child psychosexual development can be found in Maccoby and Masters' *Attachment and Dependency* (1970).

While we do not know all the reasons why most girls learn the feminine and boys the masculine behavior of their culture, we can describe to some degree the stages as they unfold year by year. Sigmund Freud and his daughter Anna (Freud, 1952) were pioneers in pointing out that sexuality does not arise suddenly as puberty is reached but starts during infancy when the baby reaches for and explores his sex organs. Thereafter the sex role is learned bit by bit, as so well described by Money and Ehrhardt (1972). A boy learns by example and by praise and punishment that certain activities are OK for him, e.g., acting tough, competing, imitating his father. At the same time he learns that certain other activities are not OK, e.g., crying, playing with dolls, wearing dresses. The little girl in the same manner learns that just the opposite activities are OK and not OK for her. However, both boys and girls make good use of learning what not to do because it serves as a guide of what to expect in the opposite sex. The sex-OK behavior is the one in which the individual becomes truly proficient in all its major and minor details. Throughout history, styles in feminine and masculine OK and not-OK behavior have changed, including some major ones in the 20th century which we hope will give both girls and boys a wider choice in developing gender OK behavior.

The early postnatal years, while the infant and young child are so attached to the parents, are critical ones for the establishment of gender identity, that is, knowing for sure whether one is a boy or a girl. For example, if a boy is reared as a girl in the first 2 years of life, it is very difficult to change him into a person who will later enact comfortably the male role that our society expects (Money & Ehrhardt, 1972). As language develops in the second year of life, the little girl begins to imitate her mother and pretend various feminine roles and the boy his father. Both sexes dramatize the mother-baby relationship and thereby start to become detached from the mother (Gesell, Ilg, & Ames, 1956). At 2½ to 3 years the child can say his/her correct gender when asked, and at 3 years verbalize sex differences between boys and girls going to the toilet. At 4 years there is marked interest in bathrooms in other people's houses and questioning about where babies come from. At 5 years, the child develops modesty about exposing himself but may giggle and act silly in going to the toilet. They may wonder why father doesn't have breasts or sister a penis. At age 6, children investigate each other, thus getting practical answers to questions about sex differences. By this age the basis of most of what the individual will ever know of being a woman or a man has already been learned at mother's and father's knee.

The next developmental stage is called the latency period by Freudians because they believe sexuality goes into a relatively underground state during grade school years. Other theorists believe, however, that the learning of gender identity from agemates continues unabated and that without peer friendships, the school-age child cannot learn to become proficient in his adult sexuality and gender role. After age 7, when children stop playing with members of the opposite sex, they nevertheless remain ever alert to what "the enemy" is doing, continuing their education in sex-OK and not-OK behavior. Gradually the walls break down so that by puberty girls and boys intermingle socially and sexually, ready to begin the courtship rites of their culture if all has gone well in childhood.

Unfortunately for the autistic child, nearly all phases of the childhood learning of sex-OK and not-OK behavior have been upset. While autistic infants are probably more attached to their parents than most of us have been programmed to believe, that infant-parent bond is not a normal one. Their learning in this aspect of development is delayed as in all others. They cannot imitate the roles of their parents or participate in the role play so necessary to learning their gender role. Nevertheless, it is my impression that many autistic children at adolescence do have an appreciation of sex differences and that the higher their social skills in general, the more adequate their gender identity. Sadly, in all but about 2 or 3%, their gender role is not secure enough to be expressed in marriage or parenthood.

Parents' Views on Masturbation and Family Nudity

We were interested in how the interview parents viewed early expressions of child sexuality. We asked whether they had started sex and modesty training with the index children, how much the children masturbated or handled their genitals, and about parental handling of this activity and nudity at home. While nearly all parents said they either had started little or no modesty training, it was obvious that most parents were nevertheless imparting their views to their children by encouraging some behaviors and punishing others.

It proved somewhat difficult to learn how many children masturbated as opposed to merely touching their genitals. Our question was asked with the assumption that the two acts were about equivalent; but on reading the responses it became evident to the raters that many parents made a distinction. As one mother said, "I think masturbation and touching genitals for curiosity are different but it is sometimes hard to tell when." More autistic than normal children were reported to masturbate (autistic, 63%; normal, 45%). About 6% of the autistic were described as doing it very frequently or most of the time, while no normal child did so.

Table 62. Parental Attitudes toward Masturbation and Touching Genitals

Attitude	Autistic		Normal	
	N	%	N	%
Important to stop and do stop	6	18	9	27
Say it's natural and to be expected but stop it	16	48	17	51
Make little or no effort to stop	7	21	5	15
Questionable	3	9	2	6

In trying to explain this difference we looked at parents' views on the importance of stopping masturbation. There were no significant differences between parent groups (Table 62).

The most common type response is illustrated by the following:

Interviewer: How important do you think it is to stop masturbation in children?

> Mother: Well, I think it's a natural thing to do, especially in little boys.
>
> Father: Yes, but I wouldn't want it to go too far. I wouldn't want it to happen very much.
>
> Mother: About the only times any of them do it is when they're undressed or bored. But I'm not sure whether it's masturbation or whether they're just curious—just handling themselves.

Interviewer: Do you try to stop it?

> Father: I don't want to put too much emphasis on it—it might get to be too much. I take their hands away and get them interested in something else.
>
> Mother: I might slap their hands away and say it's not nice but mostly I get their clothes on and divert their attention.

Many parents (autistic, 48%; normal, 51%) like the ones cited above said masturbation was natural, to be expected, and not harmful to the child; but also they stopped it in a way that they hoped would not overemphasize the activity to the children. It was as if these parents were uncomfortable in seeing their children masturbate but also were respectful of their children's sexuality and did not want to make them feel overly ashamed. Most normal children seemingly learned, if not to stop, at least to masturbate in private while autistic children more often continued to masturbate openly.

Family Modesty

One of the ways children learn about sex differences is by seeing other members of the family nude. Whether an individual grows to view the naked body as natural or with some anxiety depends largely on his parents' attitudes. In both autistic (58%) and normal (57%) households, most parents allowed little or no nudity in any family member except in the bath and bedrooms (Table 63). However, in these households there was also a relaxed attitude toward the children seeing each other and the parents undressing, bathing, or going to the toilet. Parents with four or more children practically hooted at the questions: "How much do you allow your children to come into the bathroom when you are there?" "Do you allow them to see you undressed?" One mother exclaimed: "You've got to be kidding! Our bathroom is practically the family room."

The second most common attitude (autistic, 16%; normal, 21%) was that parents did not habitually allow children to see them undressed even in the bathroom but neither did they try to "cover up" nor "get hysterical" if a child came in. Typically such parents would deny that the child wanted to see the parents nude but would say: "Oh, I think he just wants to ask a question or get some help but I do notice he kind of looks at me close." Only a few families in either group took great pains to avoid any nudity. Likewise, only a few were extremely relaxed about family nudity in all parts of the house. One routine exception to the "no nudity rule" was in children about 18 months to 2½ years of age. Here parents reported that they allowed them to run naked through the house a few minutes after bathing or at bedtime. Several parents said they enjoyed seeing their young child's body at such times as much as the child enjoyed the romp. Most parents knew about and accepted young children urinating outside at least one time. As one mother said:

> I don't think there is a little boy alive that doesn't urinate outside at least once. Mine all did and so did the neighbor's. I tell them it's all right once but that we have a bathroom for that sort of thing. I always know when it happens—all the other kids, including the neighbors, rush in to tell me.

Table 63. Parental Attitudes toward Nudity at Home

Attitude	Autistic		Normal	
	N^a	%	N^b	%
Very modest; actively avoid undressing before children	1	3	3	9
Modest	5	16	7	21
Little nudity at home but relaxed attitude toward children seeing parents bathing and dressing	18	58	19	57
Home nudity allowed (all family members)	2	6	1	3
Parents divided about how much nudity allowed (or questionable regarding attitude)	5	16	3	9

[a]$N = 33$.
[b]$N = 31$.

Parents also knew that most normal 5-year-olds wanted privacy in the bathroom and were respectful of this wish. Most autistic children 5 years of age did not seem to notice that any one was looking. Kim's father said, "It wouldn't matter if the President of the United States was there. Kim would still pull his pants down."

Puberty and Psychosexual Adjustment

The years from about 12 to adulthood, the period of adolescence, are a time of enormous change and stress for normal boys and girls in our society. At about 11 years of age, the average girl, and at about 13 years, the average boy, start to grow rapidly in height and weight and soon achieve about 90% of adult height. Not only do muscle and bone size increase quickly but there is a rearrangement in body configuration; for example, facial bone structure becomes more defined, and, in girls, the pelvic girdle broadens. Of course, the increase in sex hormones also stimulates the growth of the genitals and body hair in both sexes. Puberty comes at age 12 in the average girl and at age 14 in the average boy. Puberty is the earliest age when the girl (woman) or boy (man) are capable of bearing or begetting children. With all this bodily change comes an upsurge in sexual feelings and urges to release them. For our forebears, this was a more simple matter than for the youth of today. To preserve the race it was a necessity to mate and produce an offspring a year or two after puberty was reached because infant death rates were extremely high and early adult deaths were common. Today, it is often disastrous to both parent and child if conception occurs in the teens. Life now is longer and infinitely more complex. After puberty it takes about 10 years of additional bodily, mental, and psychological growth for a normal individual to produce physically and psychologically healthy offspring.

During this 10-year adolescent period, the individual has some of the strongest sexual cravings of his entire life. The teenager must learn how to control sexual impulses so that they can be expressed behind closed doors and in a responsible way for himself, his partner, and society. I think none of us forget the strain we were under as we uncertainly groped our way to expression of one of our main reasons for being—our sexuality. The average individual, commencing at age 11 (Gesell, Ilg, & Ames, 1956), begins to develop outlets for his sexual and psychological tension, and these change in character over the years. For example, the average 11-year-old has stomach aches and headaches, bites his nails, twitches his face, and sometimes breaks out in anger. He shows spurts of intense activity, embarrassed giggling, and laughter. These kinds of tension releasers continue through adolescence, but gradually, beginning at about age 14, the verbal outlets increase in frequency. At age 16, general tension diminishes as the normal youth becomes more comfortable with his sexuality and with social relationships in general. Masturbation and nocturnal emission, the most direct and physiologically normal releasers to sexual tension, unfortunately are heavily encrusted for most normal adolescents with feelings of doubt and guilt. Fortunately the sublimation of direct sexual expression also takes place in art, music, dancing, and sports.

For the parents of the normal teenager, stress also is great as they worry about extramarital pregnancy, alcohol and drug abuse, and early marriage. It is also a time when the adolescent is preparing to leave home. In the normal scheme of things, parents can then look forward to a freedom from these responsibilities and to a time of self-development.

The natural timetable is upset in every way but in physical growth and sexual development when the teenager is autistic. As autistic teenagers reach nearly adult height and weight, they may retain or increase their aggressive impulses. No longer can parents restrain them to keep them and the environment secure. Mothers become even more physically tired and sometimes fearful of body harm. The normal teenager has many places to go, friends to see, interesting things to do. Not so the autistic. Sexual tensions must be released in increased physical activity (rocking, picking at the body) and in frequent masturbation. In all too many cases, the autistic teenager does not masturbate privately but does it everywhere. Some develop tic-like habits of frequently and quickly touching their genitals. There is little hope that even higher functioning adolescents can become psychologically ready for parenthood, or that they can relate in a rewarding and comfortably platonic way to members of the opposite sex. Parents with great grief come to realize that the autistic child will remain intellectually and socially a child in an adult's body.

How to handle sexuality of autistic teenagers is a tremendous problem for many parents. Most parents report that the autistic male probably does not have the drive to consummate a full sexual act, but the autistic female can passively accept the sexual attention of males and become pregnant. In past years, parents could forestall biological parenthood by securing tubal ligation or vasectomy. Recent ideas concerning patients' rights have made such operations more difficult for parents to arrange. It seems that society has become blind to an unborn child's right to responsible parenting, a condition most autistic individuals cannot supply. The possibility of genetic involvement in autism makes it imperative that we learn more about the genetics of the condition. Society should not condone the imposition of double jeopardy on any segment of its unborn population.

Rubbing genitals against other people causes great concern. These activities are more prevalent in males. One divorced father related his problem:

> Mickey (age 18) lives with me now. He has been very affectionate for many years, and it's been no problem. Lately, though, he has started rubbing against some girls and women who come to the house. I am afraid he may do this in a store and get into real trouble. Also, I have a woman friend that Mickey likes a lot. He likes to hug and kiss her, but it gets him too excited. I'm not sure what to do about this.

The interviewer and the father worked out a plan that would forestall any physical contact between Mickey and girls and women. In the case of the father's special friend, she was told to maintain her friendliness to Mickey by talking to him, which he liked, and to refrain any physical shows of affection. It was desirable to place Mickey in a program with other adolescents of his chronological and mental age so that he could have peer relationships on a level that he could sustain and feel comfortable about.

Institutionalization

Obviously, many autistic teenagers could be cared for longer at home if appropriate programs in education, socialization, and work were available. Many communities are devising such programs. However, the time comes when an estimated 75% of autistic adults will need full residential care, and many of the remaining 25% will need special help and supervision to remain in the community. Programs to accomplish such help should be near the home community so that parents and other relatives can remain an active force in the autistic adult's life.

To "give up" during their child's teenage and adult years seems just as painful to parents as to do it earlier, and if the child goes into an institution, it seems just as necessary that the institution be perceived as a "good one" where care will be as attentive and loving as in the parental home.

> Mimi had been diagnosed as autistic at 3 years of age. In the residential treatment centers and in outpatient clinics she proved to be hyperirritable and unable to get pleasure or benefit from any of the programs. At age 18, her parents had some medical problems as well as the usual psychological weariness which prompted them to hospitalize her. The treating psychiatrist found her at age 24 still among the most difficult of his patients to treat, but Mimi's parents remained interested and provided as many home visits as her symptoms allowed.

Not all parents remain as close as Mimi's because time and continuing social isolation of the patient gradually tend to blunt interest. Reliable estimates are unavailable of the number of institutionalized autistic adolescents who gradually lost contact with their families. State hospital records tend to identify them as schizophrenic or severely mentally retarded with a dim prognosis that envisages lifetime hospitalization. Kanner's (1973) follow-up of 4 of his classical 11 autistic patients who "spent most of their lives in institutional care" sums up their fate as follows:

> They yielded readily to the uninterrupted isolation and soon settled down to a life not too remote from a nirvana-like existance. If at all responsive to psychological testing, their IQs dropped down to figures usually referred to as low-grade moron or imbecile.

Suitable Residential Facilities

The lack of residential facilities for lower and middle functioning autistic adolescents and young adults has already been mentioned. In the United States, with some variation in some states, handicapped people generally are not entitled to free education after reaching the age of 21. State mental hospitals are the only available facilities outside of private psychiatric clinics, which few can afford. They are, justly or unjustly, identified by most parents as "human warehouses" or "snake pits." Halfway houses organized by groups of parents tend to be more suitable for adolescents and adults in the middle or higher functioning categories than for those in the lower group who require more daily care and supervision.

A possible way of providing adequate and suitable residential care is the addition of units (beds with suitable daily activity programs) for adolescents and young adults to existing schools and treatment centers for younger children. Although some communities are struggling mightily to fund and organize units on the model of halfway houses for all their autistic adolescents and young adults, it seems that most such units would have to be continuously dependent on the reliability and dedication of residential staff and service personnel. For example, a unit organized around a normal family that is initially enthusiastic about managing it, living in it, and taking care of it might fall apart if the family decided to quit.

The advantages of planning residential units for autistic adolescents and young adults as integral components of schools for younger children are numerous. The more obvious ones are:

(1) Problems of funding and administration would be managed by an existing school apparatus.

(2) Staff supervision, training and treatment can be relatively easily organized within the framework of the school's program.

(3) There would be no dependence on permanent house mothers or fathers.

(4) School staff and service personnel could be rotated to provide a

welcome respite from concentration on young children with more severe problems.

(5) Residents of the adolescent-young adult unit could be, in some cases, integrated with supporting staff for such chores as cleaning, yard work, and even more complex assignments.

(6) Parents would less often be called upon to deal with emergencies of the kind that arise in halfway houses and similar facilities.

Needless to say, legislation to secure adequate and reliable funding at the state or federal level is essential to secure the kind of residential facilities we are suggesting.

The problems and stresses in autistic adolescence may vary considerably from one family to another. However, since similarities exist within the three groups of autistic adolescents (higher-, middle-, and lower-functioning), the following three case histories merit presentation.

The Higher-Functioning Adolescent: Aaron

The plight of the higher functioning autistic adolescent, comprising about 15 to 20% of the entire autistic population, is poignant. Some get very near to normality, and yet to themselves and to their parents they remain painfully different, outside the social and employment mainstream.

At the threshold of puberty, Aaron had progressed a long way from the isolated little boy I first saw at the age of 5 years when he could relate to adults only if they read him telephone book numbers and had no interest in other children. At that young age he could speak but not in a give-and-take conversation and never played a pretend game. At age 13, Aaron could converse about some things in a stilted way and got along fairly well with adults. When he saw me, he greeted me happily and seemed to understand the role I played in his life. However, he had no friends and his older brother, away at an out-of-town college, was like another adult to him. He longed for friends his own age but had no appreciation of how his overriding interests in mathematics and geography and his frequent temper outbursts turned off others his own age. He could not converse with them in the lingo of the adolescent or understand their social relationships. Aaron had been in a normal classroom for 4 years and had gained the respect of his classmates only in regard to his knowledge of facts. He was treated as an outsider because he was "different."

His parents enrolled him in therapeutic group programs in his own community and at distant summer camps in an effort to increase his social skills. At first enthusiastic about entering such groups, at the end of his first summer in a therapeutic camp, he told everyone he wished he hadn't come and was angry at his parents for placing him there. His counselor noted that throughout the summer Aaron screamed, cried, and physically attacked both peers and adults. Some outbursts were triggered by peer teasing, while many others were not. The boy could not differentiate when he was being teased and when other campers were merely laughing about something that had no bearing on Aaron. Gradually, however, his screaming spells became somewhat shorter and by the end of summer he recovered from them. At the end of summer, recalled the counselor, he had sometimes begun feeling delighted at the few times Aaron smiled broadly and enjoyed himself.

Aaron returned to his home and junior high school. Having visited him there, the camp counselor could point out the tactics that seemed to help Aaron deal in a better way with other youngsters. Aaron's clumsiness in sports was handled by giving him, in addition to physical training, jobs in which he excelled, such as statistician for the basketball team and mover of the yard marker at football games.

Aaron made more progress. At the end of his third summer in camp his counselor had this to say:

> Aaron is now standing up for himself, at times in a realistic way, with the others. He speaks up for himself often without screaming and he will never withdraw for hours as he did before. He still has some fears about leaving the adults to go in groups with the other boys. He tries new activities, but he still has a deep fear of losing, is still physically weaker than the others, and projects his own fears onto anyone else who is handy. All in all he is about 75% better.

Aaron's father saw him at age 17 as follows:

> His major difficulties are in mental and physical concentration and in social maturity. He has made some notable achievements in the last 2 years: had a good friend for a few months, won a scholarship contest, and stuck to a paid job for several weeks. I wonder if any of the medicines, like Ritalin, might help his concentration. He still has trouble being interested in English class although his grades are good. The eye doctor noticed abnormal eye movements ("micro-movements"), especially when he was tired. Could these movements be used to monitor his response to medicines or give insight into his cerebral disturbance? What are the advantages and limitations of further examination and treatment at this time? These are the kinds of questions I ask myself as I worry about moving him into a self-sustaining situation within the next few years.

For Aaron, there is indeed hope, but the question still remains whether his high intelligence will compensate for his uncertain emotional control and difficulties of concentration. Also, his lack of social savvy may be quite handicapping when he has to deal with others without the sustaining influence of his father.

The Middle-Functioning Adolescent: Elly[2]

It may well be that the happiest autistic person is one whose development stops short of the higher-functional level. In treating an intellectually handicapped child one aims at the highest possible level of consciousness and mental development. With the autistic it may be well consciously to stop short of this goal although this may not be possible as the drive to learn once set in motion is difficult to stop. Autistic people seem to be unusually poor at asking questions. If they ask questions, they frequently cannot use or understand the answers. This failure may represent a saturation of the imagination by the complexities of the environment, leaving no room for the autistic to wonder about things not presented to him directly.[3]

Elly's development to age 7 has already been reported (Park, 1967). She is now 20. Though slim and shapely and possessing great physical strength, Elly moves with a child's awkward grace. She lives with her parents in a home from which the other three children have graduated. She is devoted to her mother and father and deeply happy when her brother and sisters come back, but her life is solitary nonetheless. Her boyfriend, like herself in her high school's special class, comes over sometimes on weekends to play records and talk. For many years her parents brought a young woman to live in the house to be her friend and teach her skills of ordinary living, but this is no longer judged necessary. Elly herself has said that she does not need this kind of friend anymore. She has learned from them what they could teach her about housekeeping and manual arts. She cooks, bakes, weaves, and makes clothes and pottery with taste and skill, but her speech is slow and halting and her understanding of human situations, including her own, is about that of a normal 5-year-old. She knows that she is "special," has had severe problems in learning to talk and even now often fails to control herself, but she has never expressed any curiosity about herself. She has often heard the word autism but never connected it with herself or tried to find out what it means.

Elly's mind, when not bent on practical matters, runs in patterns which she can recognize and describe but scarcely control. If you give her something, she lowers her gaze and mumbles in great discomfort. She knows she must be "polite," but if she looks into another person's face and says one of the "politenesses," she knows she will see the "hang-man," not a hallucination but no less real, a little imaginary man who hangs by his hands or jumps up and down when "please" and "thank you" are said. For over 10 years her parents have been aware of a long string of powerful and involuntary associations of ideas which have brought her both pleasure and pain, and which may have existed before she could talk about them. These ideas may be the principal barriers between her and the kind of relaxed human contact that a child can have with an adult.

Elly's IQ, tested at ages 11 and 12 on the Wechsler Intelligence Scale for Children, measured 87 and 76, respectively. At 17, on the Wechsler Adult Intelligence Scale, she scored 101 to 106, computed from a performance (Q of 119 and a verbal IQ of 88 to 95. Her mental age had accelerated, but her performance, like her intellectual development, was exceptionally uneven. At age 15 she could give at once the prime factors of any integer up to about 1,200 or identify it as a prime; and though her attention has now moved elsewhere, she still calculates quickly and accurately. Like several children mentioned earlier, she has a good sense of pitch but a poor sense of rhythm and enjoys music most when it is simple and popular. She types accurately and, since she makes little attempt to understand what she reads, she can type manuscripts in foreign languages almost as easily as in English.

What is Elly's probable future? From any practical point of view, in spite of her islands of almost normal functioning, Elly is retarded. One after another, she learns the skills of living at a delayed pace. At the age of 20 she has suddenly started to check the pantry after school to see whether it contains the necessaries for dinner and breakfast, and to go downtown to buy anything that is needed. A small accomplishment intellectually, but a step towards being able to live some kind of helpful and responsible life in a sheltered environment when her parents are no longer around.

Autistic adolescents and young adults differ just as widely among each other as normal ones do, but this description may give some picture of what is possible for a young adult whose autism is in the middle range of severity, who is able to understand some of her psychological compulsions and other disabilities and cooperate in behavioral strategies aimed at relieving them, but who is not able to see herself as an adolescent or adult among others or to appreciate the true gravity of her situation.

The Lower-Functioning Adolescent: Kirk

Kirk is now 15, a handsome, tall boy with a disarming smile. His self-educated intelligent father and socially prominent college graduate mother married in their mid-40s. Kirk, their first child, was followed by a daughter who is normal though somewhat of an underachiever in school. "The boy cried almost incessantly," recalled the father, "clinging to mother, rocking back and forth, always tense, extremely anxious and utterly miserable." Kirk slept very poorly, frequently awakening in the middle of the night. He began to walk at the age of 13 months and developed a limited amount of speech (mostly expressive) by his 2nd birthday. The child "kind of disintegrated" after the birth of his sister, regressing to muteness, head-banging for hours at a time, spinning his tricycle wheel, and listening repetitively to fractions of recorded music.

Diagnosed as autistic, Kirk continued to live at home, contrary to the diagnosticians' recommendations, receiving daily treatments from a psycho-dynamically oriented child psychiatrist. The latter suggested similar treatment for the parents, recommending a colleague who proceeded to treat the mother. At first unwilling to submit to psychiatric treatment, the father eventually proceeded to consult a clinical psychologist (also a Freudian) for a few months.

"Thus for a while, with two psychiatrists and one psychologist directing our lives, our stately suburban house became a mental institution with three patients and an increasingly bewildered housekeeper who quietly cared for Kirk. My sister," continued the father, "mercifully took our youngest to live with her while we were immersing ourselves deeper and deeper in painful guilt feelings prompted by gentle, and not so gentle, indictments of our three pontificating therapists. These were directed at our allegedly pathogenic personalities, for which *our* parents were to be blamed, and to Kirk's traumas, of psychogenic origin, for which our inadequacies as parents were, in their opinions, directly responsible. Meantime Kirk continued to deteriorate, bewildered by play therapy to which he could not respond and drugged by phenothiazines which were prescribed to improve his hyperactivity. Finally, our pediatrician convinced us to send Kirk to an out-of-state treatment center for autistic children which offered a mixed program of eclectic behavior therapy and special education. We parted with the psychiatrists, sold my share in the family business, and bought a large farm with a spacious house near Kirk's treatment center. Kirk slept at home, with much help from a warm lovely couple who also managed the farm. He was finally toilet trained at age 7 and learned to dress and undress himself with relative ease. Within a year, our daughter came back to us to live on the farm."

Kirk's progress at the treatment center was at first rather substantial. He began to sleep well, eat heartily, and smile more frequently than cry. Gradually, the crying spells and fierce temper tantrums became rare. Fragmentary eye contact developed into more or less steady contact with parents and teachers. Persistent echolalia was substituted by occasional words, at first just by a few and more recently by many, though still with pronominal reversals. But, at 15 years of age, Kirk still functions most inadequately. At the treatment center he participates in some recreational group activities, likes to visit the local zoo (identifying and naming some of the animals), rides his two-wheel bike with almost age-appropriate skill, swims a bit, and uses eating utensils. However, he masturbates a lot, occasionally rubbing his genitals against men and women alike, rocks, licks books and some other objects, listens to bits of repetitive recorded music, and tensely raises hands above his head in a repetitive motion accompanied by lusty emissions of infantile-like squeaks.

"There is more to Kirk than meets the eye," explained his mother to the interviewer, "for he understands more than he lets us know and has more skills than he is ready to demonstrate. For example, he can communicate in brief sentences his cherished desires, such as going for a car ride or eating several helpings of his favorite dish. He can count to 100 and clumsily scribble a few letters when someone gently guides his hand. He also begins to watch TV and recognize a baseball game, concentrating on it for as long as 10 minutes at a time. We try to enjoy his coming home every night and on weekends, and our son responds with warm, spontaneous hugs and kisses. We have taught ourselves to perceive his life in installments. Not in weekly or monthly time intervals as with normal children, but in long installments of undetermined duration. We add up a few visible signs of progress (sometimes waiting a year or more for evidence) and look back at the strenuous periods of our lives when there were none. We also look at many other autistic children and their struggling parents and try very hard to count our mixed blessings. Kirk is better off than many others and is slowly progressing; he is still young and we do not expect his progress to stop. We can cope with our pain, but are acutely concerned about the long future."

Perpetual Parenthood

From an ethological viewpoint, even the most advanced primates have a limited capacity (in terms of time) to take care of their offspring. On a much longer and more diversified continuum, this is also a human trait. The changing pattern of care, from infancy to late adolescence, brings to the human parent of a normal child a variety of different stresses and compensating satisfactions that are relatively short in duration and destined to change and end. Save for the proverbial "Oedipal mother," there is also a time when an average parent looks forward to letting go of the grown-up child and terminating his basic parental obligations. In the case of the lower- and middle-functioning autistic adolescents and adults, parents who keep them at home are exposed, in addition to other stresses, to *perpetual parenthood* of a child at a mental level of, say, 2 to 3 years of age. No major developmental change is in sight and there is no light at the end of the tunnel.

Mrs. L., a courageous mother of two lower-functioning autistic adolescents (both kept at home) and three normal children, described perpetual parenthood as "increasingly debilitating monotony." The only relief which she could distinctly remember and identify as developmental progress was successful toilet training around the ages of 7 and 9. Improvements in behavior (in her opinion quite minor) in such areas as sleeping, eating or hypoactivity did not seem sufficient to modify her feelings of "being stuck with endless mothering of 2-year-old adult babies."

The impact of perpetual parenthood on mothers and fathers of autistic adolescents and young adults is difficult to assess. What prompts some with adequate financial means to resist institutionalization in private psychiatric clinics or schools where care is reportedly quite satisfactory? What prompts those with limited means to reject state hospital facilities which in some states provide relatively adequate care? The answers can come only through assessment of each individual parent's capacity to withstand stress in the long run and cope with the deepening depression that these stresses can produce as time marches on.

Notes

[1] Anna Freud (1965) cautioned that the child analyst "must exercise great care . . . not to confuse the effect of a child's abnormality on the mother with the mother's pathogenic effect on the child, as is done easily, especially with autistic children." However the experience of many parents with psychoanalytically oriented therapy of being blamed for "all the child's problems" shows that many therapists did not heed Miss Freud's caution (see the case history of Kirk in this chapter).

[2] Verified case history contributed by Professor David Park.

[3] I look upon the failure to ask and answer questions as a failure of the autistic person to grasp the abstractions of language which usually persists into adulthood.

REFERENCES

Brenner, C. *An elementary textbook of psychoanalysis.* New York: International Universities Press, 1974.

Freud, A. *The psychoanalytic treatment of children.* London: Imago Publishing Co., 1952.

Freud, A. *Normality and pathology in childhood.* New York: International Universities Press, 1965.

Gesell, A., Ilg, F. L., & Ames, L. B. *Youth: The years from ten to sixteen.* New York: Harper & Row, 1956.

Kanner, L. *Childhood psychosis: Initial studies and new insights.* Washington, D.C.: V. H. Winston & Sons, 1973.

Maccoby, E., & Masters, J. C. Attachment and dependency. In Paul H. Mussen (Ed.), *Carmichael's manual of child psychology.* New York: John Wiley & Sons, 1970.

Mischel, W. Sex typing and socialization. In Paul H. Mussen (Ed.), *Carmichael's manual of child psychology.* New York: John Wiley & Sons, 1970.

Money, J., & Ehrhardt, A. A. *Man & woman, boy & girl.* Baltimore: The Johns Hopkins University Press, 1972.

Park, C. *The siege.* New York: Harcourt, Brace, & World, 1967; Boston: Atlantic-Little, Brown, 1972.

Chapter 14 *

BEYOND ADOLESCENCE: AUTISTIC ADULTHOOD

Continuing Progress in Late Adolescence and Adulthood

Most autistic people show the form of their adult adjustment by early adolescence and make minimal social and intellectual progress thereafter. A few, however, continue to make progress that is gratifying to parents even though normality is not achieved.

Charlton at the age of 26 was quite different from what he was at 15 years of age and younger, when he was frequently negativistic, yelling and destructive. His father had this to say about his son's adult development:

> I was almost certain when he was younger that he would not bring any joy to any of us and that maybe we would have to put him away. Fortunately, when he was about 8 years old, my wife involved herself in some community affairs that took her mind off our troubles with Charlton. With some good household help and a day program, we managed to keep him at home. Then somewhere along the way he quieted down and became happier. Now my wife can give him little chores to do around the house. He still has his upset moments but nothing like before. Eventually, when we get old, he will have to live—I suppose in a nursing home—but my wife feels

*With contributions by Dr. David Park.

better about it because wherever he goes she thinks at least he can be happy.

Another boy at an age of 12 had continuing problems in school with inattention, unhappiness, and failure to achieve in school work at the level of his tested intelligence. His mother described how in late adolescence his mood brightened and he developed a drive to achieve both academically and in sports. His teachers reported how he caught up in his classroom work so that he finally graduated from high school. His high school program was geared for slow learners, but nevertheless, his achievements at the age of 19 years were much above those at 12 years, and his adult prognosis considerably improved.

How can we explain these late-blooming autistics? While their parents were supportive and diligent on their behalf, so were the parents of others who failed to make such progress. Any biological explanations would be guesswork. However, we do know that although the brain completes most of its biological growth by the age of about 15 to 16 years, some brain growth continues until the age of about 18, which is important for maturing of intelligence to its adult levels. After that time any increase in measured intelligence comes from continued learning and experience. The best guess is that those autistic people who show continuing intellectual, emotional, and social growth in late adolescence and adulthood probably have both a favorable biological and social matrix that allow them to make increasing use of their experiences. After all, the late blooming, normal adult is not too uncommon. Grandma Moses was well into her eighth decade of life when she started to create her series of remarkable paintings.

Charlton cannot be taken as typical. Nobody can. Autism exists in different degrees of severity and people make different adaptations to it, following the problem-solving strategies that nature or nurture have produced in them, until the spectrum of their characteristics is, within the severe limitations placed on them, a small replica of that of the rest of the world.

The High-Functioning Adult: Terry[1]

The high-functioning autistic adult sometimes gives us valuable insights into the autistic child. Terry, aged 21, speaking on his life and experiences before a meeting of the National Society for Autistic Children (1973), stressed the frustration of being unable to talk.

When I was 3 years old I felt awful because I could not talk and for that reason I screamed for hours when frustrated. I was becoming able to talk at 4½ years, but was not able to talk correctly, which also made me mad . . . A doctor once showed me a tape recorder and he and I recorded a two-sided conversation and played it back. I was fascinated but was disgusted to hear the poor sounds of speech on my side of the conversation compared with the doctor's words. This apparently made me wish I could talk as correctly as other people . . . I kept having funny stuff on my mind when I was little; I used to laugh out loud all the time too . . . one thing that made me giggle a lot that I remember clearly, when I was 8 years old some funny thing went through my mind about a record player . . . I called it the milk record player because it didn't play records, it played milk. That sounds like kid stuff but I was of the age for it.

At the time he spoke Terry had been employed for 3 years in an electric firm but had recently lost his job. While looking for another he was being helped by a local mental health rehabilitation center.

Similar retrospective narratives by other autistic people with formerly severe behavioral and cognitive problems might have a valuable research purpose in distinguishing the autistic experience from that belonging to other forms of disability.

Self-Assessment: Mr. A.[2]

Although it cannot be emphasized too often that autistic people differ among themselves almost as widely as the normal population, there are some difficulties of social orientation that seem to be almost universal. The following interview with a self-aware and articulate man is a good illustration. The case of Mr. A., now in his fourth decade of life, illustrates how poor emotional control and inability to read the nuances of social situations override the influence of his superior intelligence. He has difficulty holding a job, and he has continuing problems in starting and maintaining friendships. In an interview, Mr. A. described in vivid detail his social problems. "I lack intuitive capacity . . . which makes it difficult to perceive the subtleties that other people find easy . . . I tried to learn on a conceptual basis what different kinds of situations called for." Unfortunately, Mr. A. said he was only partially successful, and he felt he suffered continuing social rejection. He believed that professionals have failed the autistic adult who makes much progress but stops short of normal social understanding. He said:

When the autistic child gets through the early stages of treatment that the professionals are now concentrating on, there is a long and hard road ahead of him; that is, after he has learned to wash himself, to talk, to not wet his pants, not to scream.

Mr. A. told of bitterness and humiliation when he found a young woman who was not sincere in an invitation.

She invited me to visit her. Well, when I went to see her, she couldn't have been less interested, and her attitude seemed to be "What the hell are you doing here?" I'm still struggling with the rejection problem. Not so long ago it was complete rejection without exception and I was in a hopeless situation. People would say then "Oh, you're too selfish. Try being less selfish and people will like you more . . ." People have to maintain the self-concept of being compassionate people, and that is a rationalization for not getting involved . . . They use meaningless pleasantries but aren't really interested . . . .

Interviewer: Tell me about your feelings when you first started being aware of people as people to relate to.

Well, of course after age 5 and after I started first grade, I was relating to other people, but from age 2 to 5 I did as much screaming as any of them. From school on though, I was just as much of a handful for my parents to handle as the more severe cases. The only difference was that their aspirations for me were a little bit higher than the aspirations for some of the others. Like, I met one autistic who is still screaming and nonverbal at age 20. His mother said that with the greatest of effort, he might some day live in a halfway house. So the difference as far as my parents were concerned was in the level of aspirations, but it was really no less of a struggle for my parents than for the parents of that other young man.

Interviewer: How do you feel you were a handful? In what ways?

Well, in the sense of at first, in grade school, it was the matter of the other kids being able to do me a bad turn, and I tried to put my case to the authorities. No one would listen to me, then I'd get more enraged, and start behaving very badly. Well, you know that's the problem the blacks had before the civil rights movement. They were people whom others could feel superior to, people to whom others could assign the jobs that no one else wanted to do, people they could lash out at with impunity. Well, that was what I was up against from 6th grade on.

Interviewer: Do you feel that other children picked on you? "Yes." Did adults do this too?

Yes, later on, adults did it too, and well, like just last summer for instance, I was out on the road. I stopped in a bar to make a phone call and somebody who was entertaining the people with the guitar said to me, "Ah, you're so cute!" and I said to him, "Shut up over there!" and he chased me out with an iron pipe. I got into my car just in time, and then he began hitting my front windshield with that pipe and fortunately that windshield didn't break. What enraged me there was the same thing that enraged me back in 6th grade, that I could be lashed out at with impunity and nobody cared.

Interviewer: When people have said these things to you, have you had any occasion to try to use humor to answer them, or haven't you learned this kind of response?

Sometimes, a little bit, later. But not at that time, not unless I thought by doing so I could get a sympathetic hearing from somebody.

Interviewer: Does humor come easily to you, or is it difficult? "When I'm angry, it's difficult, of course." How are things going on your job?

Oh, pretty well. Now, for instance, I seem to get along with the top people in the organization, and as for the other people, it's sort of the usual kind of office situation of superficial courtesies, and well, there are some cross moments. The situation leaves a bit to be desired, but I'm so glad to be going somewhere. I'm so glad to be off dead center, really, that it hardly occurs to me to even complain about it too much, except during a few angry moments.

Interviewer: Then it's the social relationships you're talking to me about now. How about the actual work itself?

Well, as for the work itself, I seem to be very good at it. You know that autistic children in some cases are incredibly brilliant, and for those who have gotten far enough along to take a job, they find they are very loyal to their employers because they are very grateful to be employed, and are able to give themselves completely to their job.

Interviewer: How about your use of language? You speak and use words very well. Do you remember a time when you had problems understanding abstractions?

Not really. As a matter of fact, some of the people at the National Society for Autistic Children convention were intrigued by that, and were especially intrigued that I had even learned foreign languages.

Mr. A. and the interviewer had a conversation about low-functioning autistic children, and Mr. A. went on:

> The professionals seem to be concentrating on helping the low-functioning ones, but there hasn't been much done to help the high-functioning ones live in the community and maintain their dignity . . . . That's my immediate problem for myself. And as more of these low-functioning ones get through the developmental stages which people like you are trying to bring them to, that will be their concern too. And so I think it might be well to at least start laying the ground work for organizations to help them; of course I can talk for hours about how someone can live with his own problem, how others should see him, how other people should relate to him, and deal with him. I have written a part of what might be considered a book, and of course when people show interest in what I've written, it will encourage me to write more.

Interviewer: Well, I'd be very interested in reading whatever you'd like to share with me because I know a few youngsters who are coming up, not yet grown, but I still try to get help for them and their parents, and I can see some of them struggling with the same problems that you are talking about.

> I understand from the National Society for Autistic Children that there are quite a few high-functioning and intermediate functioning ones. When I first made my acquaintance with the organization, they were completely uninterested in helping me. Then, a little while after I got my job and had been working at it for a month or so, that was when this last annual convention came up and they wanted me to be on the panel, which was quite a switch from their previous refusal to give me any kind of help or recognition whatsoever.

Interviewer: You've noticed that people often do change over time and have changes of heart or changes of goals.

> And so, as I see some concrete evidence that that was a genuine change and not just another pleasantry, when I see people in the organization showing levels of interest in me that previously were not shown, or if people like you show interest in what I've written, that would give me the encouragement to go on.

Interviewer: I would like you to continue to write, because, you know, it's not only a grown-up autistic who has these problems, but other adult mental patients often find the same kind of rejection. One of their own talking about it can be quite useful to them. They'll listen harder to somebody who has been there than to somebody who has merely looked on.

> On the other hand, I've been on a psychiatric ward a couple of times and found that the other patients there made more fun of me than people on the outside world, so ... whether they'd really consider me one of them, I don't know. Those mental patients had girl friends and I don't.

Interviewer: And this eats on you?

> Oh, sure, because it still is a case of nobody being willing even to give me a chance to show what I can do. I know as a matter of fact from one puppy love affair that I had at age 12 that I'm capable of taking pleasure in pleasing a woman. I remember when I took this one out, we both ordered the same thing. There was only one portion left. I let her have it because I got a greater enjoyment from bringing forth that smile on her face than from having the portion that I wanted. Now, I feel, that if some woman would give me a chance she'd find that I perhaps have a higher form of love to offer.

Mr. A. ended the interview with a discussion of how he had recently made two good friends.

> You've heard, I think, of the people who've been in a concentration camp and then can never trust anybody. You can imagine that I had suffered from the same thing. A while back I lived in a sort of a communal household with O. and H. and another young man. You know, for a long time I didn't really believe they had genuine friendship to offer me. Finally when the summer was over and they invited me to visit them in their home far away, then I realized that I really had a couple of good friends. I only realized it as the summer went on, because due to my suspicions I was ugly to them at times, but they always went out of their way to show me that nothing had changed between me and them. And for that reason you will always hear me say that they are my two best friends.

The Institutionalized Adult: Bobby[1]

A case study of a child has a time dimension little more than that of a snapshot. On reviewing the life-span of an adult, one can begin to see autism in its full extent. Because Kanner identified the syndrome only in 1943, we merely have glimpses of the life histories of autistic people born long before that date, but it will complete the picture of what autism means to the sufferer and his family if we present, with necessary lack of detail, some cases of long standing disability.

Bobby was born in 1940 to a professionally trained father and a mother who later completed a teacher's education. While Bobby never has shown behaviorally that he can hear any sound, a galvanic skin resistance test indicated that his bearing is apparently unimpaired. In addition Bobby has insensitivity to pain and has not cried since infancy. In adulthood, if a bee stings, he grunts and goes for the baking soda. He was toilet-trained at the usual age. At age 5, after 1 year in residence at a school for the deaf, he was returned home as "unreachable." His mother then returned to school, earned a Master's Degree in special education and subsequently she started a class of special children in which to educate her son.

She found him negative in his response to the world but physically strong and active. He could do difficult jigsaw puzzles easily and quickly but had no sense of the symbolic meaning of toys. To him a toy was simply a thing, without any bearing on the rest of his life, to be put into a box and put away. His life was full of compulsive routines. When he came downstairs he would go back up and then down again a dozen times. When he went through a door he would open and shut it endlessly. He developed no conversational speech but learned to read and acquired a vocabulary of 1,000 to 2,000 words, mostly nouns, referring to specific objects. Currently he reads and understands simple information quickly and clearly but has never tried to communicate with another person, either by words or by writing. To express his needs he grunts and points. He is skillful with hammer, screwdriver, and electric sewing machine, but not to make anything. Just as in childhood he did not use toys to simulate reality, he does not use any of these instruments to shape it. The screwdriver means as little to him as the toy car.

Bobby's father died when Bobby was 31. In adulthood the family grew smaller with the other children leaving and his father dying. Bobby's life in his fourth decade became a series of sterile routines. When he was young he had often enjoyed visitors; later he endlessly rearranged the furniture and things in the yard. In a mute way he became increasingly dictatorial and compulsive. Finally his mother, approaching 70, placed him in a conscientiously run institution where he undergoes behavior-modification treatment but shows no progress, and in fact probably is in regression. He has made no significant progress in any direction since he was in his teens.

Bobby's sex drive is low and he does not distinguish between men and women. His behavior becomes steadily more ingrained and repetitive. He understands the watch and the calendar but money means nothing to him. He writes words to show their patterns and similarities but not to convey meaning, though he can fill in a single missing word in a sentence.

For almost 40 years Bobby's family tried to help him. They relocated in the country and his mother had to forego other careers while she and his father worked hard and successfully to provide a life of activity and social contacts for Bobby and the other two children. What is there to show for it? For Bobby, little. He is capable of caring for himself in an institutional setting; that is about all. But his family reports they have one great consolation: "We know we tried."

For outsiders who have not had a handicapped child in the family, such knowledge may appear to be a hollow victory considering the sacrifices each family member has to make. Not all parents can make such sacrifices. Not all brothers and sisters on reaching adulthood look kindly on their childhood or on their autistic sibling. Ken's younger sister said this:

> I know it's probably selfish but I'm resentful of everything I had to give up as a child for him. My mother won't admit it but I think she has to say she's glad she tried so hard. I think it was a waste. She and my father are separated largely because she still wants all of the energy and family money to go into a person who is 22 and not able to speak.

A Functioning Woman in Her Mid-40s: Jean[1]

She was described when she was a child by Erik Erikson (1950) but is now a woman of 45, living at home with her mother. When she was 6, Erikson observed that her eyes were "like peaceful islands within the anxious grimace of her face" while she ran through the house, uncovering beds to find the pillows. When she found them she hugged them and talked to them in a hoarse whisper. Of her avoidance of contact with him, he wrote, "She focused on me negatively."

Jean's mother was in bed with tuberculosis when Jean was 9 to 13 months old, and Jean was kept out of the sickroom by a nurse who was stern though good-natured. When at last Jean could visit her mother again, she was no longer the normal appearing baby she had been. She was afraid of the pattern of a rug, of a ball rolling on the floor, of the sound of crackling paper, of a bit of dirt. She learned to walk and to feed herself at the usual time but "gradually became sad and silent." She loved only instruments and machines: the egg-beater, the vacuum cleaner, radiators. She smiled at them, whispered to them, and hugged them. She was uninterested in people as wholes, but was fascinated by parts of their bodies, especially those ordinarily not on view. By age 6 she could read and write, though with little comprehension.

At 5½ she was placed in a residential school. Reunited with her family after a separation of a year, she began to relax and play. For the first time she used a toy dog as a toy: "Go to sleep, dog, stay under covers, shut your eyes, have to spank you, dog." She taught herself to play several tunes on the xylophone and enjoyed her family's praise as she played for them. Later she taught herself to play on the piano the first page of a Beethoven sonata "with understanding and authority," but made little progress in music beyond that point.

When Jean was 11 her parents moved near a well-known psychiatric clinic. There she lived in the children's ward and received psychoanalytic therapy for 18 years. During a trial year spent at home at age 18 she was often violent, scratching her mother so as to leave permanent scars.

At age 28, Jean was transferred to a state hospital. Returning the next week, her parents found that she had repetitively turned on lights at night and had been moved to a "back ward" where she remained for 4 years, "heavily drugged." Having no use for speech she virtually lost it, and the parents believed that the hospital staff never knew that she could read and write.

When Jean was 33 her mother used Social Security aid for the totally disabled to hire university students to help care for her in the home. The mother felt that Jean's life "began again." Although her mannerisms were, and remain, strange, her aggressiveness had moderated sufficiently that the students could teach crafts to her. Later, as she grew used to them, they took her into the community.

Jean, now in her mid-40s, is small and serious, with an intent gaze and halting speech adequate enough to meet her immediate needs. Her other infrequent conversational attempts are bizarre and repetitive. She rides city buses alone, and with sufficient encouragement makes jewelry. She sews her own clothes, cooks, and tends the garden. While her erratic behavior prevents placement in a group home, occasionally she visits friends for a few days. Recently her explosions of temper have returned and she is occasionally violent, but recently also she has suddenly started to paint. Her works, some literal and some impressionistic, are "beautiful and people buy them." Though she does not impress an observer as happy, she has partial control over her life and has achieved a degree of self-respect. Her recent achievement reminds us once again what a parent said, "We should never forget that even those quite severely affected can surprise us with their progress," even in their fourth and fifth decades of life.

A Functioning Man in His Late 30s: Mark[1]

The last case history is about Mark, one of the fortunate one-third of "schizophrenic children" reported in Bender's long-term study (1974) as having "adjusted more or less well to society." Mark has been selected for description because his was initially a classic, severe case of autism which has moderated greatly over the years.[3]

Even as an infant Mark held himself stiffly. He did not adjust comfortably in his mother's arms or demand any special attention. He started speaking in his second year, but only to express immediate needs. He reversed his pronouns, and distressed his parents by crying inconsolably for no apparent reason and by being unable to relate to other children. He was described as "hugging" other children but he did not know how to play with them.

At age 3 Mark developed intense anxiety and fears, biting his arms and household objects, and a psychiatrist was consulted. The symptoms became more severe until, at age 6, Mark was extremely anxious and unhappy and used virtually no speech. Even when his affliction was at its worst and his family was offered a prognosis so grim that they were urged to "put him away," he paid attention to music, recognized and remembered tunes, and put together complicated picture puzzles.

At age 6, after electroconvulsive treatments eliminated his anxiety and moderated his severe obsessive-compulsive symptoms, Mark began to learn. His first sign of intellectual awakening was an interest in dates. He recalled the dates of events in his life and described the weather on any given date. At age 7 he could give, instantaneously, as he still can, the day of the week corresponding to any given date. Mark currently describes how this is done, but it is almost inconceivable that anyone can go so quickly through the chain of reasoning he describes.

Also, at age 7 Mark was enrolled in a residential school where he learned neat habits, good manners and how to read and write. He wrote, and writes, English without sentence errors but with a choice of words which is not that of instinctive speakers of the language. According to his parents, "He speaks English the way we speak a learned foreign language."

From ages 10 to 16 years Mark was enrolled in a year-round residential program. Vocational-aptitude tests suggested training in office work, and this was begun. At 16 Mark could speak clearly, was somewhat ritualistic in his politeness, knew when to talk and when to be quiet, and showed in general a pleasant personality. He had learned to travel in his city and was ready for employment. Aided by a state vocational program he learned to type 60 words per minute and at 19 found a job in the supplies department of a manufacturing company. He was trustworthy with valuable materials and remembered the number of every order. Ten years later when the factory closed, Mark studied for the Civil Service examinations which he passed with high ratings. Currently he is a mail and supply clerk in a state office. He lives with his parents who have decided together that the comfort and security of this arrangement are worth more than a job which would make greater use of his talents.

Mark is studying the recorder. After initial difficulties in mastering rhythm, he has learned to transpose at sight into any key and enjoys ensemble playing with his friends, who are mostly handicapped people like himself. His friendships are affectionate and apparently deep but he shows no sexual urge. His understanding of human motivations remains at a simple level: He can recount the events of a film he has seen but has little insight into plot. His language is concrete, but he has little understanding of abstractions. His social life involves bowling and attendance at concerts and sporting events, about which he is knowledgeable.

Mark is now in his late 30s and his parents are still considering the future. While competent to take care of the mechanics of life, Mark is so "unsophisticated and gullible" that they hesitate to consider his living alone. Perhaps a devoted and responsible brother and sister will look after him; perhaps some pleasant and minimally supervised community for the handicapped can be found.

It would be idle to assume that Mark's improvement just happened. While most autistic adults remain disinterested in life, some, like Mark, acquire a steady and methodical determination and these people to some degree "make it." In Mark's case, the parents give credit primarily to his "relentless efforts to progress."

The Outlook for an Autistic Adult

Leo Kanner (1971) reported on the status of his 11 original cases when they were in their fourth decade of life. One had died suddenly of unknown causes in a state hospital at age 29, and two could not be located. Of the remaining eight, all but three lived in a state mental hospital where they participated marginally or not at all in structured activities. Two had self-help skills, but all were socially withdrawn or socially inept and at a low level of speech development. The two who functioned best held paying jobs where they performed well, and both had learned foreign languages. However, both stopped short of normality in social relationships, in ambition, and in ability to assume a life independent of their parents. One of his former patients lived in a foster home where he could perform some rather skilled chores. He could cut wood with a power saw, but without either speech or initiative he never held a paying job.

Thus, we see in the longest follow-up study yet on record that autistic adults show the same wide range in social and intellectual function as they did in preschool years. Unfortunately most remain in the low-functioning categories despite years of special schooling and therapy.

There is no evidence to show that autistic people have a different average length of life than normal groups, but since the subject remains as yet unstudied, we cannot know for sure. It seems clear that the adult life of most autistic people is neither fulfilling for the individuals nor productive for society. We must find a better treatment than is currently provided for them and their parents. We must find a prevention.

Until that day, we must strive as professionals to study and understand each individual and each family so that we can help them plan ahead in a way that will allow positive growth for each family member. We must be knowledgeable, open-minded, and compassionate, returning expressions of anxiety and anger with equanimity and patience. For their part, parents must give the professional time and candor so that (s)he can become knowledgeable about the help they can and cannot use. Each one of us has our own methods of coming to grips with sorrow and frustration. A professional can be of real use in such a complicated problem as autism that brings so much sorrow only if the parents will let the professional see the dimensions of their personalities. Also, for their part, parents must be willing to explore new ideas and new ways of looking at themselves and their child, not with the idea of hanging unusual amounts of guilt on themselves but with the idea of becoming stronger and more flexible.

Parents must also realize that not all of their guilt "comes from the doctor." In Chapter 10, I shared my observations how mothers come to the consultation room with much self-generated guilt. The task of both parents and the doctor is to find out what parental practices should and can be changed and how to free themselves of paralyzing guilt and anxiety. Only then can they begin the long task of caring for such a "different child" in a way that will be fair to themselves and their normal children.

Notes

[1] Verified case history contributed by Professor David Park.

[2] Mr. A. started to talk and use speech to communicate at the age of 5 years.

[3] The reader should note, however, that Mark had several splinter skills in preschool years which he never lost even when at his worst. It is from such high functioning groups that most of the better outcome cases originate.

REFERENCES

Bender, L. The family patterns of 100 schizophrenic children observed at Bellevue, 1935–1952. *Journal of Autism and Childhood Schizophrenia,* 1974, 4(4), 279–292.

Erikson, E. *Childhood and society.* New York: Norton, 1950, 1963.

Kanner, L. Follow-up study of eleven autistic children originally reported in 1943. *Journal of Autism and Childhood Schizophrenia,* 1971, 1(2), 119–145.

National Society of Autistic Children, *Proceedings of the 4th Annual Meeting,* Flint, Michigan, June, 1972. DHEW Publication No. (ADM)72-2, 1973.

Chapter 15 *

PERSPECTIVES ON PARENTS AND CHILDREN IN AUTISM

In this final chapter, I sketch what we know and don't know about autism and describe some of the most interesting and pressing prospective avenues for research. With Dr. David Park as a parent advocate, we present the parents' perceptions of the benefits that come from direct involvement in their child's therapy and supportive organizational activities as well as some of their basic needs to alleviate excessive hardship.

Perspectives On Our Knowledge About Autism

Parents of autistic children, as a group, do not have extreme personality traits such as coldness, obsessiveness, social anxiety, or rage. No specific parental defects in acceptance, nurturing, warmth, feeding, and tactile and general stimulation of their infants have been identified. They show no more signs of mental illness than parents of other children with organic or emotional disorders. Twin and other sibling studies support the idea of some genetic inheritance in some autistic children which may not produce the complete syndrome of autism but mainly the language-cognitive components. The foregoing conclusions were developed by McAdoo and DeMyer (1977) in a review of recent research related to family factors in autism.

*With contributions by Dr. David Park.

245

Type and location of brain defect. The best available evidence to date strongly supports a neurobiological irregularity in the central nervous system that accounts for the language and perceptual motor deficiencies found in autistic people (DeMyer, 1975; Hingtgen & Bryson, 1972). In 60 to 80% of them we found pathological EEG tracings. We also found a greater number of soft and hard neurological signs than in normal children. Such findings show us that the central nervous system has suffered some kind of untoward event but do not allow us to define its exact nature. Because it is not yet possible to study directly the functions of the central nervous system, our knowledge of the site and type of brain dysfunction must be inferential. The parts of the brain most seriously affected in most cases seem to be the language and auditory-speech centers and certain visual-motor connections. Because gross motor performance such as walking and stair climbing is so often intact (although generally below age level), we would infer that the motor centers of the brain are less seriously affected.

In most cases the nature of the brain dysfunction is probably static; that is, a primary traumatic event caused certain brain cells to die or not to develop at all or to maldevelop; then the traumatic event passed leaving an imperfect brain but also one that was capable of anatomic growth (myelination and dendritic branching) except for replacing the dead or nonexistent brain cells. Hence we see in most autistic children, as in most nonpsychotic brain-dysfunctional children, a steady increase in mental age as time progresses. In most children this growth does not accelerate sufficiently to allow them to catch up to normality. When anatomical brain growth ceases at about age 18 years, as it does in everybody, whether organically normal or abnormal, then we see the end of this progress in mental age due to anatomical brain growth. By the age of 12 to 15 years, we can clearly see the eventual adult outcome of an autistic child, and in about 97% of cases it stops short of normality. As detailed in the following section the prognosis for about three-quarters of the autistic population is either poor or very poor.

Prognosis. When a clinician makes a prognosis for an autistic child, the reactions vary from one parent to another. Parents of younger children tend to be considerably more optimistic than those of adolescents. In earlier years, even when symptoms are at their worst, many parents refuse to abandon hope; this nourishes their courage and determination to persevere. But in later years a certain resignation sets in, and many parents become interested in programs and organizations focused on the retarded rather than on autism. As mentioned earlier, clinical experience indicates that most autistic children face a poor future in adolescence and adulthood. They make unsatisfactory social adjustment and verbal expression remains poor. They do not succeed in school and do not become self-sustaining. While a small minority ultimately make a normal or quasi-normal adjustment to life, the vast majority, about 75%, spend their later years in institutions or in virtually complete dependence on their parents.

It should be noted that in a few cases of moderate severity, transformation can take place as the older autistic continues to learn. There are speech milestones which the normal child passes so quickly that only a trained observer notices them at all. Later, perhaps by many years, the autistic person may pass them too (if he gets that far), slowly and much delayed, but in much the same sequence as a normal child does. Pronouns and verb tenses may begin to straighten out in late teens or early twenties. In a few cases, rapid unexpected advances are also possible as in the case of a boy who had no useful speech whatever until age 15 when in a few months he developed language that met his immediate needs.

Knowledge of the specific factors which predict a good or poor outcome might facilitate management of the child and counselling of the parents. For example, if early identification of autism correlates with a good outcome, every effort should be made to obtain early diagnosis. So far we have no hint that such early diagnosis can change the outcome to any great degree. In the future, research may locate causes. In that happy event, early diagnosis plus knowledge of the cause in a given case may make all the difference between a good and poor outcome. Meantime, parents and professionals alike will have to make do with the following knowledge about making a prognosis early in the life of an autistic person.

According to Rutter and Lockyer (1967) speech and intelligence quotients were the best predictors of outcome in autistic psychosis. The exact predictive ranges and value of other measures, however, remained unknown in their study.

In order to learn the best indices for how an autistic child will fare later in work or school, the same kinds of measurements should be made at both initial and at follow-up evaluations. Our study at the Clinical Research Center was the first one to use this principle in studying the course of autism. In following 126 autistic children (mean age 12 years), using 36 subnormal children as controls (DeMyer, Barton, DeMyer, Norton, Allen, & Steele, 1973), we found the best predictor of functional capacity in a work-school setting was a child's rating at intake. Performance IQs and severity of illness were next to best predictors. In other words, the children with higher performance and fewer symptoms at intake performed better at follow-up 6 years later than the low functioning, severely ill children measured at the same time periods. Furthermore, treatment did not change these observations materially except perhaps in the higher functioning group. In the lowest functioning autistics (initial IQs below 40), the outcome was without exception poor.

We also compared our own findings on outcome with those of three other

Table 64. Comparison of 4 Follow-up Studies[1]

Outcome variable	Percent distribution of autistic (psychotic) population by study			
	DeMyer	Rutter	Eisenberg	Kanner
Overall outcome				
Good and very good	10	14	5	18
Fair	16	25	22	27
Poor and very poor	74	61	73	55
Speech				
Normal	6	16		
Useful (communicative)	49	46	51	
Develop useful after age 5	11	11		
Worsening	11	11		
None	32			
Education				
Age appropriate (within 2 years)	10			9
Regular school (2 or more years)	70	2		
Other variables				
Gainful employment	3	2[4]		18
Loss of autism	5	14		
Long-term institutionalization	42	44	54	54
N of autistic (psychotic) subjects	126	63	63	11
Mean CA at follow-up (years)	12	15	15	35

Notes:
[1] Sources which detail the diagnostic criteria and procedures are identified in the Reference section on page 261.
[2] Less than 50%.
[3] Over 15 years of age.
[4] Over 16 years of age.
[5] 20 to 75% depending on diagnostic group.

investigators whose follow-up studies lent themselves to meaningful comparison (Table 64). The three studies (Rutter & Lockyer's, Eisenberg's, and ours) showed fairly close agreement about the poor chance of the autistic or early-psychotic child to become completely normal. Only 1 to 2% improved to a point where there was little difference between them and children who had never been diagnosed as autistic, and only 5 to 15% reached the borderline of normality. The three studies also agreed that the proportion of autistic children with a fair to poor outcome is high. Thus, about 16 to 25%

have a fair outcome, and 60 to 75% a poor to very poor outcome. Although there were differences in the authors' definitions of good, fair, and poor, the similarities are remarkable. Kanner (1973) did not rate his follow-up subjects with respect to overall outcome. However, his case vignettes indicated that one could roughly estimate that 18% had a fairly good outcome, 27% a fair one, and 55% poor.

Since the prognosis that parents receive depends also on a clinician's competence and his predisposition to share it with them at a given time, the prognostic "verdicts," which most parents perpetually seek, frequently prove to be somewhat noncommittal and elusive. Given the uncertainty of the outcome in some cases, it is probably premature to formulate a definite prognosis for a very young child. However, for the lower and middle functioning autistic adolscents and adults whose parents continue to cling to the hope of "full recovery," it is wise for a thoughtful professional gradually to prepare and confront the parents with a dim prognosis. Even at an early date responsible people looking into the future with an autistic child have to make choices: where to live, in what size house, and they may need to make these choices while balancing in their minds the question of whether the child will be in a residential institution—and where that would be—or live at home. These are difficult choices, and the autistic member of the family is far from being the only one to be taken into account. The clinician owes it to these parents to be very clear in his own mind as to the distinction between evasion and honest doubt.

Need for additional follow-up studies. The need for such studies, partly to advance our ability to formulate prognoses, has been consistently emphasized by Leo Kanner (1973):

> ... [our effort] is an attempt to set up a sample for follow-along and follow-up studies hopefully to be conducted in clinical and research centers as the intervals between childhood and adulthood of autistic patients keep lengthening ... Continual follow-up or even better follow-along, will prove in the long run to be of great importance ... There has been a hodge-podge of theories, hypotheses, and speculations, and there have been many valiant, well-motivated attempts at alleviation awaiting eventual evaluation. It is expected, with good justification, that a next 30- or 20-year follow-up of other groups of autistic children will be able to present a report of newly obtained factual knowledge and material for a more hopeful prognosis ...

Autistic persons whose intelligence makes accelerated progress should be intensively studied neurobiologically. Is the progress due to the amelioration of a metabolic or allergic problem, for example, or is it due to the anatomical growth of subsidiary neurological pathways which then can be substituted for the primary lost pathways? The new brain localization techniques mentioned in the second following section could make follow-up studies very valuable for elucidating the neurological system's involvement in the improvement of certain symptoms. Multiple factors including training and therapy may be responsible for accelerated intellectual progress. However, since such progress so seldom happens in preschool children whose IQs are 40 or below, I think it most likely that the anatomical growth of subsidiary pathways in the higher-functioning autistic individuals accounts for most cases of accelerated progress. We would logically expect, and additional follow-up studies may substantiate this, that low IQ is a sign of more extensive neurological damage that would impede later development of extensive nerve tracts.

Pressing need to study causes. The history of medicine contains examples of accidental discoveries or strokes of genius which in one step have changed the entire clinical picture of a disease. In the present state of research on severe brain disorders, however, it is both more prudent and more realistic to rely on persistence and expanded efforts to achieve, in good time, the same goal. Clearly, our most pressing need is to discover the causes and prevent the onset of brain disorders because treatment, as now practiced, is not effective. Searches for efficacious treatment, both biological and psychological, should continue however, and we may find a treatment that helps certain kinds of autistic children. There is evidence, as in other learning disabilities, that any agent capable of injuring the central nervous system may be at fault in individual cases of autism. Viral diseases during gestation including maternal rubella (German measles), genetic inheritance, maternal alcohol consumption, birth trauma, postnatal "silent" brain infections, and dehydration during severe diarrhea all can be suspected. These putative causes must be prevented as they result in irreversible damage to brain cells.

New ways to study brain function. New techniques by radioisotope methods can localize which areas of the brain function with certain body activities (Lassen, Niels, Ingvar, & Skinhoj, 1978). For the first time it is possible to think we soon may be able to localize the points of neurological defect in the brain of autistic and other brain dysfunctional individuals.

Recently a line of inquiry into brain processing of speech and other sounds may, if used with autistic people, give us more insight into the brain location of their auditory processing difficulties. Audiologists such as Willeford (1977), Keith (1977) and others have devised tests using auditory evoked potentials that are beginning to uncover why certain children, even those who have average to above IQs, learn poorly in school. These tests can uncover defects at any one of the several auditory processing centers in the brain. Certain remediation techniques are being tried. Hopefully in at least middle- and high-functioning autistics those testing and treatment procedures may be of value. I advocate much research in the processing of auditory stimuli in all forms of learning disability in children. It is quite possible that some high-functioning autistic children who now develop fair to good language skills later in life could be helped at an early age by changing the ways that speech is taught to them. For example, some children may need to have sound blocked from one ear as they cannot use or "process" sounds heard by both ears. Others may need to have all distracting sounds eliminated. This research is in its infancy but shows much promise.

Possible extent of neurological dysfunction. Many features of autism that need to be explained can only be conjectured about in our current state of knowledge. As we learned from interviewing parents, the vaso-vegetative functions of most autistic children are abnormal, especially during the early years of life. These disturbances include sleeplessness, dietary peculiarities, less than normal caloric intake, and digestive disturbances. The most parismoniuos explanation, or guess, would be that the damage to the central nervous system is usually so extensive that it extends even to the vaso-vegetative system. Supporting this view is the finding that the nonpsychotic subnormal control children in our study had a similar incidence of the same dysfunction. The first year of life was the best in this regard, both for autistic individuals and for the handicapped control groups. While such finding makes it even more likely that the causes of disability are alike in the two groups, it means that explanations for vegetative symptoms may come from factors outside of neurological disregulation which improve as the child's nervous system matures.

Possibility of metabolic or allergy problems. Not all traumatic events have to result in a fixed and static lesion. Some autistic individuals may have a metabolic defect such as in serotonin metabolism or in other neurotransmitter systems. The relatively high incidence of constipation in our autistic population during early years of life should be investigated thoroughly. There may be some relation between constipation, mental subnormality, and dysfunction of thyroid and serotonin metabolism. As Coleman and Hur (1973) pointed out, cases of infantile hypothyroidism are often marked by mental abnormality and constipation. In Down's syndrome (previously called Mongolism) serotonin abnormalities and constipation are common. Well designed sleep research studies, coupled with metabolic studies early in life, might tell us more, not only about basic causation but about the relationship between the highly prevalent disturbance of sleep and any possible metabolic disturbances.

Dietary peculiarities and decreased caloric intake also should be studied early in life when these disturbances evidently are most severe. Possible causes of dietary irregularities include improper absorption and food allergies. The autistic infant or child may attempt to limit or avoid certain foods that are unmetabolized or abnormally metabolized or that cause digestive discomfort. One mother reported to me that when she kept her autistic son from eating "allergenic" foods, he was less hyperactive and in better emotional control. In this family, two siblings have mild learning disabilities and allergies; the mother was late in talking and believes herself to have poor emotional control when she eats foods to which she is "allergic." If there is a metabolic defect or specific allergies, could we ameliorate the functional and intellectual disability by counteracting the defects in the first year as can now be done in cretinism and phenylketonuria?

Sensory inattention. Sensory functions are also disturbed in a significant percentage of autistic children. Hyperacusis or oversensitivity to sound is found in about 42%, as born out by parental reports of discomfort from or fear of certain high-pitched or loud sounds. Hyperacusis can follow lesions at various levels in the auditory system, including defects in the middle and inner ear, auditory nerves, the central auditory pathways or in the reaction of the individual to sound. It can have an organic or psychological basis. The complaint of an exaggerated reaction to sound also is common in nonpsychotic brain impaired children if the examiner will specifically ask the mother, "Does your child show any unusual responses to sounds?"

Inattention to pain sensations and failure to notice distant objects are reported. While we can invoke various explanations for these phenomena, we do not know the exact neurobiological mechanisms involved. Vestibular function in autistics has been extensively studied by Ornitz, Forsythe, and de la Pena (1973), who have a theory that vestibular dysfunction underlies most of the symptomatology of autism. We might also see vestibular dysfunction as just another sign of a disordered central nervous system with difficulty in many forms of integration. We need a research program in which all sensory modalities are studied as directly as possible, such as exploring cerebral evoked responses to visual and auditory stimuli and connections between language thought process and auditory perception as begun by Small (1971). Research on sensory systems and perception is tedious, time consuming work full of pitfalls, especially with young, noncooperative, inattentive subjects such as autistic children. Nevertheless, it should be pursued.

Possible neurological basis of social intelligence. We need to learn much more about autistic social disabilities. In some measure we can account for them by the poor communication skills, both verbal and nonverbal. We know that verbal disabilities in autistic individuals exist on a continuum from moderately severe to extremely severe. We also know that the lower the verbal intelligence, the lower the social skills and the more profound the social isolation. However, I have frequently seen individuals with an IQ of 40, for example, who are friendly and relating and in no sense considered autistic.

How does the non-autistic child with IQ 40 differ in neurological function from the autistic with the same IQ? In the absence of evidence that autistic parents handled their autistic infants less competently than parents of nonpsychotic subnormal children, I am tempted to think that the distinctive autistic social disabilities may be based in part on a particular type of neurobiological dysfunction. Other evidence gives some support to this idea. For example, Mr. A., Mark, and Aaron all "outgrew" their language disabilities, and yet retained social disabilities. While none was socially isolated, their social "intelligence" remained on a much lower level than their verbal skills. Conversely, a number of autistic children in our study improved greatly in social skills but retained severe language disabilities. These observations suggest that social "intelligence" and verbal abstract intelligence may have a related but partially separate neurological basis which should be explored for the advancement of our grossly inadequate knowledge of these matters.

Attention deficits. As the years have passed I have become increasingly aware of the significance of attention deficit in the autistic. While clinicians usually attempt to explain it on a psychological basis, there is much evidence that the attention mechanism has at least one separate neuroanatomical locus in the reticular activating system. As in other neurobiologically handicapped children, attention deficit in autistic children exists on a continuum of severity from mild to severe. Attention generally improves with time but tends to remain subnormal. In the normal child, attention capacity also increases with age. In the autistic child, attention powers may improve at a rate different from that of language improvement. For example, Aaron's continuing attention deficit did not cause him much trouble in mathematics because he was so strong in that subject. He could catch mathematic instructions efficiently and quickly. In other matters such as working with his hands where his perceptual motor handicaps demanded concentrated attentiveness, Aaron was less successful. In fact, attention disability remained a major handicap for him in everything but mathematics.

In connection with attention deficits, I often hear from teachers that certain autistic children could learn more or score higher on intelligence tests "if they would just pay more attention." In most cases, the teacher or parent assumes that inattentiveness is a voluntary act, a sign of negativism. In other words, if the child were more motivated, he could and would attend. We must remember that attention has a neurological basis. Since there is so much evidence of other neurological dysfunction in autistic children, it is logical to assume that attention difficulties also may be due in large part to organic dysfunction. My psychologist colleagues remind me that attention is a part of general intelligence. Like all intellectual functions, attention can be shaped by environmental forces as well as anatomical ones. We learned that when an autistic person is given tasks that he can master, motivation and attention improve. Nevertheless, the underlying neurologically based attention deficit may persist and prevent him from making good use of other intellectual strengths. Attention in autism has been neglected and should be intensively studied.

Abnormal speech. In connection with improvement in language, I have observed that seldom do all elements of language become normal in those 15% of autistic people who progress in accelerated fashion but stop somewhat short of normality. There are autistics whose vocabularies contain many words but whose understanding and expression of verbal abstraction remains below average. Harold, for example, had excellent auditory memory and developed adequate powers of attention for school work so that with hard work he finished the eighth grade in a normal classroom. He memorized long passages of literary works and was thought capable of attending a high school for advanced college-bound students. The high school principal called me at the end of the first semester to talk about Harold. He was not able to understand the meaning of literature or of history, and his performance in abstract mathematics was low. Examination papers contained word-for-word quotations of the text books but seldom answered the questions. The principal concluded that Harold "was not able to think." After the second semester, Harold was transferred to a general high school program where he earned passing grades. Harold retained a rapid staccato speech which conveyed little expressive intonation.

Mr. A. and Aaron both grew to think at least as well as their normal age mates in mathematics and in language arts, and yet both retained elements of abnormal speech. Mr. A., for example, spoke in a slow measured way, almost as if he were reading a passage from a book. His speech lacked expressive changes in intonation and rhythm. Nearly all autistic people who develop conversational speech retain this kind of speech (technically called dysprosody). While disturbances in speech rhythm, tone, and emphasis may be mildly or not at all handicapping in and of themselves, they may be the hallmarks of other defects of integration that are connected with the lack of emotional control and the social ineptness that plagues the adolescent and adult lives of high-functioning autistics.

Future Research Centers

Where and how should future reserach on autism be conducted? I strongly advocate that society establish several centers in the country for the study of all learning and intellectual disabilities in infancy and childhood. While much valuable work has been done by investigators using small populations of autistic children and studying small or isolated aspects of the problem, the questions that we now must answer demand large populations and teams of investigators. For example, it seems clear that many forms of learning disability including autism start with the genes and intrauterine insults. It is practically impossible to study this time of development after the fact. We must begin with early pregnancy to study virus illnesses contracted by the mother, dietary effects, and maternal metabolism. Effects of troubled labors and deliveries must be studied on the spot. That all-important first year of life must be monitored to see the effects on parents of having an abnormally developing infant. Both in nonpsychotic subnormal and in autistic children parents perceive a change for the worse in the social-emotional development as well as in perceptual-motor development. We must monitor that change. What physical and environmental events accompany it? Is the "change" a function of parental perception in some cases? Is physical illness or metabolic irregularity responsible in such or other cases?

We must study the initial development of sleeping and eating problems. Traditionally, these are viewed as signs of "bad parenting." I think we must review these concepts especially since we found an equal number of these problems in both the autistic and nonpsychotic subnormal groups. In fact, every sign of disturbed physiology and disordered neurobiological dysfunction was found in about the same concentration in these two different diagnostic groups, suggesting that they have highly similar underlying biological problems. The important question to answer is why one group is socially isolated and the other has a social age commensurate with the overall general intelligence.

In view of the fact that so many investigators have insisted that autism is an entity separate from other forms of learning disability, both general and specific, it behooves us to prove or disprove this belief. We can do so only by studying autistic infants and children alongside other groups such as aphasic, cerebral-palsied, minimally brain-damaged, mentally retarded, and normal. Ritvo and Freeman (1977) point out how far we have to go to understand the basics of biochemistry and neurological function in all groups of children, both healthy and handicapped.

Learning disability centers would need to have at least a three-generation charter, for we need to study the genetics of all intellectual and learning disabilities and follow many lives from gestation through adulthood to learn about prevention and the best programs of management. The cost of such centers would be in the high millions, but in the long run they would save society more in monetary terms that we now pay. The savings in human productivity and sense of personal achievement would be incalculable. We could then turn more attention to the education and upbringing of all of our youth, including normal children who in our present educational and cultural system are woefully inadequate in arithmetic and score on the average 14 general IQ points lower than their parents' generation. Each child's birthright in this rich country should be a well-functioning central nervous system and the services of professional groups that can provide all children and their parents with the best that educational and health sciences have to offer.

Selected Accomplishments

While the many goals for research in autism tend to emphasize the relative paucity of significant gains, much has happened in the field since Kanner described his 11 patients in 1943. The *Journal of Autism and Childhood Schizophrenia* (its name has been recently changed to *Journal of Autism and Developmental Disorders*), together with other periodicals, brings us the evidence of intensive study in many fields of research related to autism. The investigators work in dozens of more or less specialized centers of the kind that simply did not exist a few years ago. Here and there, some parents and their children are the direct beneficiaries of their activities; but the major accomplishments can be traced to the development of parental self-help in the form of constructive participation as cotherapists and members of a dynamic supportive organization.

Parents as cotherapists. It took a while to live down the old superstition that parents are not to be trusted either to understand their children and evaluate their progress or to aid in their therapy and education. Common sense suggests now, and might have suggested a decade ago, that the circumstances of the clinical examination are not ideal for getting to know about a psychotic child, and that as observers, parents may well make up in familiarity and interest what they lack in expertise. Seven years ago, Schopler and Reichler (1972) published a study in which parents, especially those of severely affected children, were shown to give estimates of their child's function in all areas of development which coincided closely with conclusions based on standard psychological testing.

Schopler and Reichler also found that it was possible to train parents to be effective cotherapists for their own children. The method used (Schopler & Reichler, 1971) involved initial observations in which the staff learned the difficulties parents were having, followed by a training program directed at reducing these difficulties. Parents were instructed in the principles of behavior modification and allowed to observe through a one-way screen a therapist's work with their child, while accompanied by a consultant who helped them to see what was going on. It is worth quoting the advantages claimed for this form of parental training:

(1) It avoids the mystique and unfounded authority of the therapist who reports to parents from only private observations of the child.

(2) It guards the parents against recommendations which are more easily made than carried out.

(3) It provides stimulation stemming from constructive competition between parents and therapists and also affords a realistic opportunity for parents to use the therapist for modeling behavior.

(4) Direct demonstrations have a more immediate impact than verbal interpretation. They are more easily understood, especially by unsophisticated parents, than are eloquent verbal explanations.

(5) When parents are allowed to see the therapist's struggles, frustrations, and occasional mistakes, they become less self-critical and are better able to resume responsibility for the bond with their own child.

Attention was paid in these efforts to the manifold disabilities of autism: contact with other people, motivation, receptive and expressive skills in communication, perceptual and motor functions. Parents were aided in developing programs for education at home and aided and encouraged in carrying them out. The North Carolina State Program for the Treatment and Education of Autistic and Related Communications Handicapped Children (TEACH), which developed (since 1970) from these efforts, is a model of enlightened aid to autistic children and their families.

In fairness to the detractors of parental training, we must state some of their views:

(1) Not all parents have the "knack" to become cotherapists although many can be supportive of the treatment program administered by professionals. In such cases parents should not be made to feel inferior or guilty because they cannot become cotherapists.

(2) Not all children can accept training from their parents.

(3) Many children need to have vacations from treatment techniques, especially over weekends. Autistic children can be "over-treated." They need time to do just what they want to do, as does everyone.

Organizational self-support. In Chapter 12 *The National Society for Autistic Children* was mentioned in connection with parental group influences. But while some possible organizational influences may create individual problems, NSAC is gradually becoming the most important source of organizational support for the parents of autistic children, adolescents, and adults.

With a growing membership of over 5,000 families and more than 100 local chapters scattered throughout the country, the Society is now headquartered in Washington, D.C. Founded by Dr. Bernard Rimland, it rose in the 1960s when parents banded together to support each other in their problems, aggravated in some cases by the ignorant hostility of local mental health professionals to whom they had gone for help and comfort. The ignorance and hostility are largely gone now, but professionals in contact with the Society are conscious that even though an active Professional Advisory Board includes some of the most eminent names in the field, there is still a certain wariness on the part of the parents who organize and administer NSAC, an intention to keep control in their own hands.

But it is just this sense of being a parent-dominated organization that gives it its greatest supportive strength. At the annual meetings, where often more than a thousand parents, grandparents, and professionals gather to listen to distinguished speakers and practically-oriented educational programs, there is a kind of cheerful and humorous solidarity that can be felt by those who have been dealt out the utmost in hardship but who have weathered the storm and are now gathering together to tell of their experiences and gain strength for the future. In addition to organizing regional and national meetings, lobbying on behalf of the developmentally disabled, and supplying the organizing potential for local chapters, NSAC operates a remarkable Information and Referral Service. From this center parents can learn what autism is, how to take the first steps in dealing with it, and what facilities are available to help them. Teachers faced with an autistic child can get technical assistance and suggestions for reading, and professionals can obtain the latest research results. NSAC publishes a newsletter, the *Advocate*, and a journal called the *Communicator* which is aimed at teachers of the autistic.

Selected Needs of Parents

While accomplishments such as parental self-help represent a significant step forward toward alleviation of some pressures (Atwood & Williams, 1978), the experience detailed in preceding chapters shows that our society is not yet responsive enough to the basic needs of parents of autistic children, adolescents, and adults. Such needs can be as great as those of a family on the West Coast with two congenitally blind autistic boys who could neither find a school for the blind equipped to cope with autism nor a treatment center for the autistic equipped to cope with blindness. More often they can be traced to financial hardships that are severely aggravated by the presence of an autistic member in the family.

I mentioned earlier the prolonged stress that rearing an autistic child imposes on parents. Divorces are common and it seems likely that the rate may become higher among some groups. How can parents learn to cope with the stress so that family health can be maintained or bettered? In my experience, families need vacations from the problems of coping with an autistic child, but to take these vacations parents need to know the child is being cared for with affection and skill. Child care institutions and foster homes could be used for therapeutic vacations as well as for periods when residential treatment is required. It is apparent that respite care, in which the patient is briefly cared for in his home or in an institution, is a humane alternative to institutionalization, although it cannot alleviate materially the problems faced by parents who see themselves growing old.

Respite care. In several states steps are being taken to help families care for old or handicapped members. Such respite care takes the form of services provided by the community to help make it possible for the disabled person to remain in the family. Several arguments point towards the advisability of such services:

(1) They keep intact the bonds of love within the family.

(2) They spare the family the horrors, real or imagined, or the "snake pit."

(3) They are economical. It costs an estimated $50,000 per year to support one person in an institution, and a small part of this sum will provide a large amount of skilled and welcome respite care.

(4) They are in accord with the laws of the United States which are bound to provide citizens, however handicapped they may be, with conditions of life which are to the least possible degree confining and restrictive.

Such care can take the form of a trained worker who stays with the autistic person for a few hours while the family goes shopping or to see a show, or for a few days while the others take a vacation. The autistic person may need a vacation too, and a change of scene into another private house or into a suitably equipped section of a nursing home or other institution can provide welcome respite for him or her.

In most communities respite care is in its infancy or has not begun, but it is bound to spread as providers of services become aware that it offers a flexible alternative to those who can use it, in a way which is generally cheaper and more pleasant for all concerned.

Many families need uninterrupted residential placement (rather than respite care) for the autistic member for the remainder of his life. Unfortunately, this kind of placement is becoming very hard to obtain for all but the very wealthy because it is the fad now to empty our hospitals of chronic patients, which sadly for most leads to a life of miserable neglect. This practice should be discontinued as it is a disgrace to our society.

Unimpeded access to special education. Parents who resist institutionalization of their autistic child and those whose child does not require residential placement have one very distinct need in common. It is the pressing need to secure suitable educational facilities for the autistic, still scarce for the young and virtually nonexistent for the older.

Now that it is no longer believed that there is some psychotherapy that can fundamentally modify autism, the problem remains of educating the autistic to make the best possible use of their abilities within the context of the families in which they will have to live. Severe though this problem is, it is often alleviated by the relatively simple, honest, and unimaginative autistic personality. This personality may be clouded by obsessions, lack of self-control, and a greater or lesser degree of retardation, but within its limitations it is generally open to special education.

Public Law 94-142, the Education of the Handicapped Act, specified that every handicapped person up to the age of 21 or 22 (depending on the state law) shall receive an individually designed education at public expense. Every such person is to receive professional evaluation and be provided with an Individualized Educational Program (IEP), which it is then mandatory for the local educational authorities to carry out. Where the number of autistic children is small the difficulties of mounting such a program can be great, and much time may be wasted while parents argue with school authorities about this or that detail of an IEP when the real problem is quite simply compliance or noncompliance with Federal Law.

Parents dealing with the educational establishment on these questions often find themselves in an adversary position which they are ill-equipped to occupy. Here the local parents' organization can be of great practical help and support, but the professional counsellor has an authority that, when properly exercised, can "move mountains." It is, however, necessary that professionals concern themselves with the education of their clients, that they know the law, and that they be informed about the best procedures for educating autistic people.

In dealing with families these professionals should bear in mind the following:

(1) The parents have been struck by misfortune and they are ordinarily under terrible stress. But misfortune and stress are easier to bear if they are treated with sympathy and respect and if it is freely recognized that it is they who are and should be ultimately responsible for decisions which affect their own lives.

(2) Each family has its own particular set of strengths and liabilities, professionals should learn to "accentuate the positive and eliminate the negative" and not try to impose their own expectations on parents who have a firm set of values and for various reasons cannot or need not acquire the values of other individuals.

Concluding Note

This book traces the clinical course of autism from birth to adulthood and parental reactions and behavior from the mother's pregnancy through life with an "adult child." Empirical data are supplemented by case histories to illustrate some of the most typical features of the disorder. I have tried to show the many facets of normal and autistic development by using the eyes and the words of parents whose observations are too often underemphasized in psychiatric writings. While some parental reactions and personalities seem either extremely pathological or heroic, most parents demonstrate, like the rest of us, a mixture of the strengths and weaknesses generally found in the human condition. While some extreme situations are described, my intent has been to focus most frequently on the mainstream where most autistic families can be found. A few like Terry or Mr. A. who could assess their own autistic childhood have spoken up here. My own observations, suggestions, and recommendations, based on many years of concentrated research, are interwoven with the valuable suggestions of other investigators and of parents. It is my hope that this book imparts some new insights to those who try to help parents and children in autism.

REFERENCES

Atwood, N., & Williams, M. E. D. Group support for the families of the mentally ill. *Schizophrenia Bulletin*, 1978, **4**(3), 415–425.

Coleman, M., & Hur, F. Platelet serotonin in disturbances of the central nervous system. In M. Coleman (Ed.), *Serotonin in Down's Syndrome.* Amsterdam: North-Holland, 1973.

DeMyer, M. K. Research in infantile autism: A strategy and its results. *Biological Psychiatry*, 1975, **10**(4), 433–452.

DeMyer, M. K., Barton, S., DeMyer, W. E., Norton, J. A., Allen, J., & Steele, R. Prognosis in autism: A follow-up study. *Journal of Autism and Childhood Schizophrenia*, 1973, **3**(3), 199–246 (cf. *Table 64*).

Eisenberg, L. The autistic child in adolescence. *American Journal of Psychiatry*, 1956, **112**, 607–613 (cf. *Table 64*).

Hingtgen, J. N., & Bryson, C. Q. Recent developments in the study of early childhood psychoses: Infantile autism, childhood schizophrenia, and related disorders. *Schizophrenia Bulletin*, 1972, **5**, 8–54.

Kanner, L. *Childhood psychosis: Initial studies and new insights.* Washington, D.C.: V. H. Winston & Sons, 1973 (cf. *Table 64*).

Keith, R. W. Synthetic sentence identification test. In R. W. Keith (Ed.), *Central auditory dysfunction.* New York: Grune & Stratton, 1977.

Lassen, N. A., Ingvar, D. H., & Skinhoj, E. Brain function and blood flow. *Scientific American*, 1978, **239**, 62–71.

McAdoo, W. G., & DeMyer, M. K. Research related to family factors in autism. *Journal of Pediatric Psychology*, 1977, **2**(4), 162–166.

Ornitz, E. M., Forsythe, A. B., & de la Pena, A. Effect of vestibular and auditory stimulation on the REMs and REM sleep in autistic children. *Archives of General Psychiatry*, 1973, **29**, 786–791.

Ritvo, E. R., & Freeman, B. J. Current status of biochemical research in autism. *Journal of Pediatric Psychology*, 1977, **2**(4), 149–152.

Rutter, M., & Lockyer, L. A five to fifteen year follow-up study of infantile psychosis. *British Journal of Psychiatry*, 1967, **113**, 1169-1199 (cf. *Table 64*).

Schopler, E., & Reichler, R. Parents as cotherapists in the treatment of psychotic children. *Journal of Autism and Childhood Schizophrenia*, 1971, **1**(1), 87-102.

Schopler, E., & Reichler, R. How well do parents understand their own psychotic child? *Journal of Autism and Childhood Schizophrenia*, 1972, **2**(4), 387-400.

Small, J. G. Sensory evoked responses of autistic children. In D. W. Churchill, G. D. Alpern, & M. K. DeMyer (Eds.), *Infantile autism: Proceedings of the Indiana University Colloquium*. Springfield, Ill.: Charles C Thomas, 1971.

Willeford, J. A. Assessing central auditory behavior in children: A test battery approach. In R. W. Keith (Ed.), *Central auditory dysfunction*. New York: Grune & Stratton, 1977.

INDEX